PUBLIC SPEAKING MADE EASY

Magic Key to Success

Originally Titled
The Power of Eloquence

THOMAS MONTALBO

Melvin Powers
Wilshire Book Company

12015 Sherman Road, No. Hollywood, CA 91605

Printed in the United States of America

What This Book Will Do for You

IF YOU WANT TO SPEAK IN PUBLIC or need to improve your speeches, this book is for you. Reading it is like having all the advantages of one-stop shopping in a supermarket with everything under one roof. Geared to both experienced and inexperienced speakers, this book includes all you need to know to prepare and deliver any type of speech for any occasion or audience.

Here in complete step-by-step detail, right at your finger tips, you have all the techniques and tools necessary for harnessing the power of eloquence. Packed with examples from actual speeches, this book shows the powerful effects that eloquence generates, pinpoints its key elements and takes you through the entire process of building them into your speeches.

Some may think a speech can be eloquent only when the subject is a mighty issue like slavery or a compelling event like war. Yet today's turbulent times cry out for eloquent speakers. Besides, the famous Roman orator Cicero said, "He is an eloquent man who can treat humble subjects with delicacy, lofty things impressively and moderate things temperately."

You may say, "A speech is a transient thing that quickly passes into and out of existence. Words vanish into the air as we speak them. Why, then, take the time and effort to strive for eloquence?" By definition, eloquence is vivid, forceful, fluent, graceful and persuasive expression. Now wouldn't that make your speeches much more effective? By conveying thoughts and feelings clearly and impressively, eloquence brightens up flat and colorless speech material and lifts it out of the ordinary category. Why be an average speaker when you can be one of the best?

Of course, you need to support your words with substance. That's what Ralph Waldo Emerson must have had in mind when he defined eloquence as "the art of speaking what you mean and are." What eloquent speakers say is heartfelt and they want it to be equally meaningful to their audiences. So with substance and conviction, strong diction, and distinctive word patterns, your speech will glow with eloquence and you'll stir your audience.

This book takes you through the entire process of making eloquent speeches. The process starts when you're asked to speak, goes through several preliminary steps, continues to assembling, organization and rehearsal steps, and ends when you stand on the platform to deliver your speech.

Encompassing what I call the "COD of Speechmaking," this book deals with public speaking as a threefold subject: content, organization and delivery. All three are necessary to make an eloquent speech. Unless you have something to say, choose the right words and arrange them effectively, the speech conveys little or nothing, no matter how well delivered. On the other hand, no matter how superb your content and organization may be, it's through the skillful use of your voice and body that you sustain audience interest and communicate your ideas.

So I devote separate chapters to content, organization and delivery. To these basic elements I've added findings and impressions from my own experience that will throw a fresh light on them. In addition, I provide individual chapters on the introduction, body and conclusion because each step is important, even though the body makes up 80 to 85 percent of the speech.

In discussing speech techniques and tools, I first explain them, then I cite my own examples and those from other speakers. Throughout its pages this book is studded with sentences or paragraphs which begin with "Here's how . . ." to describe and illustrate methods and devices used by eloquent speakers. That's one of the unique features that make this book special.

This book also highlights and explores in depth: creating eloquent speech titles; selecting the right words and grouping them in powerful sentences; avoiding roadblocks to eloquence; making smooth transitions; fulfilling a variety of functions with quotations; building impact with the rule of three; weaving in wit and humor; and analyzing the anatomy of a master speaker.

Thomas Montalbo

ACKNOWLEDGMENTS

For permission to quote from the indicated sources, grateful acknowledgment is made to the following:

City News Publishing Company, entire text of speech "Good News About Failure" by Eugene W. Brice and excerpts from these other speeches all published in *Vital Speeches:* "Freedom to Know" by Harvey C. Jacobs; "The Dimensions of the Oppression of Women" by Phyllis Jones Springen; "A Question of Ecology" by A. L. Jones; "The Press and Its Responsibilities" by Katherine Graham; "Democratic Convention Keynote Address" by Barbara Jordan; "The Backlash Phenomenon" by Helen B. Wolfe; "A Look at the Fundamental School Concept" by James K. Wellington; "The Future of Capitalism" by Milton Friedman; "Communication" by Ernest L. Boyer; "What Did Abraham Lincoln Stand For?" by Ralph Y. McGinnis; "Digging Up Parson Weems" by Robert G. Gunderson; and "Teaching Who We Are" by D. Bruce Lockerbie.

LeRoy Collins, excerpts from speech delivered on December 3, 1963, before the Greater Columbia Chamber of Commerce in Columbia, South Carolina.

Crown Publishers, Inc., quotations by Joseph Rickaby and Thomas Merton from *The Crown Treasury of Relevant Quotations* by Edward F. Murphy, copyright (c) 1978 by Edward F. Murphy.

J. William Fulbright, excerpt from speech "The Two Americas" delivered on March 22, 1966, at the University of Connecticut.

Anne Morrow Lindbergh and Pantheon Books, a division of Random House, Inc., excerpt from *Gift From the Sea*, copyright 1955 by Anne Morrow Lindbergh.

Sol M. Linowitz, entire text of speech "Let Candles Be Brought" delivered on March 8, 1977, before the Religion in American Life organization.

Time Inc., excerpts from Douglas MacArthur's farewell speech to the Corps of Cadets published in *Reminiscences* by General of the Army Douglas MacArthur, McGraw-Hill Book Co., copyright (c) 1964 by Time Inc. All rights reserved.

W. W. Norton & Company, Inc., except from *Man's Search*

for Himself by Rollo May, copyright 1953 by W. W. Norton & Company, Inc.

Norman Vincent Peale, quotation on "Hope."

Prentice-Hall, Inc., quotation on "Manners" by Amy Vanderbilt from *Treasury of Great American Sayings* by Leonard & Thelma Spinrad, copyright (c) 1975 by Leonard & Thelma Spinrad.

The author used *The World's Great Speeches* edited by Lewis Copeland and Lawrence W. Lamm, 1973, Dover Publications, Inc., NY as source for texts of speeches "On Woman's Right to Suffrage" by Susan B. Anthony; "New England Weather" by Mark Twain; "Washington's Birthday" by Jane Addams; and "A Day of Infamy" by Franklin D. Roosevelt.

Some material in this book appeared in articles by the author in *The Toastmaster* magazine, published by Toastmasters International, Santa Ana, CA.

CONTENTS

CHAPTER 1

Eloquence: The Neglected Aspect of Public Speaking

THE POWER OF WINSTON CHURCHILL'S ELOQUENT SPEECHES had so great an impact on the hearts and minds of the British people that they rallied to his call to save their nation when the Nazis threatened invasion after having conquered most of Europe. Here's an excerpt from one of his speeches:

> "We shall not flag or fail. We shall go on to the end. We shall fight in France. We shall fight on the seas and oceans. We shall fight with growing confidence and growing strength in the air. We shall defend our island, whatever the cost may be. We shall fight on the beaches. We shall fight on the landing grounds. We shall fight in the fields and in the streets. We shall fight in the hills. We shall never surrender."

That statement demonstrates the power of eloquence. Those words reveal Churchill's great sincerity and earnestness. His firmness and assertiveness aroused his people's spirit and determination to defy the enemy. His eloquence also stems from the words he used and how he put them together. The words—short, simple and specific—are clearly and easily understood. By using rhetorical devices in arranging the words, he grabbed the listeners' attention and got his message across forcefully.

The alliteration of "flag" and "fail," the refrain of "We shall . . . ," the parallel structure of his sentences, and the repetition of "fight"—all create a pattern of rhythm, reinforce his thoughts and feelings, and stir the listeners' emotions. Each time he repeats "fight" he points up the thought more and more strongly until the cumulative emphasis reaches the climax in the last sentence.

John F. Kennedy said of Churchill: "In the dark days and darker nights when Britain stood alone . . . he mobilized the English language and sent it into battle. The incandescent quality of his words illuminated the courage of his countrymen."

The words Churchill chose and the way he grouped them were never a matter of chance with him. He always prepared his speeches with much care because he believed that audiences have the right to expect the best from speakers. But today the best falls short.

Nobody seems to talk about eloquence today, and eloquent public speaking has almost disappeared. There was a time when speech anthologies always included "eloquence" in the title, as in *Crowned Masterpieces of Eloquence* and *Modern Eloquence*. Today they substitute "great" for "eloquence," as in *The World's Great Speeches* and *A Treasury of the World's Great Speeches*. Significantly, the old collections of eloquent speeches consisted of multiple volumes; the new collections of great speeches are complete in a single volume.

If you read current issues of *Vital Speeches, Representative American Speeches*, and the *Congressional Record*, chances are you won't find one eloquent passage in thousands of words. The number of speeches delivered today is probably greater than ever. But we hear less and less eloquence as more and more people give speeches. As quantity increases, quality seems to decrease. "Years ago things were made to last," consumers complain, "but not now. People don't put their hearts into their work. You can tell by the way things are made." Is that what's happening to speeches, too?

USING GHOSTWRITERS

Politicians, government officials, business executives and other leaders claim they're too busy to prepare speeches, so they hire ghostwriters to write them. Too busy? Abraham Lincoln, Woodrow Wilson, and Winston Churchill—to name just a few eloquent speakers—undoubtedly had as much on their minds and as much to do as today's speakers. Though busy with wars and other crushing responsibilities, when the occasion arose they took pains to prepare their own speeches. Wilson would often write a speech in shorthand. "This done," he once said, "I copy it on my own typewriter, changing phrases, correcting sentences, and adding material as I go along."

Theodore Roosevelt, perhaps the busiest man of his time, prepared his speeches with great care, even making changes on the final copy before he delivered them.

No matter how skillful, ghostwriters are only substitutes. How can they capture the speaker's innermost thoughts and deepest feelings? "Great speeches are as much a part of a man as his eyeballs or his intestines," author E. B. White once said. He took a dim view of a college course designed to teach potential ghostwriters "to put words into somebody else's mouth." The course instructor called ghostwriters "indispensable artisans."

It takes more than artisans, however, to create eloquent speeches. In ghostwritten speeches the speaker's individuality, if it exists at all, is not that of the actual speaker but of the ghostwriter. And a ghostwritten speech is often the prefabricated product of a group of speechwriters or collaborators, each contributing separate fragments.

So the speaker's individuality in both substance and form is lost in a ghostwritten speech. Although the speech may be carefully assembled by skilled artisans, it will sound contrived rather than natural when delivered by the speaker who didn't write it.

No ghostwriter could have written the eloquent words Lincoln spoke in his Farewell Address at Springfield before leaving for Washington to become president:

> "My friends: No one, not in my situation, can appreciate my feeling of sadness at this parting. To this place, and the kindness of these people, I owe everything. Here I have lived a quarter of a century, and have passed from a young man to an old man. Here my children have been born, and one is buried. I now leave, not knowing when or whether I may return, with a task before me greater than that which rested upon Washington. Without the assistance of that Divine Being, who ever attended him, I cannot succeed. With that assistance, I cannot fail. Trusting in Him, who can go with me, and remain with you, and be everywhere for good, let us confidently hope that all will yet be well. To His care commending you, as I hope in your prayers you will commend me, I bid you an affectionate farewell."

No ghostwriter could have written Barbara Jordan's eloquent keynote address at the 1976 Democratic convention. Jordan, the first black woman elected to the Texas state senate, was a U.S. Congresswoman from Texas when she delivered this speech. She began:

> "One hundred and forty-four years ago, members of the Democratic Party first met in convention to select a Presidential candidate.

> Since that time, Democrats have continued to convene once every four years and draft a party platform and nominate a Presidential candidate. And our meeting this week is a continuation of that tradition.
>
> "But there is something different about tonight. There is something special about tonight. What is different? What is special? I, Barbara Jordan, am a keynote speaker. A lot of years passed since 1832, and during that time it would have been most unusual for any national political party to ask that a Barbara Jordan deliver a keynote address, but tonight here I am. And I feel that notwithstanding the past that my presence here is one additional bit of evidence that the American Dream need not forever be deferred."

No ghostwriter could have written the eloquent words spoken by Douglas MacArthur in his Farewell to the Cadets speech at West Point. Then 82 years old, an honor graduate and a former superintendent of the U.S. Military Academy as well as a national war hero, MacArthur said:

> "The shadows are lengthening for me. The twilight is here. My days of old have vanished—tone and tints. They have gone glimmering through the dreams of things that were. Their memory is one of wondrous beauty watered by tears and coaxed and caressed by the smiles of yesterday. I listen vainly, but with thirsty ear, for the witching melody of faint bugles blowing reveille, of far drums beating the long roll. In my dreams I hear again the crash of guns, the rattle of musketry, the strange, mournful mutter of the battlefield.
>
> "But in the evening of my memory always I come back to West Point. Always there echoes and re-echoes: duty, honor, country. Today marks my final roll call with you. But I want you to know that when I cross the river, my last conscious thoughts will be of the Corps, and the Corps, and the Corps. I bid you farewell."

REVEALING INDIVIDUALITY

In the above quotations from speeches by Lincoln, Jordan and MacArthur, the individuality of each speaker is clearly present. The audience can be sure that the sentiments and words are really the speaker's, not a ghostwriter's. The speakers are believable because their speeches reveal them in a personal way. Each speaker comes across as a sincere and a warm human being. What they say not only reflects their personality and character but also blends with both the occasion and audience.

Lincoln's farewell message plainly shows his thoughts and feelings as he was about to leave his long-time home and friends to assume the burden of his tremendous task as president of a nation agitated over slavery and facing possible civil war.

Jordan began by directly referring to herself, commenting on her unique situation and asserting that her presence there helped to prove that the American Dream can be attained despite obstacles.

MacArthur, in his personal reminiscences, undoubtedly enjoyed full credibility with his audience because of his distinguished record both at West Point and on the battlefield as well as for his commitment to the cadets' motto, "duty, honor, country."

The audiences listening to Lincoln's, MacArthur's and Jordan's speeches, according to eyewitness reports, were deeply stirred and responded with the same warmth and goodwill which the speakers reflected as they spoke from their hearts.

Those audiences were moved because the speakers themselves were moved. The speakers talked with impressive force about something they personally knew and felt. That's eloquence. William Jennings Bryan defined eloquence as "the speech of one who knows what he is talking about and means what he says." "Eloquence," said Ralph Waldo Emerson, "is the best speech of the best soul."

What Bryan and Emerson said about eloquence spells out the reasons for the success of Lincoln's and MacArthur's farewell speeches and Jordan's keynote address.

The widespread use of ghostwritten speeches is only one reason why eloquence in speechmaking has declined. Another is television.

DUAL-AUDIENCE SPEAKING PROBLEM

To be effective, a speech must be tailored to a specific audience. But a politician, business executive or professional addressing a televised meeting is speaking simultaneously to two audiences. One is the immediate audience and the other consists of thousands or millions of TV viewers at home. A speaker compared this dual-audience situation to "having one bullet and having to shoot north and south at the same time."

The immediate audience at the meeting is specific and visible to the speaker, who can thus speak in ways to gain their interest and motivate them. The huge TV audience at home is vague and unseen, consisting of persons with a vast range of different backgrounds and opinions. So a large percentage of the TV audience is bound to disagree with the speaker, no matter what he or she says.

To cope with the two-audience problem and avoid alienating or offending the unknown TV viewers, the speakers tend to pull their punches rather than strongly proclaim the things they really believe. The English author George Orwell wrote that political speeches consist chiefly of "euphemism, question-begging, and sheer cloudy vagueness."

Structured to appeal to great masses of home viewers, speeches on television sound dull and lack qualities that interest, stimulate or challenge audiences. Edwin Newman, television broadcaster and author, says, "Advertising, public relations and polling techniques create attitudes that are designed to appeal to a large number of people. These attitudes tend to flatten out a speech."

Television also shows political candidates substituting 30-second spot announcements for speeches to convey their messages. What can the candidates say of significance in half a minute?

COMMERCIALISM AFFECTS ELOQUENCE

Still another factor in the neglect of eloquence in today's speechmaking is its commercial aspect. Speakers who have a burning desire to say something worthwhile are more likely to say it eloquently than those who are motivated to speak mainly for money.

Thousands of present and former government officials, television and radio personalities, columnists, politicians, and professional speakers are hired to give half-hour or one-hour speeches at conventions; professional, business and trade associations; corporations; colleges; and clubs. Most of the speakers develop a few set speeches which they deliver to different audiences.

The speakers receive enormous fees ranging from $2,000 to $20,000 a speech. Nearly all speakers hire agents who take a cut, usually one-third, of the lecture fee. In most cases, speakers are paid the fee plus expenses, including transportation, lodging and meals. Not so long ago speakers were happy just to have the chance to speak before prestigious organizations. Fees then ranged from modest to nonexistent. Going back to Emerson's time we find that his fees as a professional speaker ranged between $10 and $40 for his eloquent lectures, some of which are still read today a hundred years after his death.

Why can today's speakers command four and five-figure fees in today's lucrative business on the speaking circuit? One reason is the law of supply and demand. Many thousands of audiences gather every day in large cities at meetings sponsored by a variety of organizations. They all want speakers. The heavy demand exceeds the supply of speakers. Another reason is that the celebrity speaker draws people into the auditorium, the increased attendance helping to defray the costs of the meeting. A third reason is that organizations earmark large amounts in their budgets for hiring speakers.

Does today's plain speech style lend itself to eloquence? By all means. "If men would only say what they have to say in plain terms, how much more eloquent they would be," said the English poet Samuel Coleridge. Ben Jonson, an English dramatist and poet laureate whose poems reflect a plain yet vigorous style, said, "Talking and eloquence are not the same: to speak, and to speak *well* are two things."

The oratorical style slips into empty talk when it uses too many big words and long, complex sentences. On the other hand, the plain speech style falls flat when overloaded with short, simple sentences, commonplace words and cliches. But by avoiding these excesses, either style can generate eloquence.

Is eloquence necessary? Certainly. The English statesman and writer John Morley, in his *Life of Gladstone*, wrote, "To disparage eloquence is to depreciate mankind." Cicero put it this way, "If truth were self-evident, eloquence would not be necessary."

But truth is not self-evident and speeches deal mostly with the needs and wants that motivate people. Human nature being what it is, the public speaker, said Emerson, "plays upon the assembly of men as a master upon the keys of a piano." Not only must speakers discover the truth, but they must express it eloquently to others, appealing to listeners' emotions as well as to their intelligence.

Technology and mass communication systems may change the way speeches are delivered but not the way they're created. Principles of rhetoric, like human nature, have remained essentially the same from ancient to modern times. To be eloquent, you don't have to wave your arms, shout, rant and rave. You can be eloquent standing still and speaking conversationally.

Back in the 1800s, Wendell Phillips, one of the most eloquent speakers of all time, used the conversational delivery while his great contemporaries, Henry Clay and Daniel Webster, orated eloquently in the traditional manner. More recently, such modern speakers as John Kennedy, Martin Luther King, Adlai Stevenson, Winston Churchill, Will Rogers and Franklin Roosevelt delivered eloquent speeches.

St. Augustine, who earned his living for some years as a teacher of rhetoric, said, "The power of eloquence—so very effective in convincing us of either wrong or right—lies open to all." And he was right. This is not to suggest that everybody can become a Lincoln or a Churchill. But if you study and apply the language elements used by eloquent speakers, your audience will understand and remember what you say.

To create eloquence in your speech you must first have something worthwhile to say and be able to say it with sincerity and conviction. If you say what you truly believe, you'll find it easier to be eloquent. That has been the experience of all effective speakers. Mirabeau, the French orator, said of the revolutionist Robespierre, "That young man will go far as a speaker. He actually seems to believe what he is saying."

WATCH YOUR RHETORIC

But you must also pay attention to the two elements of rhetoric that are the most crucial in expressing your ideas and feelings both clearly and distinctively: (1) choice of words and (2) rhetorical devices. These elements are covered in detail later in this book.

A speech is something more than a rambling group of sentences leading the audience from nowhere in particular to nowhere in general. Yet too many speeches sound disorganized and dull. Sometimes speakers improvise their speeches and even admit, "I don't know what I'm going to talk about until I go before the audience," or "Oh, I never know until I get up there. I could talk for hours and wing it as I go along."

Churchill never made speeches on the spur of the moment. Nor did Lincoln. Mark Twain said he needed three weeks to prepare for an impromptu speech. Preparation is the foundation of successful public speaking. Eloquent speeches don't just happen. They must be carefully planned and organized before rehearsal and delivery.

That's what this book is all about—how to achieve success in public speaking with the power of eloquence, the power that causes audiences to pay attention, to listen and be inspired. This book contains everything you need to know to be eloquent. If you were to take a course in public speaking, the tuition would cost you hundreds of dollars more than the purchase price of this book. More than a theoretical guide to eloquence, this book tells you not only *what to do* but exactly *how to do it*. This is a practical "how-to" book that gives you techniques and tools you can use right away.

Succeeding chapters identify, describe and explain numerous techniques and tools and illustrate them with many examples from actual speeches that are models of eloquence. The chapters take you step-by-step in the process of making a speech from the time you're invited to speak to the point of actual delivery.

The first step (Chapter 2) is to get a catchy or compelling title for your speech. If it sounds odd to start with the title, think of how it:

1. Condenses your entire speech into a few words.

2. Forces you to keep on target—your topic—during the preparation of your speech.

3. Sets the tone of your speech.

4. Contains the first words your audience sees in advance notices or programs and hears from your introducer, so the title should arouse the curiosity of prospective listeners. One speaker, for example, used as his speech title, "Does Two Plus Two Equal Five?" Everything in his talk amplified the message conveyed in his title—that people should look at statistics skeptically and evaluate what's behind the numbers.

Developing the content of your speech is the next step (Chapter 3). The next three chapters (4, 5, and 6) deal with the organization of your material: one chapter on the body of your speech, a second on the introduction and a third on the conclusion. The reason for separate chapters on the introduction and conclusion is that these parts require almost as much care as the body itself, since an eloquent introduction compels attention at the beginning and a stirring closing leaves an enduring impression.

Chapter 7 is devoted to the important subject of transitions, which are often overlooked by speakers, yet are designed to tie together everything in your speech both for you and your audience. The next two chapters (8 and 9) cover in depth many rhetorical devices that can transform ordinary statements into vivid and forceful expressions. A whole chapter is devoted to one of the devices—the magical rule of three—because it's a fascinating and remarkably effective technique which can be used in a number of ways: as a pattern of expression; as a process for thinking and developing ideas; as a formula for organizing speeches; as a tool for constructing wit and humor; and as a method for creating speech titles.

Chapter 10, on the delivery of a speech, provides numerous

specific suggestions for effective coordination of voice, gestures, bodily action, pauses and visual aids to reinforce your words. With the delivery of your speech, the step-by-step process reaches the last step. The next four chapters then dig deeply into different subjects, each referred to in previous chapters but now requiring concentrated treatment.

Chapter 11 is devoted entirely to the power of quotations—their functions, ways to use them, where to find them, how to select them, and how to deliver them. Chapter 12 delves into how to choose the right words and avoid words that block communication.

Still another chapter (13) provides a searching analysis of Winston Churchill's theory and practice of speechmaking, resulting in seven lessons for all public speakers. Chapter 14 covers humor, describes its ingredients, gives techniques for using it in both serious and humorous speeches, and analyzes in detail one of Will Rogers' after-dinner speeches.

The last chapter (15) summarizes the preceding chapters and deals with the need for the practice of delivery in front of an audience and how to obtain it. Following the final chapter you'll find two appendixes containing supplementary material useful for your ready reference:

Appendix I—Eloquent Quotations

These are memorable sayings from ancient and modern times that apply to life today on various subjects, arranged alphabetically for your easy use in helping you to develop or illustrate ideas as well as to liven up your speeches.

Appendix II—Models of Eloquent Speeches

Actual speeches delivered by yesterday's and today's public speakers, these masterpieces of eloquence will demonstrate many speech techniques and inspire you to greater effort and excellence. Although you cannot learn delivery skills in printed speeches, you can profit from a study of their content, organization of material, sentence structure, and language.

CHAPTER 2

How to Create Eloquent Speech Titles

MOST SPEAKERS UNDERESTIMATE THE IMPORTANCE OF A SPEECH TITLE. They work long and hard to research and write their speeches. Then at the last minute they realize they must give a title to the program chairman.

So what do they do? Chances are they just jot down the first thing that comes to mind. Few take the time and devote the effort needed to create titles that are worthy of their carefully prepared and rehearsed speeches.

Yet the title may be the most crucial part of your speech. That's because the title can help or hurt your speech in five ways:

1. The title makes the first contact with your audience.

You may gain or lose listeners before you even begin to talk. Why? Because the title contains the first words the audience sees in programs or advance notices and hears from the person who introduces you. An eloquent title can attract a large and receptive audience while a bad title can leave you with empty seats or indifferent listeners. You've heard people say, "I'd like to hear that speech," or "That speech doesn't sound promising." All this happens before you stand at the lectern or on the podium to greet the audience and start speaking.

Just as titles help sell books and attract readers to magazine articles, just as headlines catch the eye of newspaper readers, and just as advertisers lure potential buyers with tantalizing captions, so can the speech title arouse the curiosity and interest of prospective listeners.

One speaker who recognized the importance of a title used this one for a speech on excessive government regulation of business:

"Pardon Me—Your Knee Is On My Chest." Another speaker, criticizing the high cost of political campaigns, called his speech "Our Gold-Plated Democracy." A third speaker, defending large corporations, titled his speech "Who Needs the Biggies?"

2. The title puts your speech in focus.

When you're preparing your talk, a title can help you focus your thoughts, guide you in pulling material together, and keep you from drifting away from your topic. Condensing your entire speech into a few words, the title keeps you on target. If formulating a title proves difficult, this may be a sign you don't have any single strong idea or central concept in your speech.

3. The title organizes the speech itself.

The title is a superb tool for organizing a speech. In a speech titled "What Are We Trying to Do?" a speaker began, "I have chosen as a theme a simple question," and repeated in his introduction the same question as in the title. He threaded this question through the body of his speech with each of a dozen illustrations. Finally, he closed his talk by posing the same question as he summarized and drove home his message.

Another speaker used the same technique in a speech titled "Whose Ox Is Being Gored?" In his introduction he indicated that, if the title suggested he was going to show inconsistencies in perceptions of issues, "that is exactly right." After each of several examples in the body of his speech, he remarked that it did seem to matter "whose ox is being gored." In his conclusion he said, "We need to put our oxen out to pasture. We need to act responsibly in ways that no longer make goring them necessary."

4. The title provides you with a refrain.

The title can be subtly used as a refrain throughout your speech. As in the above examples, repeating as an echo the question, "What Are We Trying to Do?" or "Whose Ox Is Being Gored?" helps listeners to follow the speaker's train of thought. Remember, nobody listens all the time. But an audience would be hard-pressed to forget your title or the theme it suggests if you skillfully repeat the title as a refrain in the introduction, body and conclusion.

5. The title leads to other speech ideas.

Searching for an attention-getting title, like researching for a speech, will often spark ideas for other speeches. Authors have made the same discovery. One book almost invariably leads to another, thanks to research. As we explore facts and theories we stumble on material that stimulates our imagination for still another speech or book.

Likewise, an eloquent title itself can motivate a speaker or writer to develop supporting material that matches the title. One author who knows the importance of titles says she has been successful in writing for the confession magazines "by starting with the title, and then writing a suitable story to go with it."

If you try to figure out catchy titles for your speeches, you'll find that your efforts will yield a number of irresistible titles. And some of the extra titles will inspire you to prepare speeches to fit.

WHAT'S IN A NAME?

Shakespeare's Juliet is wide of the mark when she says to Romeo, "What's in a name? That which we call a rose by any other name would smell as sweet." Poet Thomas Moore was more on track. He said, "Oh, call it by some better name/For friendship sounds too cold."

That's the trouble with too many speech titles. They're as cold and unexciting as package labels or identification tags. They lack the power to grab attention, awaken interest, arouse curiosity or stimulate feelings.

What makes a title eloquent? Three factors must be considered:

The first factor is length. No rule exists that specifies how long or how short a speech title should be. When Lincoln was asked how long he thought a man's legs should be, he answered, "Well, I should think a man's legs ought to reach from his body to the ground." So it is with a title—it should be long enough to do the job.

If Life Is a Bowl of Cherries—What Am I Doing in the Pits? wasn't too long a book title to prevent it from becoming number one on the best-seller list. In *Vital Speeches*, which twice a month prints current speeches, you'll find titles such as "Trade Union Power Brings Britain to the Brink," "After You Get Where You're Going, Where Will You Be?" and "The Black Hole in the Businessman's Perception of His Problems."

Here are some long titles from *Representative American Speeches*, collections published each year: "Cowboys, Indians and the Land of Promise: The World Image of the American Frontier," "Global Interdependence: Life, Liberty, and the Pursuit of Happiness in Today's World" and "In Pursuit of Equality in Academe: New Themes and Dissonant Chords."

Although those headings are gripping enough and their unusual length attracts attention, most eloquent titles are short, so it's safe to assume that short titles are preferred over long ones. Surely it's easier to remember short titles.

The second factor to consider in creating eloquent speech titles is appeal. That means a title should be vivid, imaginative and stimulating. Don't depend on the subject matter of a title to provide the punch that compels attention. Even the rare subject that has built-in impact or excitement may not be enough to guarantee interest. Besides what the title says, how it says it is important. The title should stir audiences to want to listen.

Here are some examples of intriguing titles:

Where Death Delights is a book on courtroom medicine and how autopsies can exonerate the falsely accused, determine the recipient of a fortune in insurance, and smoke out likely suspects. The title is derived from the following inscription on the wall of a city examiner's office: "Let conversation cease. Let laughter flee. This is the place where death delights to help the living."

Bring on the Empty Horses narrates an actor's memoirs. The title is taken from an anecdote about a movie director who started a scene involving 100 riderless horses by shouting, "Okay, bring on the empty horses!"

All My Patients Are Under the Bed is the title of an autobiography whose author is a cat doctor who makes house calls.

Elephants in Your Mailbox is a book about the secrets of mail-order marketing. The title comes from a catalog that once offered an elephant ladder, which was pictured leaning up against the animal it is normally used to mount.

The third factor needed in constructing eloquent speech titles is relevancy. A title must relate to your subject. Nobody wants to be misled. If your title purposely confuses people or seems absurd to them, they won't like it and may stop listening to you.

But you don't have to give your entire speech in the title. Nor does your title have to describe the speech. Some inkling, suggestion or clue may be enough to convey your main idea indirectly.

One speaker's subject was the public debt, yet he titled his talk "The Greatest Danger To Be Feared." The relevancy of the title was made clear when the speaker began his speech by saying, "The title of this talk is taken from a letter by Thomas Jefferson . . . Here's the opening line: 'I place economy among the first and most important virtues, and public debt as the greatest of dangers to be feared.'"

The title of Russell Conwell's classic speech "Acres of Diamonds" only indirectly explains his theme. Conwell told the story of a man who sold his farm to travel all over the world searching for a diamond mine but didn't find it. Later, one was found underneath his farm. Had he stayed home he could have had acres of diamonds. All he had to do was dig for them in his own backyard.

NINE TECHNIQUES FOR SPEECH TITLES

How do you create an eloquent title? Conceivably it may just come to you, emerging suddenly from your subconscious mind. But you can't rely on chance. Use one or more of the following nine techniques:

1. Experiment with tentative titles.

Start your experiment by asking yourself such questions as: "What am I really trying to tell the audience? What's different about my thoughts or approach? What single idea ties my speech together?"

Answer those questions as simply and clearly as you can. Your answers will undoubtedly trigger some ideas for a title. You might call this process "solitary brainstorming."

While brainstorming allows a group to come up with bright or foolish suggestions for solving a problem, solitary brainstorming is played all by yourself. But the end result is the same—some useful ideas turn up. Jot them down and choose a tentative or working title.

Now, is the title too broad? Try narrowing it down. "That's better," you say to yourself. But don't be satisfied yet. Maybe there's still a better way to say it. Turn the words around. Add or take out words. Will alliteration or rhyme help?

Try again, and then again, and once more, and over and over—until you've made the title eloquent. That point is reached when you can say your title is brief, forceful, conveys a strong message about your subject or theme—and really pulls the audience into your speech.

2. Take a phrase from your speech.

This technique has the advantage of a ready-made title and built-in relevance to the speech. In a stirring speech appealing for all-out aid to the democracies fighting Nazi aggression, Franklin D. Roosevelt said, "We must be the great arsenal of democracy." From that sentence came the title of the speech, "The Arsenal of Democracy."

In Roosevelt's speech to Congress asking for a declaration of war on Japan, he said, "Yesterday, December 7, 1941—a date which will live in infamy—the United States of America was suddenly and deliberately attacked by naval and air forces of the empire of Japan." From that sentence was derived the speech's title, "Day of Infamy."

Lincoln, in his first inaugural address, said, "The mystic chords of memory, stretching from every battlefield and patriot grave, to every living heart and hearthstone all over this broad land, will yet swell the chorus of the Union, when again touched, as surely they will be . . . by the better angels of our nature." The phrase "mystic chords of memory" would have made an eloquent title of that speech if custom didn't dictate that it be simply labeled "Inaugural Address."

"Blood, Sweat and Tears" is the title of Winston Churchill's speech in which he said, "I have nothing to offer but blood, toil, tears and sweat." Martin Luther King's best-known speech "I Have a Dream" got its title from the text in which he skillfully repeated that phrase several times. Thomas E. Dewey, launching his first try at the nomination for president, said in a speech, "We seem to be on our way toward a rendezvous with despair." That sentence gave him the title of his speech, "Rendezvous with Despair."

Douglas MacArthur, in his farewell speech to Congress said, "I still remember the refrain of one of the popular barracks songs of that day which proclaimed most proudly that old soldiers never die; they just fade away." "Old Soldiers Never Die" was the title of his speech.

Robert G. Gunderson, professor at Indiana University, titled a speech, "Digging Up Parson Weems," taking the title from his text. His theme was that each generation invents its own heroes and mythology of success. "This explains," he said, "why geriatric types are fond of digging up Parson Weems (architect for the success mythology of the early Republic) . . ."

3. Use alliteration.

The device of alliteration works wonders in making speech titles come alive. Alliteration occurs when the same letter starts successive words, as in this sentence itself. One of language's oldest rhetorical devices, alliteration is still popular today.

So alluring is alliteration that people continue to relish many trite expressions. Here are some examples: pretty as a picture, bold as brass, brain and brawn, hale and hearty, part and parcel, dead as a doornail, right as rain, fit as a fiddle.

Good As Gold is the title of a novel that became a best-seller. *The Power of Positive Thinking* is an all-time best-selling nonfiction book and "Bewitched, Bothered and Bewildered" is an all-time song hit.

WHY ALLITERATION APPEALS

Why is alliteration so appealing? What are its delights that can make even nonsense sound wise? Language is primarily a system of sounds. That's why alliteration, though a simple technique, tends to attract attention and strengthen the power of speech.

As alliteration harmoniously links suitable words together, it produces a sound pattern with a rhythmic swing and a lilting tune. This sound pattern emphasizes the words and makes them eloquent.

That's why many speakers use alliteration in speech titles. One speaker discussing environmental problems titled his speech "Progress, Pollution and Parallel Technologies." Another speaker, dealing with the dangers of mass media, called his talk "Liberty, Leadership and License" instead of using a humdrum title such as "The Mass Media."

Browse through *Vital Speeches* and *Representative American Speeches* and you'll see plenty of other alliterative titles.

4. Try rhyme.

Just as people respond to alliteration because of its rhythm, so do they react to rhyme. The poet uses rhyme to heighten the readers' experience as they feel the stimulus of rhyming sounds. Functionally, the poet's use of rhyme goes even beyond its sound qualities. Rhyming words interrelate with one another, emphasize and reinforce their meaning and establish the tone of a phrase, sentence or passage.

For all those reasons rhyme is an effective device in formulating intriguing speech titles. One speaker titled his speech "Communicate or Suffocate." His theme was that fallacious charges by business critics go unanswered because companies fail to communicate with the uninformed public and that unless management presents the facts well "the continued wave of discontent will change the system beyond its capacity to survive." So the speaker used rhyme in his title not merely for the sake of conscious rhyming effect but in consideration and relevance of his theme.

To that end, several other speakers used rhyme in their speech titles: "Is There a Spy in the Sky?"; "Quality and Equality"; "From Pariah to Messiah."

5. Use key words.

Certain words attract people irresistibly. Among such words are "how," "power," "magic," "secret," and "miracle." Use these words in your speech titles and you'll strike a responsive chord in your audiences.

Because people want to know, they're attracted by book titles such as *How Adults Learn; How Do We Choose?; How Doctors Diagnose You; How Do You Face Disappointments?* A title like *How Does a Poem Mean?* surprises the readers because they would expect *What Does a Poem Mean?* The unusual title intrigues them. What's it about? The book stresses not *what* a poem means, but *how* it says what it means.

Often the titles begin with "How to," as in these examples: *How to Use Your Time to Get Things Done; How to Become the Person You Want to Be; How to Be Happy No Matter What; How to Get Action: Key to Successful Management.*

By nature people are interested in developing and exerting the power of their physical, mental and spiritual abilities. So they're drawn to titles like *Power Is You; Power: How to Get It, How to Use It; Executive Power: How to Use It Effectively; Power Ideas for a Happy Family; Power of Total Living.*

Any message spoken or written with the word "magic" in it seems to cast a spell on people. Titles tantalize if they contain "magic," as in the title of the book *Magic Moment* which transforms a tiny portion of time into a moment of enchantment. The book title *Magic Journey* makes a trip sound adventurous and thrilling.

Pleasurable expectation or visualizing a happy future implied in the titles pulls readers toward these books: *Magic Power of Self-Image: The New Way to a Bright Full Life; Magic of Thinking Big; Magic of Herbs in Daily Living; Magic in Your Mind; Magic Power of Command Selling: How to Take Charge of the Sale.*

The word "secret" often appears in titles of magazine articles and books because that word is as magical as "magic" itself. "Secret" promises something specific that will help people attain a desired goal—achieving improvement, excellence or happiness. Hence the appeal of such titles as: *Secret of Success; Secret of Happiness; Secret of Perfect Living; Secret of Abundant Living; Secret of a Spirit-Filled Life.*

By definition, a miracle is an extremely outstanding or unusual accomplishment. The word "miracle" in a title, therefore, raises expectations that something wonderful or amazing will happen. That explains the appeal of such titles as: *Miracle of Instant Memory Power; Miracle Success System: A Scientific Way to Get What You Want Out of Life; Miracle Power of Transcendental Meditation; Miracle Diet for Fast Weight Loss; Miracle Power for Infinite Riches.*

Titles of book jackets and magazine covers show those key words in abundance. Authors and editors know such titles begin the process of selling books and magazines. The promise reflected by the titles pulls in the readers. What they read in the books and articles will help them in some practical way or teach, inform, persuade, entertain or inspire them—and change their lives for the better.

By using one or more of the key words, as shown in the examples above, you can create a speech title that will persuade audiences to listen to the speech itself.

6. Ask a question.

Glance through *Vital Speeches* and *Representative American Speeches* and you'll find that speech titles are often questions. Here are some examples:

"Who Is Wise?"

"Frustration or Fulfillment?"

"Can We Better The 'Bitter Society'?"

"Who Is Going to Deliver the Bad News?"

"Does Two Plus Two Equal Five?"

"Television Can Show and Tell But Can It Listen?"

"Money—Or Is It?"

"Can We Afford to Be Honest?"

"Which Future for Tomorrow?"

"How Much Is Enough?"

"Can Free Enterprise Survive Success?"

Why do speakers frequently use a question as a speech title? Well, it's easy to change a label title into a question. For example, instead of labeling your speech "Noise Pollution," you could ask "Who Needs Noise?"

But there's another explanation. Coincidence or not, the question mark looks like an inverted hook. That hook in a speech title catches and holds the attention of listeners, pulling them into the speech. That's because a question is almost impossible to brush aside. Listeners instinctively find themselves thinking of an answer. Meanwhile they're drawn to the speaker to hear his or her answer.

7. Choose a quotation.

Good quotations also make first-rate speech titles. When appropriately selected and used, quotations add both charm and substance to your message. French essayist Michel de Montaigne put it this way, "I quote others only in order to better express myself."

Even familiar quotations are usable again and again because, as German philospher Friedrich Nietzsche said, "A good aphorism is too hard for the tooth of time, and is not worn away by all the centuries, although it serves as food for every epoch."

USE ONLY KEY WORDS

But you might well ask, "Isn't a quotation too long for a title?" Yes, so use only key words. For example, one speaker used this Biblical quotation in his speech: "And they shall beat their swords into plowshares and their spears into pruning hooks: nation shall not lift up a sword against nation; neither shall they learn war anymore."

From that quotation the speaker pulled out two words for the title—"Of Plowshares and Pruning Hooks."

Lincoln's "A House Divided Against Itself" speech received its title from the Biblical quotation, "And if a house be divided against itself, that house cannot stand," which Lincoln also cited in his text and added, "I believe this government cannot endure permanently half slave and half free." This is only one of many examples from his speeches that show he used the Bible as a principal source of inspiration and quotations.

The Uncertain Trumpet, an actual book title, is derived from the Biblical quotation, "If the trumpet give an uncertain sound, who shall prepare himself for battle?" This metaphor, if aptly applied, would make an impressive speech title.

Besides the Bible, quotable phrases for eloquent speech titles are available to public speakers from a number of sources.

SHAKESPEARE IS A SOURCE OF ELOQUENT TITLES

Shakespeare's writings contain a gold mine of phrases that make eloquent speech titles. Hundreds of quotations from his plays have been used by modern authors as titles for their books. Remarkably, in the following ten-line passage from Shakespeare's *Macbeth*, the italicized phrases became the titles of nine books:

> *Tomorrow, and tomorrow*, and tomorrow
> Creeps in *this petty pace* from day to day,
> To the last syllable of recorded time;
> And *all our yesterdays* have lighted fools
> The way to *dusty death*. Out, out, *brief candle!*
> Life's but a *walking shadow*, a *poor player*
> That struts and frets his hour upon the stage,
> And then is heard no more; it is a tale
> *Told by an idiot*, full of *sound and fury*,
> Signifying nothing."

A speaker gave his speech this short, provocative and relevant title "One Man In His Time," which he excerpted from Shakespeare's *As You Like It*:

> All the world's a stage
> And all the men and women merely players:
> They have their exits and their entrances;
> And one man in his time plays many parts . . .

Many of Shakespeare's quotations are of course well-known and widely used, but many other less familiar quotes are perfectly suitable for titles. For example, in Hamlet's death scene, Horatio says, "Now cracks a noble heart. Good night, sweet prince, and flights of angels sing thee to thy rest!" Gene Fowler used *Good Night, Sweet Prince* as the title of a biography of his friend, the actor John Barrymore, who had played Hamlet.

TRY FAIRY TALES

Fairy tales yield intriguing titles. Inspired by Lewis Carroll's *Alice's Adventures in Wonderland*, Lilli Palmer, actress and author, titled her autobiography *Change Lobsters—and Dance*. She tells of her life from the early years when her promising acting career in Germany was cut off by Hitler's regime, to her cabaret work as a refugee in Paris, small roles in British movies, marriage, Hollywood and Broadway stardom, divorce, remarriage, and a new career as writer.

She continually "changed lobsters," that is, picked up the pieces and went on with the dance, as described in the following excerpts from Carroll's fairy tale: "Change lobsters again! yelled the Gryphon . . . So they began solemnly dancing round and round Alice, every now and then treading on her toes when they passed too close . . ."

CHOOSE TITLES FROM THESE OTHER SOURCES

Other sources of potential titles for speeches are proverbs and poems. They appeal because they condense ideas in language chosen and arranged to create a response through meaning, rhyme, rhythm or alliteration. They sharpen thoughts to the point of utmost brevity and eloquent expression.

Proverbs usually have a balanced structure and compare or contrast thoughts, as in these examples: "Cold hands, warm heart"; "Out of sight, out of mind"; "Feast today, fast tomorrow." Taking a cue from such proverbs, a speaker resorted to the same technique when he constructed his speech title, "Waste Not—Want Not." In his talk he discussed the impact of government regulations on the chemical industry.

In a speech on the economy, the speaker said, "We have taken the wrong road . . . The wrong road has been the road of government economic intervention. The right road would have been to permit and encourage free markets." The title of his speech was "The Road Not Taken," which he borrowed from Robert Frost's poem bearing the same title and containing these lines:

> Two roads diverged in a wood, and I—
> I took the one less traveled by . . .

The American author John Gunther called one of his books *Death Be Not Proud*, borrowing the title from the English poet John Donne, who used the phrase in both the title and text of a sonnet that reads:

> Death be not proud, though some have called thee
> Mighty and dreadful, for thou are not so . . .

8. Alter familiar quotations or clichés.

Try a clever and unexpected twist on some shopworn or old phrase to formulate original and fresh titles. This technique involves changes such as inversion and word substitution that catch people by surprise as they do a double take.

By inverting the familiar saying "Food for Thought," an author titled a book on diet and food "Thought for Food." *Time* magazine, referring to magic, called it "A Trade of Tricks," reversing the cliche "Tricks of the Trade."

A speaker's subject was the conversion of farmland to nonagricultural uses such as highways, airports and shopping centers. His theme was that we're not facing up to the costs of land-conversion today but deferring them to another generation. He called that philosophy "pave now, pay later," a takeoff on the airline slogan, "Fly Now, Pay Later." So he titled his speech, "Pave Now, Pay Later."

In a speech based on the theme that only companies telling the truth will reap the benefits of consumer patronage and loyalty, a speaker said, "Today's public is much too sophisticated (or suspicious) and far too fed up with verbal shenanigans to fall for those clever ploys that used to work so well." So in keeping with his theme, the speaker titled his speech, "You Can't Fool *Any* of the People *Any* of the Time *Any* More." The speaker had changed the actual words of Lincoln, who said, ". . . you can't fool all of the people all the time."

A speaker altered the construction of the proverb "He who pays the piper calls the tune," so that it would fit the theme of his speech. Speaking on academic freedom and the taxpayer's role in decisions concerning the university, he titled his talk "If They Pay the Fiddler, Should They Get to Call the Tune?"

Another speaker changed the slogan "Back to Basics" to "Forward to Basics." The Biblical phrase "Faith, Hope and Charity" was altered to "Faith, Hope and Clarity" as the title of a magazine article on "techno-speak," talk used in corporate life and politics.

9. Apply the rule of three.

The title "Faith, Hope and Clarity" illustrates still another method for creating speech titles—applying the rule of three, that is, saying things in threes. For example, if you were to give a talk on the affluent lifestyle, you could take three luxury items and title your speech "Cadillacs, Condos and Caviar."

Here are actual speech titles constructed by grouping three things:

"No Arts, No Letters—No Society"

"War, Transport and Show Biz"

"Sense, Courage and Professional Competency"

"Chemophobia, Politics and Distorted Images"

"Resources, Results and the Seven Deadly Sins"

The rule of three is also used for other purposes, which along with its use in speech titles, are explained in detail with numerous examples in Chapter 9, "Shape Your Eloquence With the Rule of Three."

Considering the many advantages of an eloquent title, why not dress up your next speech with one? By using the techniques shown in this chapter, you can create a title worthy of your speech—one that will please you and captivate your audience.

REMEMBER THESE POINTS

Recognize the five reasons for the importance of a speech title:

1. Makes the first contact with your audience before you even speak.
2. Puts your speech in focus.
3. Organizes the speech itself.
4. Provides you with a refrain.
5. Triggers other speech thoughts and ideas.

Consider three factors in constructing a title:

1. Length.
2. Appeal.
3. Relevancy.

Apply one or more of nine techniques to create eloquent speech titles:

1. Experiment with tentative titles.
2. Take a phrase from your speech.
3. Use alliteration.
4. Try rhyme.
5. Employ key words: "how," "power," "magic," "secret," "miracle."
6. Ask a question.
7. Choose a quotation.
8. Alter familiar quotations or clichés.
9. Turn to the rule of three.

CHAPTER 3

Have Something Eloquent to Say

YOUR ELOQUENT SPEECH TITLE, discussed in the preceding chapter, is only the packaging of your topic. Now you must develop the content to put in the package and to match the eloquence of your title.

Content is one of the three necessary elements of any speech. The other two are organization and delivery, but neither can compensate for lack of content. You must first have something to say. The speaker with nothing to say has no reason for speaking. The English novelist George Eliot put it this way, "Blessed is the man who, having nothing to say, abstains from giving us wordy evidence of the fact."

Many others agree. Louis Nizer, trial lawyer and public speaker, said, "Eloquence without substance is like a table beautifully set in all its appetizing whiteness and decorated with flowers—but no food." Preparing a recipe for cooking wild turkey, a Pilgrim pioneer wrote, "First hunt and catch your turkey." The humorist Will Rogers said, "You can't heat an oven with snowballs."

Primarily, then, a speech should be judged by its content, the vital core of your speech. Without minimizing the importance of organization and delivery, it can be stated that neither perfect organization nor masterful delivery by itself makes an eloquent speech. They certainly enrich a speech but it's the subject matter that has to be organized and delivered. The subject matter gives meaning to the speech. Woodrow Wilson said, "Thought is the fiber, the pith of eloquence. Eloquence lies in the thought, not in the throat."

What does it mean to have something eloquent to say? William Jennings Bryan said, "You must feel that you have something to say that people ought to hear." Cicero believed that "No man can be eloquent on a subject that he does not understand." Saying something eloquent, therefore, includes three factors:

1. Speaking on a worthwhile subject.

2. Speaking on a subject that you've earned the right to talk about because of your background or research.

3. Having a burning message that compels you to speak out in earnest.

A worthwhile subject is one that deserves the time and effort you spend on it as a speaker and the time and effort the audience devotes to listening to you. Here are some titles of actual speeches that deal with worthwhile subjects and promise to say something valuable:

"Who Is Wise?"

"The Five Major Forces Affecting the World Today"

"What Do We Value—How Do We Assure It"

"Today's Problems, Tomorrow's Promise"

"In Theory We Can But in Practice We Can't"

"How the Truth Becomes a Lie"

"Why Can't Government Be Run Like a Business?"

"Three Career Traps for Women"

"Driving Forces in Public Policy"

Each of the above subjects was intended and appropriate for a particular occasion and a particular audience.

EARN THE RIGHT TO SPEAK

Earning the right to speak on a subject implies a competence derived from training and practice in a trade or profession or special knowledge otherwise acquired, such as from research. It was a university president who spoke on "Who Is Wise?" at a college commencement. The president and chief executive officer of an oil company talked about "How the Truth Becomes a Lie" to an audience of petroleum landmen with whom he shared common experience, beliefs and backgrounds. A woman corporation executive with an educational background in psychology and professional experience as a management consultant addressed the American Women in Radio and Television on "Three Career Traps for Women."

An example of a speaker who rises to eloquence when dealing with a cause which enlists his whole heart is Abraham Lincoln. After several years of campaigning against the extension of slavery, he was invited to address a distinguished Republican audience at the Cooper Union in New York City. Eagerly accepting the invitation, he spoke out in earnest for an hour and a half, his words flowing readily and with intense feeling.

Beginning with a long analysis to show that the founding fathers had looked forward to slavery's ultimate extinction, Lincoln then said, "But enough!" Next he directed his stirring message to the Southern people. Here are some excerpts:

> "You consider yourselves a reasonable and a just people; and I consider that in the general qualities of reason and justice you are not inferior to any other people. Still, when you speak of us Republicans, you do so only to denounce us as reptiles, or, at the best, as no better than outlaws. You will grant a hearing to pirates or murderers, but nothing like it to 'Black Republicans'. . . . You say we are sectional . . . You say we are revolutionary, destructive, or something of the sort. . . . You say we have made the slavery question more prominent than it formerly was. . . . You charge that we stir up insurrections among your slaves. . . ."

Lincoln brought up one charge of the Southerners after another and denied each with eloquent responses. Finally, he addressed himself to his fellow Republicans. He cautioned them against yielding to threats from the Southerners and against "groping for some middle ground between the right and the wrong." Concluding his speech eloquently, he said:

> "Neither let us be slandered from our duty by false accusations against us, nor frightened from it by menaces of destruction to the government nor of dungeons to ourselves. Let us have faith that right makes might, and in that faith, let us, to the end, dare to do our duty as we understand it."

Lincoln's Cooper Union speech was so well received that it was reproduced as a campaign document and he was invited to give talks in other Eastern states. Less than three months later he was nominated for president by the Republican convention. Yet before the Cooper Union speech he had not been seriously considered for the nomination.

What did Lincoln put into his Cooper Union speech that made it so eloquent? Why did Horace Greeley, editor and political leader, say, "I do not hesitate to pronounce it the very best political address to which I ever listened—and I have heard some of Daniel Webster's grandest"? Why did H. C. Whitney, an attorney who had ridden the circuit with Lincoln, say, "Lincoln's Cooper Union speech is a far greater intellectual production than the Gettysburg speech"?

Lincoln spoke on a worthwhile subject; he earned the right to talk about it because he had researched the subject; and he had a burning message that compelled him to speak out in earnest. The subject was worthy because the problem of slavery tormented the nation and was the paramount issue of the time.

Three months had elapsed between the invitation to speak and Lincoln's delivery of the speech. During the intervening time he searched through records of congressional proceedings and delved into political history books. Examining many statutes, resolutions, speeches, letters and books on the lives of the founding fathers, he studied the subject with painstaking thoroughness.

Lincoln sought documentary proof and other pertinent information concerning the question Stephen Douglas had raised in a recent speech: What was the attitude of the founding fathers on the control of slavery in the federal territories? Douglas took the position that the federal government was forbidden to control slavery in the territories, but presented no facts to support his contention. Lincoln researched this question, devoted much time thinking about what he found, and concluded the evidence proved the opposite of Douglas' position.

So Lincoln was inspired to speak out in earnest and to buttress his message with an array of facts. After a few introductory remarks at the beginning of his Cooper Union speech, he plunged into the body of his speech with this transitional passage: "Let us now inquire whether the thirty-nine framers of the Constitution, or any of them, ever acted upon this question; and if they did, how they acted upon it."

INFLUENCE OF BOOK READING

Material for eloquent speeches, as in Lincoln's Cooper Union address, comes from knowledge, thinking and inspiration. The objectives of increasing your knowledge, making you think, and inspiring you to speak can all be achieved by reading books. Books influenced Lincoln's thinking on slavery. He read every book he could get because, as he said, "The things I want to know are in books."

Books are only one source of knowledge but they're extremely useful to speakers. You'd be wise to take the advice of Francis Bacon, the English philosopher, who wrote: "Some books are to be tasted, others to be swallowed, and some few to be chewed and digested; that is, some books are to be read only in parts; others to be read, but not curiously; and some few to be read wholly, and with diligence and attention."

Today, books are far more plentiful and easier of access or possession than in Lincoln's time. If you read good books, you'll learn how much knowledge there is in them that we don't use in coping with everyday problems. Many eloquent public speakers owe their success to the reading of books.

Daniel Webster said, "If there is anything in my style or thought to be commended, the credit is due to my kind parents in instilling into my mind an early love of the Scriptures." So often and intently did he read and reread the Bible and other books that he practically memorized them.

Henry Clay, who ranks with the most eloquent speakers, said, "I owe my success in life to one single fact, namely, that at an early age I commenced and continued for some years the practice of daily reading. . . . It is to this that I am indebted for the impulses that have shaped and molded my entire destiny."

Winston Churchill wrote in his autobiography that when he was 22 years old he felt himself "wanting in even the vaguest knowledge about many large spheres of thought . . . So I resolved to read history, philosophy, economics, and things like that."

John Kennedy read books of all kinds including biography, history and fiction.

These are only a few of the outstanding speakers whose reading of books contributed much to their success. Book authors are teachers as well as writers. They open up worlds of learning for their readers by exploring new fields of factual knowledge and providing insights into the human condition. As the English writer Thomas Carlyle said, "All that mankind has done, thought, gained, or been is lying as in magic preservation in the pages of books."

By condensing into a book the knowledge that may have taken a lifetime of study and experience to acquire, the author transfers that knowledge to you in a few hours of reading time. The information you obtain becomes material for your speeches. "A good knowledge of facts," said Churchill, "would arm me with a sharp sword." Reading feeds your mind as it provides food for thought. Perhaps that's why the English writer Charles Lamb said he felt like saying grace as much before reading as before eating.

STRETCHING THE MIND

Using the knowledge you get from books makes you think because it sets your mind working as you exercise your powers of reflection and judgment. Such exercising stretches your mind and sharpens your viewpoints. Churchill said, referring to his reading, "I hope by a persevering continuance of this practice to build up a scaffolding of logical and consistent views which will perhaps tend to the creation of a logical and consistent mind."

Besides the knowledge and thinking benefits, book reading provides inspiration. The same urges that stirred the authors to write can motivate you to speak out.

Mahatma Gandhi, Hindu nationalist leader, said that his reading of Henry Thoreau's *Civil Disobedience* left such a "deep impression" on him that he felt impelled to know more of Thoreau. So Gandhi looked up his other writings and read them "with great pleasure and equal profit." Adopting "civil disobedience" as his motto and technique for protest, Gandhi gave speeches to thousands of his followers and led them to success in their crusade for India's independence from British rule.

Thoreau's *Civil Disobedience* also influenced the civil rights leader Martin Luther King, Jr., who first read it in college. In his book, *Stride Toward Freedom,* King wrote, "Fascinated by the idea of refusing to cooperate with an evil system, I was so deeply moved that I reread the work several times. This was my first intellectual contact with the theory of nonviolent resistance." Later, talking about boycotting segregated buses, King said, "I became convinced that what we were preparing to do in Montgomery (Alabama) was related to what Thoreau had expressed . . . From this moment on I conceived of our movement as an act of massive noncooperation." King and his eloquent speeches turned local protests into nationwide concern for civil rights legislation.

FINDING TIME TO READ

Even though you may agree that reading can help you make better speeches, you may wonder how busy people find time to read. Theodore Roosevelt carried a small library with him on his speechmaking tours. As a result he managed to read a book almost every day. The British orators William Gladstone and Edmund Burke always carried a book, ready for reading during spare moments. Lincoln had the same habit. When plowing, while the horses rested, he perched on the rail fence and read a book. In the store where he clerked, he read when not waiting on customers. As president he continued to use bits of time for reading books. The eloquent American orator Henry Ward Beecher, during his lecture tours, always toted a black bag containing books which he read on the train. John Kennedy read books on plane trips and elsewhere whenever he could.

If you always carry a book or have one handy at home and office, you can turn into productive time the snippets of time that most of us waste. For example, when we have nothing to do during waiting periods, we tend to do just that—nothing. Instead, you can read a book while waiting for and traveling on planes, trains and buses, waiting in reception rooms of doctors, dentists and lawyers, and sitting in the barber shop or beauty salon. If you prefer, reserve a special time for reading books before you go to bed or when you get up. During the day, read at lunchtime or substitute reading breaks for coffee breaks. If you keep a book nearby, you'll easily find 30 minutes every day to read it, no matter how busy you are. And if your reading speed is average, you'll find you're reading a full book a week. That adds up to a lot of books for just minutes a day!

RESEARCH TO FILL GAPS

You may need material from sources other than books to fill in the gaps in your speech material and to make sure your information is accurate as well as up-to-date. Consult magazines, newspapers and other references in the public library. Look up encyclopedias, almanacs and the *Reader's Guide to Periodical Literature,* which lists most of the magazine articles published in the United States.

Phonograph discs and cassettes are available for acquiring knowledge as well as for stimulating thinking and speaking. Also obtainable are recordings of eloquent speeches taped either by the original speaker or by actors.

The reference librarian in your public library will help you locate the most profitable reading and recordings for your purposes. Although research is a necessary ingredient in eloquent speechmaking, don't dig down so deeply that you reach bedrock. Winston K. Pendleton, humorous-inspirational speaker, tells this story: "The other day a little girl went to the library and said to the librarian, 'I want to know something about the Ming Dynasty for school. Can you help me, please?' The librarian said she would be glad to help. After about 20 minutes, she had assembled a stack of books about two feet high. 'There,' she said, 'that will tell you all about the Ming Dynasty'. 'Thank you very much,' the little girl said, 'but I don't want to know that much about it'."

Whatever your subject, there's probably too much material available. So don't get bogged down in research. Determine how extensive your subject is. Will you go into it deeply, just hit the high spots or merely limit yourself to a facet or two? Generally, you'd be wise to narrow your topic. Think through what you already know about the subject. Go over it in your mind at many intervals for several days or weeks, as time allows. Dwell on it wherever and whenever you can. You'll be surprised at the ideas you'll come up with when you feed your thoughts into the pressure cooker of your subconscious mind.

Then focus on the facts you need to support your ideas. Instead of collecting data indiscriminately, zero in on what you're looking for. You may still gather more material than you'll need or use. If so, you can then choose what suits your purpose best. Arrange your collected notes in some organized manner on cards or loose sheets. This enables you to shuffle the notes later when you analyze your accumulated facts and begin to carve your speech into shape.

USING PERSONAL EXPERIENCES

Diligent research and careful thinking are not the only ways you can create material for eloquent speeches. You can also draw subject matter from your personal experiences. As William Jennings Bryan once said, "One can only be eloquent if he talks with enthusiasm about something he knows a lot about." You certainly know a lot about what you have personally lived through. That gives you a built-in subject, requiring little research or thinking.

Based on personal experiences, the speech material grows within you. Having lived with your subject, you can talk with sincerity and genuine feeling. You believe in what you say and you're involved in it firsthand. Bryan also said, "A speaker should not speak from the top of his head, but from the bottom of his heart. He must be tremendously enthused about worthwhile subjects, concerning which he is thoroughly informed."

Sojourner Truth, an American pioneer woman orator, was a former slave who never learned to read or write. But speaking from personal experiences, she spoke with emotional conviction. She lived the things she talked about, so her intense feeling flowed readily into oral expression. Her deeply felt thoughts displayed sincerity and earnest devotion without any reservation or misgiving.

Speaking out for women's rights as well as against slavery, she joined the abolitionist crusade as a featured speaker and stumped the country. Attempts by mobs to silence her only spurred her on. A common argument in her day was that woman's physical frailty made it impossible for her to do a man's work. A tall and muscular woman with a deep voice, she thundered:

> "Nobody ever helps me into carriages or over mud-puddles . . . And ain't I a woman? . . . Look at my arm! I have ploughed, and planted, and gathered into barns, and no man could head me! And ain't I a woman? I could work as much and eat as much as a man—when I could get it—and bear the lash as well! And ain't I a woman? I have borne 13 children, and seen most of 'em sold off into slavery, and when I cried out with my mother's grief, none but Jesus heard me! And ain't I a woman?"

When Sojourner Truth spoke, eyewitnesses observed that even the most unruly hecklers quieted down to listen. One eyewitness said "she turned the sneers and jeers of an excited crowd into notes of respect and admiration." Her eloquence as a speaker sometimes rivaled that of Frederick Douglass, who was a great 19th-century orator and with whom she often shared the public platform.

Douglass also was born a slave and had no educational background. As a household servant at age 9 he learned to read but at age 16 was returned to his plantation home as a field hand. When he was 21 he escaped to the North and devoted his leisure time to reading books as a means towards self-education.

Three years later Douglass delivered a speech at a meeting of the Massachusetts Anti-Slavery Society, which hired him as an agent. Within a few years he became an orator of exceptional eloquence. When he spoke on the agony of being a slave, he drew his speech material from personal experiences and twisted his face as if he were still feeling the pain. Here are excerpts from a speech to the citizens of Rochester, New York, at a Fourth of July celebration:

> "Am I to argue that it is wrong to make men brutes, to rob them of their liberty, to work them without wages, to keep them ignorant of their relations to their fellow men, to beat them with sticks, to flay their flesh with the lash, to load their limbs with irons, to hunt them with dogs, to sell them at auction, to sunder their families, to knock out their teeth, to burn their flesh, to starve them into obedi-

ence and submission to their masters? Must I argue that a system thus marked with blood and stained with pollution is wrong? No; I will not.

"What, then, remains to be argued? . . . At a time like this, scorching irony, not convincing argument, is needed . . . What to the American slave is your Fourth of July? I answer, a day that reveals to him more than all other days of the year, the gross injustice and cruelty to which he is the constant victim. To him your celebration is a sham; your boasted liberty an unholy license; your national greatness, swelling vanity. Your sounds of rejoicing are empty and heartless; your denunciation of tyrants, brass-fronted impudence; your shouts of liberty and equality, hollow mockery. Your prayers and hymns, your sermons and thanksgivings, with all your religious parade and solemnity, are to him mere bombast, fraud, deception, impiety, and hypocrisy—a thin veil to cover up crimes which would disgrace a nation of savages."

SUMMING UP

This chapter has explored the ways you can develop eloquent content for your speech—something you know so well, something you're so much interested in and something you so impatiently desire to talk about to others because you sincerely believe they ought to know.

To repeat briefly, here are points to remember.

Saying something eloquent means speaking:

1. On a worthy subject.
2. On a subject that you've earned the right to talk about because of your background or research.
3. With sincerity and conviction.

Sources of eloquent speech material are:

1. Knowledge.
2. Thinking.
3. Inspiration.

Sources of knowledge, thinking and inspiration are:

1. Books.
2. Magazines and newspapers.
3. Phonograph discs and cassettes.
4. Personal experiences.

CHAPTER 4

Organize What You Say for Eloquent Effects

WINSTON CHURCHILL ONCE COMPLAINED TO A WAITER about a dessert, saying, "This pudding has no theme." Churchill didn't like a mass of mushy, shapeless food. That's how he felt about speeches that seem like jellyfish, lacking firm structures and skipping from one thing to another. He believed the speaker should develop a theme by compactly assembling "a series of facts . . . brought forward, all pointing in a common direction." That is, a speech must hang together, with its material solidly connected. In a half-century of eloquent speechmaking, Churchill always fashioned each speech in an orderly and structured whole.

Nothing that you do when preparing a speech is more important than the way you arrange your ideas. Take these words, for example: material it be to speech must understand organized. Confusing? Sounds like gibberish? Yes, but you easily recognize each word. Besides, there's a real, intelligible message in that group of words. But lack of proper arrangement hides it. The message is unmistakable after you go through those garbled words and rearrange them like this: speech material must be organized to understand it.

Clearly, order is necessary if words are to make sense. Unless the words are fitted together in the proper sequence, the sentence means nothing. If single sentences require order, so must a whole speech. Listeners must depend on you to make them understand. It's not up to them to sort out your ideas. Nor can they interrupt you to say, "Wait a minute. I don't understand what you're saying."

To organize ideas for a speech is to put them into shapes that an audience can recognize. John Ruskin, the English writer and critic, said: "Composition means, literally and simply, putting several things together, so as to make one thing out of them . . . Thus a musician composes an air, by putting notes together in certain relations; a poet composes a poem, by putting his thoughts and words in pleasant order . . ."

ARRANGE IDEAS FOR EASY LISTENING

So it is with a public speaker. What you say should be organized for understanding. Your ideas should be arranged to make it easy for listeners to follow you. Otherwise, it's easy enough for them to tune you out, even though they may have to stay in their seats.

The philosopher and writer George Santayana once said the human mind is not rich enough to drive many horses abreast and wants "one general scheme, under which it strives to bring everything." Aware of the power of "scheme," which comes from the Latin word "schema" meaning "shape," Santayana and other philosophers think of "scheme" as a system, the careful grouping of items to form a unified whole. No speech can win audiences unless it's in good shape, that is, well-organized.

Organizing a speech is like cooking a dinner. Just as a dinner begins with an appetizer to whet the diner's appetite, so should the introduction of your speech lift up your listeners' ears and excite their desire to hear more. As a mixture of spices adds zest to the diner's appetizer, a blend of attention-grabbing remarks makes listeners eager to hear what you say next.

Like the entree of a dinner, the body of a speech is the main course—the substance. Organizing a speech relates to its substance just as cooking does to food. The cook takes raw food and makes it edible and tasty. The speaker takes mere facts and analyzes them—discovers patterns, detects similarities and differences, traces effects to causes, shows relationships, and forms opinions. Speech material should be presented in a logical arrangement so it flows smoothly in a forward direction.

LIMIT YOUR MATERIAL

But as in dining, don't bite off more than you—and your listeners—can chew. Limit your material to what's necessary to develop your story. Support your ideas with just enough details and examples to make yourself clear. Too much may give your audience mental indigestion. Be as considerate as the hostess who sees to it that her dinner guests don't become bloated.

The conclusion of a speech is like the dessert in a dinner. Both should be zestful. The dessert is the taste people leave the table with and a speaker's last words are what the listeners remember longest. To avoid having the dinner guest feel overfed, the dessert is a small portion. Similarly, a speech ending should generally be short. And just as the dessert is flavorful to the palate of diners, a speech conclusion should be sharp and stimulating to the senses of your listeners.

As a cook rates bravos for a delicious dinner, the speaker merits resounding applause for an eloquent speech. But a fine speech, like a tasty dinner, can't be hastily thrown together. Both the speech and the dinner demand careful planning and preparation. All three parts of a speech—introduction, body and conclusion—are so important that each part deserves a chapter of its own. Ingredients for the introduction of a speech will be described and illustrated in Chapter 5 and for the conclusion in Chapter 6. The rest of this chapter will discuss, with examples, various techniques for organizing the body of a speech.

You may ask, "Why not take the introduction first? After all, that's the beginning of the speech." True, the introduction comes first when you deliver the speech but not when you prepare it. Before you introduce your talk, you must see how you'll develop it. How can you introduce something until you know what it is? The body is about 80 percent or 85 percent of the total speech. All the main points and subpoints by which you explain or support your central theme are in the body. Until you know specifically what the body will contain, it's neither practical nor wise to develop the introduction or conclusion.

After you've identified and organized the main ideas and subpoints in the body, then is the logical time to work on the introduction. Then you'll have an easy time not only with the introduction but also with the conclusion.

The great Roman orator Cicero suggested this procedure 2,000 years ago, and many of today's public speakers agree with him. Here's what Cicero said: "When the point for decision and the argument which must be devised for the purpose of reaching a decision have been diligently discovered by the rules of art, and studied with careful thought, then, and not until then, the other parts of the oration are to be arranged in proper order."

Chapter 3 showed you how to develop the content of your speech. Through thinking and research, you've gathered a mass of raw material, just as the cook assembles the ingredients listed in recipes. As the cook transforms the ingredients into a tasty dinner, you must now fit your material into a shape that your audience can understand and find interesting. Merely stating cold facts and figures can make a speech dull. Cooks say a recipe by itself won't necessarily produce a delicious dish. The ingredients must be skillfully mixed. Proper use of herbs or spices can change a tasteless fish into a gourmet's delight.

APPROACH DEPENDS ON YOUR PURPOSE

Likewise, a successful speech depends not only on the material you use but also on how well you put it together. The approach you'll take in presenting your subject depends on your purpose. The same subject can be handled in different ways.

Suppose your subject is scuba diving. If you want to inform, you'll tell about such things as the self-contained underwater breathing apparatus, from which the acronym "scuba" is derived. You'll discuss other necessary gear, location of suitable diving spots, availability of lessons by professional instructors, and how to organize a scuba diving club. You'll also cover the hazards involved and ways to prevent accidents. If you aim to entertain, you'll talk about some amusing incidents that happened to you or others while scuba diving. If your purpose is to persuade, you'll describe the thrills of scuba diving and why it's the hobby of millions of people in the United States.

Many different methods exist for constructing a speech, but all must show unity, coherence and emphasis. Your speech has unity when you choose a theme and develop it by selecting and arranging your material for a single impression. Only one central thought should prevail. Everything else must relate to it and move smoothly and easily in the direction of achieving the single impression. This singleness of purpose gives your speech the quality of unity.

Coherence is the glue that holds together all the materials of a speech. As ideas are expressed one after the other, coherence cements them. Just as mortar makes bricks or stones stick together in building construction, coherence locks together ideas and sentences in the framework of a speech. By providing continuity, coherence takes your audience step by step, moving straight ahead and erecting bridges from one point to another with connecting statements, such as "That's the first point; here's another," "By way of contrast," or "Now let's consider." Such transitional phrases and sentences hook ideas together and make it easy for listeners to follow the sequence of your material as well as understand the relationship between what you've said and what you're going to say next.

You get emphasis in a speech by making something stand out like a lighted match on a blacked-out stage. In no speech are all the points equally important. Some are more important than others, even among the secondary thoughts or supporting details. Naturally you want your strongest points to attract special attention.

POINTING OUT HIGHLIGHTS

As a speaker you view the aspects of your subject in their true relations to each other. You want your audience to view them from the same perspective. To make sure this happens, you can use three structural elements, each of which serves as an index finger that points out highlights:

1. Add more material to develop the ideas you want to spotlight. Listeners are likely to remember what you talk about most.

2. Place the items you want emphasized at the beginning or end of the body of your speech. The same technique applies to the other parts of a speech—to words in a sentence, to segments of the speech and to the whole speech itself. The first and last words seem to stick longest in the minds of the listeners.

3. Vary the normal sequence. Listeners tend to notice and remember unusual structuring. A sentence, for example, usually goes from subject to verb to object. But in one of Winston Churchill's wartime speeches, he spoke of destroying the Nazi regime and then he said, "From this nothing will turn us." The usual order of the sentence would be "Nothing will turn us from this." By transposing the normal sequence he drew special attention to his solemn vow which gained added emphasis. This reverse-order technique applies to other speechmaking situations. For instance, audiences are accustomed to hearing speakers give examples after stating the point. But if you first cite examples and then state your point, the reversed order emphasizes the point.

Keep in mind these principles of unity, coherence and emphasis as you proceed to organize the body of your speech. Review several times the mass of raw material which you have collected for your speech. Then go on as follows:

1. Write a one-sentence statement of your central idea or theme, after asking yourself and answering these questions: "What am I trying

to say? What am I aiming for? What one dominant idea do I want to leave in the minds of my listeners?" You'll be surprised how eloquent your statement will sound if your answers to those questions are carefully thought out and deeply felt. The theme statement is your whole speech in a nutshell. Whether you selected your theme during the process of gathering material or afterwards, and whether you actually express or only imply it when you deliver your speech, write your theme down on paper now. The statement of your theme will prevent you from going in all directions as you develop the body of your speech point by point.

2. Choose from your accumulated material the main ideas by which you expect to explain, expand or support your theme. The body of your speech can develop with ease and effectiveness two to five main points. Three should normally be enough for listeners to get your central idea. Anyway, chances are they won't remember more than three. The main points should be more specific than your theme and each should develop a different aspect of it. List your main points on the same sheet of paper containing the statement of your theme. Leave plenty of blank space between the main ideas for grouping subpoints.

3. Jot down under the main points the subpoints with which you plan to build and support those main ideas. As in the case of your main ideas and for the same reasons, limit the number of subpoints. All your main points and subpoints are lined up on paper as chunks of related material, just as the cook goes to market with a grocery list organized according to meat counter, produce section, frozen foods and canned goods. Your main points and subpoints form the framework or skeleton of the body of your speech.

4. Flesh out the skeleton with supporting materials such as illustrations, specific instances, anecdotes, quotations, and statistics.

5. Decide how to arrange your major and minor points in some kind of a structural sequence which helps listeners to follow, understand and remember what you say. Select your structure from one of the many available patterns of speech organization and then arrange your outlined material around it. Described below are organizational patterns with examples to show how they have been applied in eloquent speeches.

TIME PATTERN

The concept of time is a dominant factor in speech organization as it is in everyday living. You hear many speeches based on the time pattern. Days, months, years and seasons occur in natural and familiar divisions of time. Clocks, calendars and timetables regulate daily life. Everybody is aware of time.

For those reasons, speakers often discuss their subjects from the angles of the past, the present and the future, that is, in a natural sequence of ideas. They say first, "Looking back . . ."; second, "Now, today . . ."; and third, "Looking ahead . . ." In the Gettysburg Address, Lincoln remembers the past, looks at the present and anticipates the future:

> "Four score and seven years *ago* . . .
> "*Now* we are engaged . . .
> "That this nation, under God, *shall* . . ."

Addressing an annual Political Action Committee conference in Washington, D.C., a present-day speaker reviewed the evolution of the American labor movement. He first went back to the beginning of the movement in 1881 and after discussing its current status, he delved into the future of organized labor.

SPACE PATTERN

Like time, space meets us at every turn. By definition, space is where all things exist. Everything occurs in specific places. So your speech material can be arranged according to its relation to space. You may use the space sequence in various ways: North, South, East, West; near to far; left to right; top to bottom; front to back.

You can talk about geographical regions; a visit to a World's Fair or Disney World from one end to the other; the structure of a skyscraper floor by floor; life in urban, suburban, and rural areas; the layouts of cities in terms of downtown, midtown, and uptown segments. Such space patterns systematize the space elements of your speech material and enable audiences to visualize, understand and remember what you tell them.

Albert J. Beveridge, widely known in his time as one of America's great orators, delivered a speech on "The March of the Flag" which gave him national recognition. In that speech he eloquently used the space pattern from East to West to show how the United States expanded from the Atlantic Ocean to the Pacific Ocean.

General Douglas MacArthur, in his famous address to Congress, arranged the middle part of his talk into four geographical divisions: (1) the world; (2) Asia; (3) the Pacific Ocean; and (4) Korea. He began the body of his talk by saying, "The issues are global, and so interlocked that to consider the problems of one sector, oblivious to those of another, is but to court disaster for the whole."

That space pattern enabled MacArthur to narrow down his subject step by step until he could focus his audience's attention on Korea, the heart of his speech. After covering the first three space elements, he went on to the fourth and linked them all together with one unifying sentence that also served as a transition: "With this brief insight into the surrounding areas I now turn to the Korean Conflict."

PROBLEM-CAUSE-SOLUTION PATTERN

The title of the Problem-Cause-Solution pattern suggests the basic structure of the body of your speech:

I. Identification of Problem—What's wrong?
  - A. Importance of Problem—Who gets hurt?
  - B. Causes of Problem
    1. Major cause
    2. Contributing cause
    3. Another contributing cause

II. Solutions
  - A. Possible alternatives
    1. First alternative
    2. Second alternative
    3. Third alternative (speaker's recommendation)
  - B. Reasons for choice of recommended solution
    1. Better than first alternative because . . .
    2. Better than second alternative because . . .

Normally this pattern is used when you advocate a change in the present policy or system of an organized group. Such a group may be your club, city, state or nation. You generate concern by the audience for the problem and then offer a solution that you think will solve it.

One present-day speaker gave a speech on urban crime. He identified the problem as a high crime rate, stating that while the population over a ten-year period increased by 13 percent, serious crimes rose by 148 percent. Granting that the causes are many, he concentrated on one that stands out. He said, "A major reason why is that just when we need more effective law enforcement the courts have set out, generally, to render it impotent." He also said the criminal's judgment is that crime does pay.

Strengthening family life, converting more people to religion, raising the standard of living, and building moral character—all would help discourage crime, but such conditions would take years to develop, the speaker pointed out. So he recommended changing the present system of criminal justice to cope with the rising crime rate. His solution consisted of ten points, some requiring court approval and others legislative action. His reason for the proposals, he said, is "that they make it much, much easier to convict the guilty and thereby protect the rights of the innocent."

ILLUSTRATION PATTERN

Organizing the body of a speech around illustrations means supporting each main point with one or more examples. Most public speakers would agree with Lincoln who said that people are "more easily influenced and informed by illustrations than in any other way." The great American orator Henry Ward Beecher once said, "Illustrations are as natural to me as breathing."

Examples clarify ideas and make them stick in the memory of the audience. Listeners remember the illustration which brings back to mind the point that the speaker made. They can easily forget an idea but carry away the example which recalls the idea. That's because an illustration creates a more vivid and concrete impression than the idea to which it relates.

You can use both real and hypothetical illustrations. The real ones carry more conviction because they tell what actually happened, while the hypothetical examples tell what may or could happen. Norman Vincent Peale says, "The true example is the finest method I know of to make an idea clear, interesting, and persuasive." Sometimes, however, no matter how hard you try, you just can't find appropriate factual examples. Then you invent illustrations that suit your purpose. Of course, when using fictitious examples, begin them with "Suppose . . ." or "If . . ." to make clear you dreamed them up. As for factual illustrations, you can choose either historical examples familiar to your audience or specific instances drawn from daily life.

Sometimes you want to explain only a single idea in a speech. Then all you need is a series of illustrations to clarify and amplify your idea. This type of organization is found in Russell Conwell's "Acres of Diamonds" speech which brought him fame and wealth. An eloquent inspirational talk, its single idea is that opportunity is in your own backyard.

To explain this idea, Conwell provides a series of illustrations which he draws from real life. With true stories he tells how all men and women can achieve success. He begins with the story of a man who sold his farm to travel all over the world searching for a diamond mine which he never found. Later, one was found underneath his farm. Had he stayed home he could have had acres of diamonds. All he had to do was dig for them in his own backyard. Conwell's examples constitute a string of beads, tied together with transitional sentences that say in effect, "Here's another illustration."

Organizing the body of a speech with one illustration after another gives you several advantages:

1. Adds strength and comprehensiveness to your single idea.

2. Provides you with an exceedingly simple structure that's easy for you to develop and easy for your audience to follow.

3. Lends itself to occasions of various time limits, making it easy to lengthen or shorten your speech by merely adding or omitting illustrations without affecting in any way its structure.

EXTENDED COMPARISON PATTERN

The extended comparison pattern involves comparing two ideas, processes, organizations, objects, events or whatever by drawing a series of parallels between them. This requires building the entire body of your speech around the parallels, examining or noting the similarities and drawing inferences from them.

Working out a somewhat detailed comparison between the idea you're proposing and the one you're comparing it with, identifies the features of each and in effect places the two concepts side by side. You tell about Idea A, the theme of your speech. You tell about Idea B. Then you compare Ideas A and B point by point. By matching your Idea A with Idea B at a number of points, you multiply and intensify the effect. Because such an extended comparison includes specific references, it anchors an idea firmly in the minds of your listeners and makes it easy for them to remember it.

Many speakers have discovered the power of the extended comparison pattern in building the body of their speeches. The eloquent speaker Henry Ward Beecher said, "I have seen an audience, time and again, follow an argument doubtfully, laboriously, almost suspiciously, and look at one another as much as to say, 'Is he going right?' until the place is arrived at where the speaker says, 'It is like—' and then they listen eagerly for what it is like. . ."

Shakespeare made eloquent use of the extended comparison pattern in his play, *The Life of King Henry V*, in which he composed a speech for the Archbishop of Canterbury based entirely on an elaborate comparison between a human society and a beehive. Shakespeare's theme in the Archbishop's speech is that in any organized community, definite divisions of authority, responsibility and function must exist. To get this idea across, the speech compares a community of people headed by a monarch with a colony of honeybees. Shakespeare could have used a metaphor or simile. But those techniques draw only a single comparison. By using the extended analogy, he compares at many points and in concrete terms the state of man with the commonwealth of honeybees.

Asserting that heaven divides "The state of man in diverse functions, setting endeavor in continual motion," the Archibishop continues: "So work the honeybees, creatures that by a rule in nature teach the act of order to a peopled kingdom." This excerpt is merely a small portion of the speech. In a series of parallels, the Archbishop says, for example, that in both kinds of societies there are officers, soldiers, magistrates, merchants and workers. The detailed comparison helps listeners to visualize and understand the multiple relationships. The analogy not only clarifies the idea but also fixes it in the audience's memory.

Booker T. Washington, a former slave who became an eloquent speaker, organized the body of his speech at the Cotton States Exposition in Atlanta by comparing his subject of race relations with a ship lost at sea:

> "A ship lost at sea for many days suddenly sighted a friendly vessel. From the mast of the unfortunate vessel was seen a signal: 'Water, water; we die of thirst!' The answer from the friendly vessel at once came back: 'Cast down your bucket where you are.' The captain of the distressed vessel . . . cast down his bucket, and it came up full of fresh, sparkling water from the mouth of the Amazon River.
>
> "To those of my race . . . I would say: 'Cast down your bucket where you are—cast it down in making friends, in every manly way, of the people of all races by whom we are surrounded . . .'
>
> "To those of the white race . . . I would repeat what I say to my

own race, 'Cast down your bucket among those people who have without strikes and labor wars tilled your fields, cleared your forests, built your railroads and cities, brought forth treasures from the bowels of the earth, and helped make possible this magnificent representation of the progress of the South . . .'"

With his extended analogy of the lost ship, Booker Washington created a powerful speech as he urged his audience to cast down their buckets among the people of all races.

Franklin D. Roosevelt, in one of his eloquent speeches, compared the United States Government with

> "a three-horse team provided by the Constitution to the American people so that their field might be plowed. The three horses are, of course, the three branches of government—the Congress, the Executive, and the Courts. Two of the horses are pulling in unison today; the third is not. Those who have intimated that the President of the United States is trying to drive that team, overlook the simple fact that the President, as Chief Executive, is himself one of the three horses. It is the American people themselves who are in the driver's seat. It is the American people themselves who want the furrow plowed. It is the American people themselves who expect the third horse to pull in unison with the other two."

As you can see from the above examples, building the body of your speech around an extended comparison gives power to your central theme by making it impressively clear and vivid.

LOGICAL PATTERN

By definition, "logical" means arriving at conclusions or inferences reasonably drawn from events or circumstances. You can organize the body of your speech around a few main ideas, using them to argue for your proposition and supporting each by two or more subpoints.

The logical pattern is broad enough to cover almost all speeches that aim to persuade. Tell your audience where you stand on an issue and then justify or support it with logical thoughts. Here are five methods of logical thinking:

1. Cause and effect

In organizing the body of your speech by cause-and-effect reasoning, describe the factors or events that explain some result. Developing a subject by the cause-and-effect sequence implies that a relationship exists between the factors or events involved, as in these examples:

a. Reading many good books (*cause*) makes a person well-educated (*effect*).

b. Large numbers of people moving to the suburbs (*cause*) brought about the decline of American cities (*effect*).

Cause-and-effect reasoning is logical when the assumed cause is sufficient to create the effect you claim. Remember, however, that sometimes it's difficult, if not impossible, to talk about relationships between a single cause and a single effect. The effect produced might be traced to many causes. In such cases, select the one that stands out as a cause but don't claim it as the only cause.

2. Deductive logic

This method is reasoning from the general to the specific, reaching a logically necessary conclusion from facts or propositions, as in this example: All virtues are praiseworthy; honesty is a virtue; therefore, honesty is praiseworthy. The first two propositions imply the third proposition, which is the logical conclusion.

Susan B. Anthony used deductive logic in her speech "On Woman's Right to Suffrage." Delivered over a century ago, that speech is as eloquent today as it was then because it's a timeless model of organizational structure and logical analysis.

Starting the body of her speech with a quotation from the preamble to the U.S. Constitution, Anthony plunged into a chain of reasoning based on facts and logic. She emphasized that "It was we, the people, not we, the white male citizens, nor yet we, the male citizens, but we, the whole people . . . women as well as men who formed the Union."

Essentially, Anthony's deductive reasoning took this form:

First premise: The National Constitution guarantees all U.S. citizens the right to vote.

Second premise: Women are U.S. citizens.

Third premise: Women have the right to vote.

That kind of deductive logic, called "syllogism" by Aristotle who first formulated it over 2,000 years ago, has been the core of Western logical thought ever since.

3. Inductive logic

This method of reasoning is the opposite of deductive logic. Inductive logic moves from the specific to the general. From specific instances you draw a general conclusion. For example, you see the sun rise and set day after day. Since the beginning of time the sun has been rising and setting every day. From these specific observations you can therefore logically generalize or conclude that "The sun rises and sets every day."

4. Analogy

Logically, the analogy compares one idea or object with another by assuming that:

a. If two or more things are the same in some respects, then they must be the same in other respects.

b. Similar causes produce similar effects.

Although the analogy compares things which are unlike in appearance, class or substance, it draws attention to likeness in relationships. For example, speakers and writers compare human society with the animal kingdom. Abraham Lincoln, in his Cooper Union speech, eloquently used the analogy of the highwayman to answer the secessionists:

> "Under all these circumstances, do you really feel yourselves justified to break up this government, unless such a court decision as yours is, shall be at once submitted to as a conclusive and final rule of political action? But you will not abide the election of a Republican president! In that supposed event, you say, you will destroy the Union; and then, you say, the great crime of having destroyed it will be upon us! That is cool. A highwayman holds a pistol to my ear, and mutters through his teeth, 'Stand and deliver, or I shall kill you, and then you will be a murderer!'"

5. Dilemma

In logic, the dilemma is an effective method of disproving something. By presenting alternatives equally unsatisfactory to an opponent, the dilemma applies logical proof that puts the adversary into a very weak position. Using the dilemma in his Cooper Union speech, Lincoln eloquently demolished the charge of the Southern leaders:

"You charge that we stir up insurrections among your slaves. We deny it; and what is your proof? Harper's Ferry! John Brown! John Brown was no Republican; and you have failed to implicate a single Republican in his Harper's Ferry enterprise. If any member of our party is guilty in that matter, you know it or you do not know it. If you do know it, you are inexcusable for not designating the man and proving the fact. If you do not know it, you are inexcusable for asserting it, and especially for persisting in the assertion after you have tried and failed to make the proof. You need not be told that persisting in a charge which one does not know to be true, is simply malicious slander."

PSYCHOLOGICAL PATTERN

This method of organizing the body of a speech is useful when dealing with an audience whose attitude is unknown or hostile. In such cases, arrange ideas in the sequence of acceptability by the audience. Begin with points of agreement, starting with the most acceptable, then the next most acceptable, and continue in the same way until you gradually lead your listeners into an approving state of mind by the time you reach the controversial points.

This sequence of organizing your points provides you with a powerful approach in directing the will or mind of the audience toward a mental atmosphere that's favorable to your purpose. In his play *Julius Caesar* Shakespeare wrote an eloquent speech for Mark Antony which illustrates the power of the psychological pattern in speechmaking. Just before Antony delivers this speech, Marcus Brutus speaks to the same audience and on the same subject.

In an earnest, straightforward speech organized on a logical pattern, Brutus says he killed Caesar for plotting to make himself an absolute dictator of Rome. Pointing out that Caesar was his best friend, Brutus defends the assassination as a sacrifice in the cause of freedom. He says, "As he was ambitious, I slew him . . . for the good of Rome" and asks, "Hath you rather Caesar were living, and die all slaves, than that Caesar were dead, to live all free men?"

By the end of his speech, Brutus has convinced his fellow citizens he acted with reason and justice. Some of them say, "This Caesar was a tyrant," "We are blest that Rome is rid of him," "'Twere best Antony speak no harm of Brutus here!"

That puts Antony in a tough situation. He wants to condemn Brutus as a traitor. But how can he do it? What does Shakespeare do?

He has Antony deliver a speech based on the psychological pattern. As Antony begins, "You gentle Romans—" he's drowned out by the hostile audience. He tries again, "Friends, Romans, countrymen, lend me your ears. I come to bury Caesar, not to praise him." Now the audience is quiet and pays attention because he starts with a point of agreement totally acceptable to the audience. Then Antony says, "The evil that men do lives after them. The good is oft interred with their bones; so let it be with Caesar." That's the next most acceptable point of agreement with the citizens, who nod as if to say, "You're right, let's bury Caesar and forget him!"

Antony continues, "The noble Brutus hath told you Caesar was ambitious. If it were so, it was a grievous fault, and grievously hath Caesar answered it." Note Antony's phrase "if it were so" with which he repeats what Brutus charged against Caesar. Not actually conceding Caesar was ambitious, Antony agrees that if he were, then he was open to blame and paid the penalty for it.

You see, Antony continues to express himself in a conciliatory fashion, which lets the citizens agree with him without his admitting any wrongdoing by Caesar and without attacking Brutus. In reminding the audience that Brutus said Caesar was ambitious, Antony adds, "And Brutus is an honorable man." Antony continues with a series of incidents about Caesar, each indicating he wasn't ambitious.

For example, Antony speaks of a generous act of Caesar's for the public good and rhetorically asks if that's what a power-seeking man would do. After citing each instance, Antony uses as a refrain variations of such questions or statements as "Did this in Caesar seem ambitious?," "Yet Brutus says he was ambitious," "And Brutus is an honorable man."

By each statement or question Antony conditions his listeners to agree with him. Cleverly stringing together short, concrete words, he lets them flow like a stream into the ears of his listeners. That makes him sound spontaneous and unpretentious. Then he says, "I speak not to disprove what Brutus spoke, but here I am to speak what I do know." In other words, Antony speaks the truth and Brutus lied.

The psychological leverage in Antony's speech is built up gradually through his series of points carefully sequenced to turn the citizens against Brutus and toward himself. By the time Antony finishes his talk, he has aroused their moral indignation and has led them to conclude that Caesar was grossly wronged and Brutus is both a liar and a traitor. By arranging his speech in the psychological pattern, Antony achieved his purpose.

TOPICAL PATTERN

When your speech material cannot be arranged easily and conveniently in any other sequence, use the topical pattern for developing the body of your speech. Books are classified by topics in libraries. The "yellow pages" of the telephone directory classify commercial, professional, and special services by topics. The supermarket arranges its merchandise by cereal products, soft drinks, cleaning products, fresh produce, baked goods, canned goods, and frozen foods, which in turn are grouped as fish, meat, vegetables and fruit juices.

Topical sequence is adaptable for all types of speeches. The natural or conventional divisions of many subjects provide the organization. As you cut a whole pie into portions for serving, you can divide almost any general subject into groups for presentation. Just as it makes no difference which wedge of the cut pie you pick up first, so it doesn't matter which classified group in your speech you take up first.

You simply break up the subject into a series of main points. Phases of a subject may be classified as political, economic, educational, philosophical, or social. If your subject is clothing, you can organize the body of your speech under "material," "workmanship," "style," and "cost." The topics give you and your audience the mental pegs from which a speech can hang.

In a speech on Lincoln's birthday observance, Ralph Y. McGinnis asked, "What did Abraham Lincoln stand for?" and answered his question by analyzing Lincoln's qualities. Using the topical pattern, McGinnis classified Lincoln's qualities in the following groups:

1. Personal Character
    a. Truth
    b. Ethical Conduct
    c. Initiative
    d. Responsibility
2. Intellectual Capacities
    a. Intelligence
    b. Constitutional Government
    c. Economic Free Enterprise
3. Emotional Nature
    a. Belief in Freedom
    b. Belief in God
    c. Forgiveness

The above outline constituted the body of the speech. Each quality was developed and illustrated by incidents and anecdotes from Lincoln's life or quotations from his speeches and letters.

A BRIEF WRAP-UP

The ideas in your speech should be arranged to make it easy for your audience to follow you as you talk.

First, organize the body of your speech. Then develop the introduction and the conclusion.

Keep in mind the principles of unity, coherence and emphasis as you organize the body of your speech in one or more of the following techniques:

1. Time Pattern
2. Space Pattern
3. Problem-Cause-Solution Pattern
4. Illustration
5. Extended Comparison Pattern
6. Logical Pattern, using one or more of the processes of logical thinking, namely:
    a. Cause and Effect
    b. Deductive Logic
    c. Inductive Logic
    d. Analogy
    e. Dilemma
7. Psychological Pattern
8. Topical Pattern

CHAPTER 5

Excite Your Audience with Eloquent Openings

As YOU LISTEN CAREFULLY TO LIVE OR TAPED SPEECHES or leaf through books of speeches, you may be surprised to notice how dull many speech openings and closings are. Too often, public speakers devote considerable time and effort in preparing the body of their speeches but give little or no thought to how to begin and end them. Yet the first and last sentences of a speech are crucial. They make or break a speech. This observation is confirmed by such proverbs as:

"Well begun is half done."

"The hardest step is over the threshold."

"A good beginning makes a good ending."

"A bad beginning makes a bad ending."

The beginnings and endings of speeches are often left to chance because the speakers expect to think of them on the spur of the moment. When the time arrives, the moment of inspiration fails to come and the result is a weak beginning or closing.

Your speech will have more impact if you plan ahead just how you'll get into and out of your speech. What the Greek philosopher Plato said over 2,000 years ago about arranging and proportioning speech material is as valid today as it was in his time. He said, "Every speech ought to be put together like a living creature, with a body of its own, so as to be neither without head nor without feet, but to have both a middle and extremities, all composed in such sort that they suit each other and the whole."

Keeping in mind Plato's image of a speech consisting of head, body, and feet, you need to plan beforehand the material that goes in the introduction (head), the middle (body), and the conclusion (feet). In addition, you must put together all three parts in the whole speech in such a way that they don't stick out as separate and disconnected segments.

How you begin your speech is as important as a smooth and fast start is to the sprinter. Like the sprinter who must not stumble at the starting block, you must avoid the handicap of a poor introduction. Your preliminary words are the first impression you make on an audience. If you capture attention and interest at the beginning, you're likely to keep your listeners with you until the end. But if you lose them from the start, when they really want to listen, you're letting yourself in for some heavy sledding in trying to get them back.

How to organize the body of a speech was the subject of the preceding chapter. The next chapter will deal with the functions of the conclusion and the various methods of achieving them, along with examples from actual speeches. The rest of this chapter covers the functions of the introduction and describes, with examples, the techniques to use.

In general, the introduction of a speech does the same thing as the words, "Now hear this," which the U.S. Navy uses to begin all shipboard messages. More specifically, the introduction of a speech should perform one or more of the following functions:

ESTABLISH CONTACT WITH AUDIENCE

This means more than just getting attention—it also means tuning the audience into the speech. After the chairman has introduced you as the speaker and announced the title of your speech, the audience naturally will look at you rise and walk to the lectern and even listen to you for a while.

In the first or second minute of a speech almost everybody in the audience yields attention to the speaker. But such voluntary attention won't last long if you take it for granted. Soon your listeners will sit back and let their attention drift to daydreaming or let their minds turn to personal matters unless you say something that rivets their attention to you. Or they may pay attention on a low level, that is, no more than a bare minimum required by common courtesy.

People normally are vitally interested in their personal and family affairs. They may be only little concerned with the issues which public speakers usually deal with in their speeches. You should want more than the mild attention audiences voluntarily give speakers at the start of their talks. Your aim is to intensify that attention with a vivid or forceful introduction that will transform indifference into aroused interest. You do that by saying something that grabs their attention and makes them eager to hear more.

ENLIST GOODWILL

Here again mere attention is not enough. Like the goodwill of a business establishment, the introduction of your speech should form a friendly relationship between you and your listeners. The idea is to quickly get on a common footing with them. They will give you a willing ear if you establish yourself in their good graces. Warm up to them and they in turn will feel the same toward you.

AROUSE INTEREST IN THE SUBJECT

If you show your listeners how your subject relates to their needs, you'll motivate them to listen to you. Psychologists say these are basic needs: survival (food, drink, sleep, shelter); safety (freedom from crime and environmental hazards); social (love, affection, and identification with groups); esteem (desire for respect); self-actualization (self-improvement and realization of one's potentialities). If your subject satisfies some such need in your listeners, they will pay attention eagerly and respond readily.

LAY THE GROUNDWORK FOR THE BODY

Give the audience a preview or bird's-eye-view of your subject. Lay the groundwork for what will follow the introduction. Tell where you're going in your talk and how you're going to get there. Lead the listeners naturally into the body of your speech. Sometimes you can do this by saying exactly what aspects of the subject you will take up.

SET THE TONE

Tone is your attitude or feelings toward the subject of your speech and tends to work on your listeners so as to induce a similar reaction on their part. Whether your attitude or feelings are serious, humorous, outraged, jubilant, casual, or otherwise, your first few words in the introduction of your speech set the tone for what is to follow.

You begin your speech by saying, in effect, "I feel very strongly about this matter because it affects the lives of all of us" or "I'm glad to be here, but I might just as well be perfectly frank with you—I'd much rather be somewhere else."

To help you set the tone of your speech, ask yourself some basic questions: "Am I primarily giving information to the audience?" "Am I trying to persuade the audience to accept my point of view?" "Am I urging action?" "Am I trying to entertain?" Establish whatever tone is required but be sure it's appropriate to both your subject and your attitude toward it.

For example, when Lincoln began his Gettysburg Address with the Biblical phrase, "Four score and seven years ago . . ." he set a dignified tone in keeping with the nature of the solemn occasion—dedicating the battlefield's use as a burial ground. Adlai Stevenson likewise set the tone for his tribute to Winston Churchill at the memorial service in Washington, D.C. with this opening sentence: "Today we meet in sadness to mourn one of the world's greatest citizens."

TECHNIQUES FOR INTRODUCTIONS

The introduction to your speech doesn't have to fulfill all the functions described above. But preliminary remarks of some kind help to get the audience tuned in with the speaker. Imagine yourself changing places with the audience. Think about what would make you, as a listener, sit up and take notice if another speaker were talking on your subject. Ask yourself, "Why should this audience listen to me talk about this topic on this occasion?" The answer to this question will guide you in preparing the introduction to your speech.

Some introductions consist of only one sentence. It could be a plain, straightforward and honest-to-goodness statement of what you're going to say—and still be eloquently expressed. For example, in a speech on fire prevention your introduction might rely on a single rhetorical question, "What would you do if a fire broke out in this room—and the exit door wouldn't open?" This short and simple sentence vividly reveals your subject; catches and holds the listeners' attention; pulls them into your speech and stirs them by appealing to their desire for self-preservation; foreshadows what's coming up; and leads you and your audience directly into the body of your speech.

When nominated for president of the United States, Adlai Stevenson opened his acceptance speech with one sentence: "I accept your nomination—and your program."

On the other hand, Henry W. Grady, a Southerner, in his speech "The New South" which he delivered to a Northern audience after the Civil War, devoted almost half of his long speech to the introduction. He faced hostile listeners and had to create a receptive attitude before he could convince them of the rewards to be gained from cooperation instead of antagonism between North and South.

Today's speeches generally don't have long introductions, partly because of radio and television time demands but also because the hectic pace of present-day living makes modern audiences impatient of elaborate introductions. Today's listeners want you to move on quickly to the substance of your speech.

Besides, for a speaker to say too much in the introduction would be like a hostess serving an overfilling appetizer and leaving little room for the main dish. A long introduction may defeat its purpose as it consumes valuable time required for the body, which is the meat of the speech. Yet a short introduction may fail to make the audience receptive to what follows.

How long the introduction should be depends on a number of factors: the occasion; how much time you and your audience have; the relationship between you and the audience; the nature of the subject; and the attitude of the audience toward the subject. Introductions average about 10 percent of the speech, although some eloquent speeches have shorter introductions. No precise length can be prescribed. Let circumstances guide you.

All of the introduction's functions shown above can be woven into a single technique or accomplished by a combination of techniques. The methods of opening a speech are numerous enough to give you plenty of choice. Here are a dozen methods described with examples from actual speeches:

1. Refer to your audience.

You can refer to your audience in three different ways, each of which will surely give you their attention and goodwill:

a. *Establish common ground with the group by personal association.* If you can, identify yourself with your listeners by saying something like, "I once lived right here in your hometown" or "I'm proud to be a member of your profession." Dwight D. Eisenhower realized how such a reference compels an audience to listen when he delivered a speech in Oklahoma. He said, "First, I should like to extend my thanks to the people of Oklahoma for this chance to share in celebrating the fiftieth anniversary of Oklahoma's statehood. Born in the Lone Star State just to your south, and reared in the Sunflower State just to the north, I have tonight a fine feeling of coming home again."

John F. Kennedy began his first State of the Union address to Congress as follows:

> "It is a pleasure to return from whence I came. You are among my oldest friends in Washington and this House is my oldest home. It was here, more than fourteen years ago, that I first took the oath of federal office. It was here, for fourteen years, that I gained both knowledge and inspiration from members of both parties in both houses—from your wise and generous leaders—and from the pronouncements which I can vividly recall, sitting where you now sit—including the programs of two great Presidents, the undimmed eloquence of Churchill, the soaring idealism of Nehru, the steadfast words of General de Gaulle. To speak from this same historic rostrum is a sobering experience. To be back among so many friends is a happy one. I am confident that that friendship will continue."

b. *Pay a compliment to the audience.* When General Douglas MacArthur was fired by President Harry Truman, Congress invited MacArthur to address them in a joint session to give his side of the story. MacArthur began his speech by promptly and eloquently establishing rapport with his audience.

With these opening words, MacArthur recognized the power and prestige of Congress: "I stand on this rostrum with a sense of deep humility and great pride—humility in the wake of those great architects of our history who have stood here before me, pride in the reflection that this forum of legislative debate represents human liberty in the purest form yet devised. Here are centered the hopes and aspirations and faith of the entire human race."

c. *Identify yourself with the special interests of the audience.* Many audiences have common interests, desires and objectives which you can relate to or identify with to gain their attention and goodwill. Say something like "You and I believe in the same things" or "These goals we aim to accomplish together."

In his first campaign for president, Franklin D. Roosevelt delivered one of his best speeches, "The Philosophy of Government," at the Commonwealth Club in San Francisco, California. Right at the beginning Roosevelt identified his own interests with those of the club members who wanted national issues discussed on a nonpartisan basis. Here's how Roosevelt began his speech:

> "I count it a privilege to be invited to address the Commonwealth Club. It has stood in the life of this city and state, and, it is perhaps accurate to add, the nation, as a group of citizen leaders interested in fundamental problems of government and chiefly concerned with achievement of progress in government through nonpartisan means.
>
> "The privilege of addressing you, therefore, in the heat of a political campaign, is great. I want to respond to your courtesy in terms consistent with your policy. I want to speak not of politics but of government. I want to speak not of parties but of universal principles."

2. Refer to the occasion.

Ronald Reagan began his inaugural address as president by referring to the occasion. He said:

> "To a few of us here today this is a solemn and most momentous occasion. And, yet, in the history of our nation it is a commonplace occurrence.
>
> "The orderly transfer of authority as called for in the Constitution routinely takes place as it has for almost two centuries and few of us stop to think how unique we really are.
>
> "In the eyes of many in the world, this every-four-year ceremony we accept as normal is nothing less than a miracle."

You can start many of your speeches by referring to the occasion. By beginning with such a reference, you give the audience a feeling of importance in being there and thus achieve rapport with them. The occasion doesn't have to be of national or international scope to be significant. Any occasion which calls for a speech is important. Audiences expect speakers to recognize holidays, anniversaries, dedications, commencements or other special events where the occasion is the central theme for the entire program.

Giving a commencement address, for example, one speaker began with these words: "I'm genuinely pleased to share with you these important moments in your lives. I'm pleased, first of all, because this ceremony of commencement represents a celebration of one of the most cherished cultural values of the human race—enlightenment. I'm pleased, second, because this ceremony represents for us all an occasion for sober reflection on the deeper meanings of life. And it is to this purpose that I wish to invite your attention for a few moments this morning."

3. Refer to yourself.

When Winston Churchill spoke to a joint session of Congress, he quickly captivated his audience by getting on a common footing with his listeners with a reference to his American ancestry. Here's how he began his speech:

> "I feel greatly honored that you should have invited me to enter the United States Senate Chamber and address the representatives of both branches of Congress. The fact that my American forebears have for so many generations played their part in the life of the United States, and that here I am, an Englishman, welcomed in your midst, makes this experience one of the most moving and thrilling in my life, which is already long and has not been entirely uneventful.
>
> "I wish indeed that my mother, whose memory I cherish across the vale of years, could have been here to see. By the way, I cannot help reflecting that if my father had been American and my mother British, instead of the other way around, I might have got here on my own. In that case, this would not have been the first time you would have heard my voice. In that case, I should not have needed any invitation; but if I had, it is hardly likely it would have been unanimous. So perhaps things are better as they are."

Note in that eloquent introduction Churchill's touches of humor which helped to make his audience warm up to him.

4. Refer to speech title.

A title that indicates both the topic and tone of your speech can serve as an excellent introduction, as it does in a speech by Phyllis Jones Springen. She repeats the title in her introduction to start a chain reaction of ideas that arouses the audience's curiosity and makes them eager to hear more of what she has to say. Here's her introduction:

> "When I was asked to speak on 'The Dimensions of the Oppression of Women,' I laughed. 'Oppression' is such an ugly word. Our

chairman must have been thinking of those Arab countries where women can't vote and where a woman can be forced to marry any man her father selects, but in the United States women are hardly 'oppressed.' But as I began to do my research, I quit laughing. There exists a tremendous amount of legal and economic discrimination against the American woman. Much of it is subtle and, therefore, hard to recognize."

By twice repeating his speech title "What Did Abraham Lincoln Stand For?" in his introduction, Ralph Y. McGinnis previewed what he was going to cover. Here's his introduction:

"If we should ask the question, 'What did Abraham Lincoln stand for?' we might receive a wide variety of answers. And some Americans today might be hard pressed to give any answer, simply because they are too caught up in today's problems to give any attention to yesterday's problems during the American Civil War. Sometimes we fail to realize that the very qualities of character that enabled Abraham Lincoln to solve the problems of his day are the same qualities of character that can help us to solve our problems today.

"What did Abraham Lincoln stand for? To answer this question we might adopt the classical Aristotelian approach of analyzing Lincoln's personal character, his intellectual capacities, and his emotional nature."

5. Refer directly to your subject.

If you know your audience already has a deep interest in your subject, you might just as well plunge into it like a diver off a diving board. Such a direct and swift approach compels the attention and admiration of your audience as it implies the speaker will promptly cover the subject.

For example, when the economist Milton Friedman spoke at Pepperdine University in Los Angeles, California, on "The Future of Capitalism," he began by quickly coming to the point, saying:

"When I speak of the future of capitalism I mean the future of competitive capitalism—a free enterprise capitalism. In a certain sense, every major society is capitalistic. Russia has a great deal of capital but the capital is under the control of governmental officials who are supposedly acting as the agents of the state. That turns capitalism (state capitalism) into a wholly different system than a system under which capital is controlled by individuals in their private capacity as owners and operators of industry. What I want to speak about tonight is the future of private enterprise—of competitive capitalism."

Katherine Graham, board chairman of the Washington Post Company, addressed a group of businessmen and their wives on "The Press and Its Responsibilities." After a bit of witty pleasantry, she speedily switched to her subject and previewed the rest of her speech. Here's her introduction:

> "I am delighted to be here. It is a privilege to address you. And I am especially glad the rules have been bent for tonight, allowing so many of you to bring along your husbands. I think it's nice for them to get out once in a while and see how the other half lives. Gentlemen, we welcome you.
>
> "Actually, I have other reasons for appreciating this chance to talk with you tonight. It gives me an opportunity to address some current questions about the press and its responsibilities—whom we are responsible to, what we are responsible for, and generally how responsible our performance has been."

6. Use "Let's Talk It Over" approach.

This approach for the introduction of a speech can be described as having a heart-to-heart talk with your audience, that is, putting heads together, reasoning things out, or thinking out loud. Such a person-to-person type of introduction is designed to put the audience at ease and in a mood to talk things over because it's worthwhile thinking together to make decisions.

LeRoy Collins, former governor of Florida and past president of the National Association of Broadcasters, was speaking on problems the South faced when it adjusted to a new system of race relations and the extension of civil rights. Collins, a Southerner, was addressing a southern audience that included old friends and associates.

Aware that his audience might be either skeptical or hostile, Collins explained in his introduction he was there just to talk out a few problems that concerned him, were unclear to him and were theirs as much as his. This is what he said in his opening remarks:

> "It is a high privilege for me to be here in Columbia, and to participate in this Greater Columbia Chamber of Commerce Annual Meeting of 1963. I like South Carolina and I always have. Yours is a state rich in history and exciting in opportunity . . .
>
> "I do not believe anyone is more genuinely proud of his southern birth and 'raising' than I am. I love this land. But some thoughts have been brooding in my mind lately . . and I think South Carolina and Columbia are good places for me to talk these out . . . not all

of you will agree with what I have to say. This does not trouble me, and it should not trouble you.

"I have tried to be a Southerner who speaks plainly on sensitive issues, and you are sons and daughters of a state which . . . has been characterized by forthright debate. Doubtless as you have detected down the years, a number of people in other neighborhoods of America have not always agreed with the forthright talk emerging from South Carolina. But debate, if it is honest and thoughtful, refines the decisions in our republic and makes them more intelligent.

"I have not come to address old grievances. It is the future of the South and of our nation that I wish to take up with you here tonight. And the one is inseparable from the other."

7. Use startling statement.

An unusual fact, an amazing assertion, or an unfamiliar statistic jars the minds of your listeners and induces them to pay rapt attention to what follows in your speech. To begin with a startling statement is to say something completely opposite to what the audience expects to hear.

Suppose you started your speech with such statements as "Education is useless," or "Civilization is stupid." Imagine the gigantic impact those words would have on your audience. You might actually hear them gasp. By using the unexpected which causes shock you focus attention on your subject. Naturally you'll have to justify your startling statement as you move along in your speech.

For example, one speaker began his speech as follows:

> "There are 31 million Americans 60 years and older. They constitute the single largest minority in the nation—more of them than there are blacks or Chicanos of all ages. This minority, since 1900, is growing at twice the rate of our total population."

At this point some members of that speaker's audience subconsciously might have asked themselves, "So what? Why should *I* listen? What's in this for *me*?" Anticipating such a reaction and to stimulate additional listener interest, the speaker went on to say in the next sentence: "The way in which these older Americans are viewed by society as a whole, by younger persons and by themselves has important implications for all of you concerned with the well-being of older Americans."

Another speaker said the following in his introduction:

"According to the Nielsen Index figures for TV viewing, it is estimated that by the time a child graduates from high school he has had 11,000 hours of schooling, as opposed to 15,000 hours of television. I would like to repeat that. By the time a child is 18 years old, he has spent more hours in front of the television set than he has in school. Over TV he will have witnessed by that time some 18,000 murders and countless highly detailed incidents of robbery, arson, bombings, shootings, beatings, forgery, smuggling and torture—averaging approximately one per minute in the standard television cartoon for children under the age of ten. In general, seventy-five percent of all network dramatic programs contain violence with over seven violent episodes per program hour. Concurrent with this massive daily dose of violence over our television screens has been a dramatic rise in violence in our society."

8. Ask a rhetorical question.

A rhetorical question is asked for its effect on the audience rather than for an answer. It's an effective way to get your audience to think of your purpose. That's why rhetorical questions are frequently used in the introduction of a speech.

One of the oldest techniques in speechmaking, it's still used today because rhetorical questions catch and hold the attention of listeners and pull them into the speech. Rhetorical questions are not "just rhetoric" or verbal embroidery. They're almost impossible to ignore. Listeners instinctively find themselves thinking of answers. Meanwhile they're drawn to the speakers for their answers.

You can ask one or more rhetorical questions in the introduction or elsewhere in the speech. An introduction relying on a single question is likely to provoke an immediate mental response from the audience. As soon as you ask, for example, "Can democracy survive?" the listeners are thinking of their answers as they anticipate yours.

You can also grab the audience's attention with a series of questions. One speaker asked three questions in a row in his introduction: "Where is the United States going? Where has it been? Where is it today?"

Another speaker introduced his topic with these rhetorical questions, using them to pinpoint the areas he intended to talk about: "What is the attitude of the average citizen toward freedom? How could we describe the climate of freedom in the United States today? How do mass media contribute to this atmosphere?"

9. Illustrate.

An illustration may be an example, a story, an anecdote, an incident or any happening, real or fictitious, which clarifies or intensifies an idea. Any of these types of illustrations is suitable for introducing your speech to catch the audience's attention, provided you show how the illustration applies to your subject.

If the subject of your speech were the structure of the United States Government, you might start off by comparing it with a three-legged stool, pointing out that the three legs are like the three branches of the government. Then you can say, "Just as the stool will collapse if any one of the legs is removed, so will the government fall if any one of the branches is eliminated."

Select an illustration for your introduction that directly relates to the central theme of your speech and enables you to move smoothly into the body of your talk. If you cannot locate the proper illustration, create your own. Use the appropriate details from the life or career of another person, living or dead, and arrange them in an interesting way to demonstrate what you want the audience to focus on in your introduction. Or put into the form of an anecdote one of your own personal experiences.

Russell Conwell began his famous inspirational speech, "Acres of Diamonds," with a personal anecdote to illustrate his theme that the greatest opportunities are in one's own backyard. Here are his opening words:

> "While traveling down the Tigris and Euphrates rivers many years ago, I found myself in the company of an old Arab guide we had hired at Bagdad. He was unusually talkative and seemed to think it was not only his duty to guide us, and do what he was paid for doing, but also to entertain us with stories.
>
> "The old guide, who was leading my camel along the river bank toward Nineveh, told me story after story until I grew weary and ceased to listen. I remember that he took off his Turkish cap and swung it in a circle to get my attention. I could see it through the corner of my eye, but I had decided not to look at him for fear he would begin again. I finally did look, nevertheless, and as soon as I did he went right into another story.
>
> "He said, 'I will tell you a story which I reserve for my particular friends.' When he emphasized the words 'particular friends,' I listened, and I have always been glad I did. The old guide told me that there once lived not far from the River Indus an ancient Persian by the name of Ali Hafed."

Conwell continued, saying that Ali Hafed was a successful farmer who sold his farm to go out and seek a mine of diamonds. After a long and fruitless search he died, poor and dejected. Later, the diamond mine of Golconda, "the most magnificent in all the history of mankind," was discovered on the farm which Hafed had sold.

Applying this story to his theme, Conwell said that the old Arab guide went on to say, "Had Ali Hafed remained at home and dug in his own cellar, or underneath his own wheat field, or in his own garden, he would have had 'acres of diamonds.' For every acre of that old farm, yes, every shovelful, afterward revealed gems which since have decorated the crowns of monarchs."

10. Refer to a historical or current event.

To get off to a good start, refer to a past or present event at the beginning of a speech. Such a specific reference can serve as a text for the main part of the speech.

Sometimes a speaker will use in the introduction both a historical and a current event. Martin Luther King began his eloquent "I Have a Dream" speech at the Lincoln Memorial in Washington, D.C. with a "then" and "now" comparison as he said:

> "Five score years ago, a great American, in whose symbolic shadow we stand today, signed the Emancipation Proclamation. This momentous decree came as a great beacon light of hope to millions of Negro slaves who had been seared in the flames of withering injustice . . .
>
> "But one hundred years later, the Negro still is not free. One hundred years later, the life of the Negro is still sadly crippled by the manacles of segregation and the chains of discrimination . . ."

A speaker on another occasion referred to current news items in his introduction to a speech on "The Real Cause of Inflation." He said: "Two newspaper stories caught my eye back in February. These stories were side-by-side on the front page of *The Wall Street Journal*. One story predicted consumer fears of inflation—*fears of inflation*—will delay economic recovery. The other story said the Administration puts a higher priority on economic recovery than on fighting inflation."

11. Use a quotation.

Using quotations is so important as a speech technique that an entire chapter in this book is devoted to it (Chapter 11, "Enrich Your

Speech With Eloquent Quotations"). Beginning your speech with a quotation has several advantages:

—Gets instant attention from the audience. Quotations from the Bible, Shakespeare, Aristotle, Jefferson, Churchill or other distinguished authors, philosophers and statesmen have high prestige value.

—Lends the weight of authority to your own views. The persons you quote as experts in their particular fields bring their knowledge and skills to bear on your side.

—Discloses your subject or theme. The quotation provides you with a springboard from which to launch your own remarks.

—Provides you with a text which forms a framework for your whole speech, as does the Biblical text for the preacher's sermon.

—Serves different purposes. The same quotation can be adapted to suit you, your subject, the audience and occasion.

When John F. Kennedy was a United States senator he delivered at Harvard University a commencement speech in which he made an eloquent plea for a better understanding of politicians by intellectuals. Here's how he began his speech:

> "It is a pleasure to join with my fellow alumni in this pilgrimage to the second home of our youth. Prince Bismarck once remarked that one third of the students of German universities broke down from overwork; another third broke down from dissipation; and the other third ruled Germany. As I look about this campus today, I would hesitate to predict which third attends reunions (although I have some suspicion), but I am confident I am looking at 'rulers' of America in the sense that all active informed citizens rule."

The same quotation from Bismarck was used by another speaker for a different subject, audience and occasion. He spoke at a membership initiation of the Western Kentucky University Chapter of Phi Alpha Theta in Bowling Green, Kentucky. Here are his opening words:

> "Once when Chancellor Bismarck faced an audience of German students in the late nineteenth century, he boldly gave the odds for their achieving fame and fortune: One third, he predicted, would break down from the relentless university discipline. Another third, he warned, would be struck down by the ravages of dissipation. The remaining third would survive to run Germany. Here tonight we see the third destined to run Kentucky, if not the country. I congratulate the new members of Phi Alpha Theta, and I am honored to be a part of this very happy occasion."

You can use quotations for the purpose of refuting them. Political speakers often use this approach. They compare the statements made by the opponent with his record. Al Smith, the first man to serve four terms as governor of New York, used to say, "Let's look at the record." Another method is to show that the facts justify a different interpretation of the quotation. Lincoln used this method in his Cooper Union speech. He began with a quotation from his opponent, Stephen Douglas, and then with facts and logic proceeded to refute Douglas' assertion.

12. Use humor.

The technique of humor in speechmaking is important enough, even in serious speeches, to justify a whole chapter in this book (see Chapter 14, "Enhance Your Eloquence With Wit and Humor").

In this chapter the discussion on humor will be confined to its use in the introduction of a speech. Most public speakers like to begin their speeches with some humor. Why? Because humor at the beginning of a speech:

—Loosens up speaker and audience, producing for both a more relaxed feeling.

—Establishes quick contact between speaker and audience.

—Shows the audience that the speaker doesn't have an exaggerated sense of self-importance.

—Puts the audience in a more receptive mood.

The idea behind the use of humor in beginning your speech is to "break the ice," to melt or soften the formality or reserve that normally exists between strangers—between you and the audience. This can be done with a few words that reveal you as a warm, good-natured, and unpretentious person. Give your opening words a light and easy touch. There's no need to tell sidesplitting tales or jokes that provoke belly laughs. Chuckles and smiles are enough.

Let's see how some eloquent public speakers have used the following techniques to achieve humor in the introductions of their speeches:

Commenting on the chairman's flattering introduction

At a convention of the American Bar Association, the chairman introduced Adlai Stevenson. When Stevenson stood up to give his speech, he said, "I was a little worried as Mr. Craig was giving that wonderful introduction. I began to think he was going to introduce Benjamin Franklin."

Poking fun at yourself

The speakers in the next two examples both belittled themselves and in so doing must have endeared themselves to the audience.

Oliver Wendell Holmes Sr., American physician, educator and author, delivered an after-dinner speech at the Boston Merchants Association. He began his speech as follows:

> "It was my intention, when I accepted the public invitation to be with you this evening, to excuse myself from saying a word. I am a professor emeritus, which means pretty nearly the same thing as a tired-out or a worn-out instructor."

James K. Wellington, delivering the keynote address at a Pi Lambda Theta annual conferience at Arizona State University, Tempe, Arizona, said in his introduction:

> "Thank you, I consider it a privilege and pleasure to have been invited to keynote the 1976 Pi Lambda Theta annual conference. Your theme, 'A Look at the Fundamental Concept,' is of particular interest and concern to me. Others know of my interest, and there have been some truths and untruths springing up. At the outset, I would like to clarify which is which.
>
> "It is true that I did introduce the fundamental school idea to the Scottsdale people while serving on the school board. It is also true that the concept had strong emphasis in the three R's, encouraged discipline and patriotism, and advocated educational standards and measuring student achievement against those standards.
>
> "It is not true that while attending a high school pep rally the band struck up a lively tune, and I marched backward across the football field. Further, it is not true that I have signed a movie contract with 18th Century Fox."

Describing a funny happening on the way to the meeting

When vaudeville was in its heyday before the advent of talking motion pictures, actors began their act by saying, "A funny thing happened to me on my way to the theater tonight" or "Something happened on my way over here." Likewise, public speakers often start their speeches by telling their audiences about something that happened to them on the way to the meeting.

Sometimes the speaker pulls a switch, that is, tries a variation of this technique by starting as follows: "Every time I go to dinner meetings, the speakers get up and start talking about something that happened to them on the way to the meeting. Well, you know, I've been going to dinner meetings for years, and believe me nothing has ever happened to me on the way . . ." The speaker pauses, waiting for the laugh. Then he says, "Until tonight . . ." and proceeds to tell about his humorous happening.

General Douglas MacArthur used this "On my way over" technique in one of his speeches. One of America's few outstanding speakers in the military, MacArthur graduated from West Point at the top of his class and later became superintendent of the academy. To accept the Sylvanus Thayer award for service to his nation, MacArthur went to West Point, where he delivered an eloquent inspirational speech to West Point cadets. He began with these three sentences:

> "As I was leaving the hotel this morning, a doorman asked me, 'Where are you bound for, General?' And when I replied, 'West Point,' he remarked, 'Beautiful place. Have you ever been there before?'"

With those few opening words, MacArthur, austere in appearance and solemn in manner as befitted his five-star general's rank, not only identified himself with the audience and place but also demonstrated he was not a stuffed shirt and gained immediate acceptance by the cadets.

Telling an amusing anecdote about yourself

At a dinner given by the alumni of Columbia University, Will Rogers delivered an address on "Education and Wealth," which he began as follows:

> "President Butler paid me a compliment a while ago in mentioning my name in his introductory remarks, and he put me ahead of the Columbia graduates. I am glad he did that because I got the worst of it last week. The Prince of Wales last week, in speaking of the sights of America, mentioned the Woolworth Building, the subway, the slaughterhouse, Will Rogers, and the Ford factory. He could at least have put me ahead of the hogs."

Identifying with the audience

Mark Twain gave a speech on "New England Weather" at an annual dinner of the New England Society. Here's his opening sentence:

> "I reverently believe that the Maker who made us all, makes everything in New England—but the weather."

With a single short sentence Twain identified himself with the audience and plunged directly into his subject.

Saying something witty

Bishop Fulton Sheen, whose reputation as an eloquent speaker spread beyond the Roman Catholic church and made him a public figure, opened one of his talks as follows:

> "Applause sums up the highest of Christian virtues. To applaud, as you just did, at the beginning of the speech, is an act of faith. If you applaud in the middle of my speech, it is an act of hope. And if you applaud at the end of my speech, it is an act of charity."

SUMMARY

The introduction of a speech should perform one or more of these functions:

1. Establish contact with the audience.
2. Enlist goodwill.
3. Arouse interest in the subject.
4. Lay the groundwork for the body of your speech.
5. Set the tone.

Those functions can be accomplished by one or more of the following techniques for beginning a speech:

1. Refer to your audience.
   a. Establish common ground.
   b. Pay a compliment.
   c. Identify yourself with their special interests.
2. Refer to the occasion.
3. Refer to yourself.
4. Refer to the title of your speech.
5. Refer directly to your subject.

6. Use a "Let's talk it over" approach.
7. Use a startling statement.
8. Ask a rhetorical question.
9. Illustrate.
10. Refer to a historical or current event.
11. Use a quotation.
12. Use humor.

CHAPTER 6

Wrap Up Your Talks with Eloquent Closings

LAST WORDS LINGER. Final impressions last. The conclusion of your speech is your last chance to make an impact on the audience. Your ending can strengthen or weaken your speech. Like a ball game, a speech can be lost or saved in its final seconds.

When a lumberjack chops away at a tree trunk, just before it's ready to topple he yells "timber!" and takes a mighty swing of the ax. Likewise, if you close your speech in a last surge of eloquence, you drive home your point of view and persuade your audience. The eloquent words you use at the end are those your listeners will remember longest. How you close can shape their total impression of your talk. Your ending can be the trigger that motivates them to act or believe as you advocate.

For those reasons many public speakers consider the conclusion of a speech its most important part. Certainly it's the part that's often quoted in newspaper stories and by other speakers. That's why it's wise to wind up with an eloquent ending—emphatic and forceful, sharp and stimulating, decisive and final.

By definition the conclusion of a speech is to say, in effect, "This speech is finished." In a motion picture or a novel the words "The End" appear at the conclusion. Porky the Pig says at the end of the movie cartoon, "That's all, folks!" The clown Canio, at the end of the opera "I Pagliacci," says, "The comedy is ended!" But public speakers must end their speeches in different ways.

Above all, don't drag out your conclusion. We all know the

guests who say goodbye inside the house and then stand outside talking for half an hour. Some public speakers tell us they're about to end but instead continue talking on and on and on.

One reason Edward Everett's speech at Gettysburg has been long forgotten and Abraham Lincoln's survives is that Everett dragged out his conclusion while Lincoln closed quickly and to the point. Everett diluted his conclusion by embellishing his closing thoughts and lingering at the areas where soldiers fell as he described the plains, fields and streams. Even when he quoted from Pericles' famous funeral oration—a logical closing point—Everett dragged on for another hundred words before he finally stopped talking.

Lincoln's simple yet eloquent final words brought his entire speech into focus: "We here highly resolve that these dead shall not have died in vain—that this nation under God shall have a new birth of freedom—and that government of the people, by the people, for the people shall not perish from the earth."

Time after time public speakers use the conclusion of a speech as a dumping ground or grab-bag for leftovers, bringing in new points or bits of information and other miscellaneous items. They say, "When I discussed such-and-such, I forgot to mention. . ." or "Let me go back for a moment to something I talked about earlier." When the final scene of a stage play comes to a climax, the curtain falls fast. A carpenter's last stroke of the hammer when he drives in a nail is a powerful, clinching blow. And so it is in closing speeches. End quickly but don't break off as if you ran out of time and words.

Besides conveying the overriding sense of finality rather than ending abruptly, the conclusion of a speech performs these functions:

—Satisfies the listeners, leaving them in the proper mood or frame of mind.
—Restates briefly in different words what was said in the body of the speech.
—Emphasizes the main points and central idea, helping the audience to remember them.
—Crystallizes the speaker's thoughts, pointing out what it all means or adds up to.
—Secures a favorable reaction from the audience, motivating them to respond to the speaker's request or suggestion.

Those functions are not necessarily separate steps. As is true of the introduction, one technique may accomplish all of the functions of the conclusion, or different techniques may be used for each. Like the introduction, no conclusion should be far out of proportion to the body of a speech. And like the introduction, no arbitrary length exists for the conclusion, but a general rule of thumb suggests from 5 percent to 10 percent of the speech.

Described below are a dozen techniques for speech conclusions, illustrated with examples from actual speeches:

1. Appeal for action or belief.

Be straightforward, specific and emphatic in asking your audience to take some step. Say, in effect, "Here's what we should do." Where action is implied or can be understood though unexpressed, you don't have to spell out the details. But you still urge the audience to believe strongly in your plea. This method assumes you've made a convincing case for your proposition in the body of your speech.

Lincoln's closing sentence in his long speech at Cooper Union strikingly illustrates this technique. His sentence shows how a few simple words can be magnificently arranged in rhythmic fashion to express eloquently an appeal to the audience for both belief and action. Here's what he said: "Let us have faith that right makes might, and in that faith, let us, to the end, dare to do our duty as we understand it."

John F. Kennedy ended his inaugural address by appealing to people everywhere to join him in the task of defending freedom. Here's his conclusion:

> "And so, my fellow Americans: ask not what your country can do for you—ask what you can do for your country. My fellow citizens of the world: ask not what America will do for you but what together we can do for the freedom of man. Finally, whether you are citizens of America or citizens of the world, ask of us here the same high standards of strength and sacrifice which we ask of you. With a good conscience our only sure reward, with history the final judge of our deeds, let us go forth to lead the land we love, asking His blessing and His help, but knowing that here on earth God's work must truly be our own."

Winston Churchill's speech, "A Time to Dare and Endure" was delivered five months after England was at war with Germany in the Second World War. Note especially the directness and vigor as well as the simplicity and clarity of his concluding words:

> "Come then: let us to the task, to the battle, to the toil—each to our part, each to our station. Fill the armies, rule the air, pour out

> the munitions, strangle the U-boats, sweep the mines, plow the land, build the ships, guard the streets, succor the wounded, uplift the downcast, and honor the brave. Let us go forward together in all parts of the Empire, in all parts of the Island. There is not a week, nor a day, nor an hour to lose."

Theodore Roosevelt's "Man in the Arena" speech contains this stirring conclusion:

> "It is not the critic who counts; not the one who points out how the strong man stumbled, or how the doer of deeds could have done them better. The credit belongs to the man who is actually in the arena; whose face is marred with dust and sweat and blood; who strives valiantly; who errs and comes short again and again; who knows the great enthusiasms, the great devotions, and spends himself in a worthy cause; who, if he wins, knows the triumphs of high achievement; and who, if he fails, at least fails while daring greatly; so that his place shall never be with those cold and timid souls who know neither victory nor defeat."

Such an eloquent appeal to high motives applies not only to persons engaged in world-shaking events but also to any person who exerts his or her efforts in a just cause, whether at a local club, a PTA meeting, a City Hall conference, or whatever.

2. Use a quotation.

Quotations open up for public speakers a tremendous resource from which to draw everything that has ever been said and written on any subject. The use of quotations is one of the best and simplest methods of ending a speech. But quotations can be used to advantage in any part of a speech. For this reason this book has an entire chapter on quotations (see Chapter 11, "Enrich Your Speech with Eloquent Quotations").

To close a speech, use a quotation that ties together the main ideas of your speech or captures its essence. For example, James K. Wellington, in his speech "A Look at the Fundamental School Concept," talked about quality education. He explained his fundamental school plan, showed how it works, and told why he felt better results must be expected from educational efforts. All this he tied together with two quotations in his conclusion:

> "Over 2,400 years ago, Aristotle said that 'all men by nature desire knowledge.' Assuming this to be true, it is the responsibility

of educational institutions to fulfill and satisfy this desire. I believe that the fundamental alternative is proving to be a highly desirable and effective educational concept in achieving such an objective. I close with a quote from Adlai Stevenson:

"'Respect for intellectual excellence, the restoration of vigor and discipline to our ideas of study, curricula which aim at strengthening intellectual fiber and stretching the power of young minds, personal commitment and responsibility—these are the preconditions of educational recovery in America today; and I believe they have always been the preconditions of happiness and sanity for the human race.'"

Speaking for the first time to the British people as their Prime Minister, when the Battle of France was raging and England was threatened, Winston Churchill concluded with a quotation that embodied the essence of his speech:

> "Centuries ago words were written to be a call and a spur to the faithful servants of Truth and Justice: 'Arm yourselves, and be ye men of valor, and be in readiness for the conflict; for it is better for us to perish in battle than to look upon the outrage of our nation and our altar. As the Will of God is in Heaven, even so let it be.'"

3. Summarize.

Using a summary to end your speech is like giving your talk in miniature. If you listen to or read a summary conclusion you should be able to tell what the speaker essentially said in the entire speech. That's probably why speakers tend to use the summary conclusion more often than any other kind of ending.

Summarizing at the end brings to bear on the audience the full weight of your speech, complete in scope yet brief in expression. So a summary conclusion suggests a restatement of your central theme or main points with no elaboration or explanation. It's like saying to your audience, "Now before I sit down, let me go over what I've said to be sure you understand me." This doesn't mean you give your speech all over again. In summarizing your speech, go over what you previously said, but do it quickly and concisely, so that as Cicero once said, "The recollection may be revived, not the speech repeated."

One way to summarize is to put the gist of your speech into one sentence. Reducing your whole speech to a single sentence may seem difficult, if not impossible, but it has been done.

Daniel Webster summarized his famous two-hour speech, "Reply to Hayne," in a single sentence with these well-known concluding words: ". . . liberty and union, now and forever, one and inseparable."

Robert G. Ingersoll boiled down his eloquent eulogy of his brother in one short sentence: "There was, there is, no greater, stronger, manlier man."

One-sentence closing summaries have impact on the audience because they tie together your speech at one swoop and are easy to understand as well as to remember. The key to close by summarizing in one sentence is to capture the essence of your speech and express it in a single thought. You can do this with any subject. And you may find a quotation that will summarize your whole speech in one sentence.

Suppose you were to give a speech on "Self-Confidence." Look up quotations and you'll run into Eleanor Roosevelt's single sentence which will eloquently summarize your speech on "Self-Confidence." She said: "No one can make you feel inferior without your consent."

Another technique for summarizing a whole speech is to focus attention on your central theme, drawing together your main points without elaboration. That is, you restate portions of your speech without details and apply them to your central idea so as to enhance it. Your last words in this summary should enable you to leave your listeners with their attention firmly fixed on the central theme of your speech.

That's what Theodore Roosevelt did in ending his speech on "The Strenuous Life." Here's his conclusion:

> "I preach to you, then, my countrymen, that our country calls not for the life of ease, but for the life of strenuous endeavor . . . If we stand idly by, if we seek merely swollen, slothful ease, and ignoble peace, if we shrink from the hard contests where men must win at hazard of their lives and at the risk of all they hold dear, then the bolder and stronger people will pass us by and will win for themselves the domination of the world. Let us therefore boldly face the life of strife, resolute to do our duty well and manfully; resolute to uphold righteousness by deed and by word; resolute to be both honest and brave, to serve high ideals, yet to use practical methods. Above all, let us shrink from no strife, moral or physical, within or without the nation, provided we are certain that the strife is justified; for it is only through strife, through hard and dangerous endeavor, that we shall ultimately win the goal of true national greatness."

In those concluding words, Theodore Roosevelt highlighted his theme by repeating without elaboration the substance of his speech, even using some of the same key words and phrases.

Still another technique for summarizing a speech is to catalog the main points in your speech. This directs attention to these points so as to reinforce them in the minds of your listeners.

To avoid the possibility that this point-by-point summary conclusion may sound like a laundry list, you should follow it with a general statement that directly or indirectly calls attention to the central theme of the speech. Such a statement could be an exact repetition of a sentence previously used in the speech, a modified restatement, or a quotation.

Adlai Stevenson delivered the eulogy at the memorial service for Winston Churchill in Washington, D.C. Stevenson's summary conclusion catalogs Churchill's many-sided achievements and virtues and is followed by a general statement coupled with a stirring quotation covering the theme of the speech as a whole:

> "The great aristocrat, the beloved leader, the profound historian, the gifted painter, the superb politician, the lord of language, the orator, the wit—yes, and the dedicated bricklayer—behind all of them was the man of simple faith, steadfast in defeat, generous in victory, resigned in age, trusting in a loving providence and committing his achievements and his triumphs to a higher power.
>
> "Like the patriarchs of old, he waited on God's judgment and it could be said of him—as of the immortals that went before him—that God 'magnified him in the fear of his enemies and with his words he made prodigies to cease. He glorified him in the sight of kings and gave him commandments in the sight of his people. He showed him his Glory and sanctified him in his faith.'"

4. Relate conclusion to introduction.

You can end a speech by returning to the beginning, thus completing the circle. This has the effect of tying up your speech with a bowknot. If you say in your introduction what you'll develop in the body, then show in your conclusion that you have done so. This technique is often used by ministers who use a Biblical verse in the introduction as a text and then refer to it in the conclusion.

By repeating at the end of your speech the idea, quotation, image or whatever you offered in the introduction, you give the audience the feeling of coming home again. Closing a speech by swinging back to the starting point causes the listeners to go through a cycle and gives them a satisfying sense of completion.

Barbara Jordan's keynote address at a Democratic National Convention ended as follows:

> "Now, I began this speech by commenting to you on the uniqueness of a Barbara Jordan making the keynote address. Well I am going to close my speech by quoting a Republican President and I ask you that as you listen to these words of Abraham Lincoln, relate them to the concept of a national community in which every last one of us participates: As I would not be a slave, so I would not be a master. This expresses my idea of Democracy. Whatever differs from this, to the extent of the difference is no Democracy."

Note how Jordan directly returns to the beginning of her speech (see text of her introduction in Chapter 1).

Katherine Graham ended her speech on "The Press and Its Responsibilities" by referring to the questions in her introduction (see text in the preceding chapter under the heading "Refer directly to your subject"):

> "So instead of seeking flat and absolute answers to the kinds of problems I have discussed tonight, what we should be trying to foster is respect for one another's conception of where duty lies, and understanding of the real worlds in which we try to do our best. And we should be hoping for the energy and sense to keep on arguing and questioning, because there is no better sign that our society is still healthy and strong."

Having set up the questions in her introduction, Graham in her conclusion brings them back to the minds of her listeners as she briefly sums up.

5. Build up to a climax.

This method of closing a speech depends on placing a series of sentences, clauses or phrases in a sequence that produces a cumulative effect. The series ranges from the least important item to the most important, which is the climax. Note how Oliver Wendell Holmes, Sr., achieves a cumulative effect in a single sentence: "I know it, I concede it, I confess it, I proclaim it."

Abraham Lincoln, in the final sentence of his "Gettysburg Address," uses a series of four clauses in crescendo fashion to build up momentum and create a snowball effect toward the climax:

> "It is rather for us to be here dedicated to the great task remaining before us—that from these honored dead we take increased devotion to that cause for which they gave the last full measure of devotion—that we hereby resolve that these dead shall not have died in vain—

> that this nation under God shall have a new birth of freedom—and that government of the people, by the people, for the people shall not perish from the earth."

The conclusion of William Jennings Bryan's "Cross of Gold" speech consists of four sentences, grouped in climactic order ranging from the lowest subordinate idea to the highest major thought. As with Lincoln's ending above, Bryan's thoughts increase in significance or intensity until they reach a point of climax—the moment of greatest emphasis. Each of Bryan's three previous sentences becomes more intense, both in thought and expression, as it moves toward the final sentence. Here's Bryan's conclusion:

> "Therefore, we care not upon what lines the battle is fought. If they say bimetallism is good, but that we cannot have it until other nations help us, we reply that, instead of having a gold standard because England has, we will restore bimetallism, and then let England have bimetallism because the United States has it. If they dare to come out in the open field and defend the gold standard as a good thing, we will fight them to the uttermost. Having behind us the producing masses of this nation and the world, supported by the commercial interests, the laboring interests, and the toilers everywhere, we will answer their demand for a gold standard by saying to them: You shall not press down upon the brow of labor this crown of thorns, you shall not crucify mankind upon a cross of gold."

6. Emotionalize.

To emotionalize is to stir the hearts and quicken the pulses of your listeners or to excite their feelings and sensibilities. Leave them with optimism and hope. Uplift and hearten them with encouraging closing words that spur them on to exert greater efforts for achieving difficult goals. Creating powerful impressions, the emotional conclusion motivates audiences and is often used to end inspirational speeches.

Listen to Winston Churchill's concluding words in a speech that inspired the British people to defend their country against overwhelming odds:

> "The Battle of France is over. I expect that the Battle of Britain is about to begin. Upon this battle depends the survival of Christian civilization. Upon it depends our own British life, and the long

> continuity of our institutions and our Empire. The whole fury and might of the enemy must very soon be turned on us. Hitler knows that he will have to break us in this Island or lose the war. If we can stand up to him, all Europe may be free and the life of the world may move forward into broad, sunlit uplands.
>
> "But if we fail, then the whole world, including the United States, including all that we have known and cared for, will sink into the abyss of a new Dark Age made more sinister, and perhaps more protracted, by the lights of perverted science. Let us therefore brace ourselves to our duties, and so bear ourselves that, if the British Empire and its Commonwealth last for a thousand years, men will still say, 'This was their finest hour.'"

Russell Conwell, in his speech, "Acres of Diamonds," opened with an illustration that suggested his theme—success is in your own backyard—and developed it by piling up example upon example until the audience could not doubt his idea was true. When he reached that point, he concluded as follows:

> "Let every man or woman here, if you never hear me again, remember this, that if you wish to be great, you must begin where you are and with what you are, now. He who can give to his city any blessing, he who can be a good citizen while he lives here, he who can make better homes, he who can be a blessing whether he works in the shop or sits behind the counter or keeps house, whatever be his life, he who would be great anywhere must first be great in his own community."

7. Visualize the future.

This technique ends a speech by describing a vision of the future or the dawn of a new day. Proverbs say "The darkest hour is that before the dawn," "The dawn will come to dispel the night," "The darkest hour breaks brightest into dawn," and "When the night is darkest, dawn's nearest." These observations show why speakers often end their speeches by painting a picture of better times to come. Audiences want speakers to end speeches on a high note—to give them a fleeting look at the land of promise. Who wants to listen to the preachers of doom and gloom?

Over a century ago the eloquent orator Robert G. Ingersoll said in a speech, "I see a world at peace . . . a world where labor reaps its full reward; I see a world without the beggar's outstretched palm . . . the piteous wail of want; and, as I look, life lengthens, joy deepens, love canopies the earth; and over all, in the great dome, shines the eternal star of human hope."

Franklin D. Roosevelt said, "I see an America whose rivers and valleys and lakes . . . are protected as the rightful heritage of all the people; I see an America where small business really has a chance to flourish and grow; I see an America of great cultural and educational opportunity for all its people . . ." In his speech asking Congress to declare war against Japan, FDR ended, "With confidence in our armed forces, with the unbounding determination of our people, we will gain the inevitable triumph, so help us God."

In an address to the French people in both English and French after the fall of France in the Second World War, Winston Churchill touched their hearts, lifted their spirits, and gave them faith by ending his speech as follows:

> "Good night, then: sleep to gather strength for the morning. For the morning will come. Brightly will it shine on the brave and true, kindly upon all who suffer for the cause, glorious upon the tombs of heroes. Thus will shine the dawn. *Vive la France!* Long live also the forward march of the common people in all the lands toward their just and true inheritance, and towards the broader and fuller age."

Martin Luther King's "I Have a Dream" speech in which he deplored the wrongs inflicted upon his race ended with a dawn-of-a-new-day conclusion:

> "So I say to you, my friends, that even though we must face the difficulties of today and tomorrow, I still have a dream . . . I have a dream that one day on the red hills of Georgia, sons of former slaves and sons of former slaveowners will be able to sit down together at the table of brotherhood . . . I have a dream my four little children will one day live in a nation where they will not be judged by the color of their skin but by content of their character . . . I have a dream that one day every valley shall be exalted, every hill and mountain shall be made low, the rough places shall be made plain, and the crooked places shall be made straight and the glory of the Lord will be revealed and all flesh shall see it together . . ."

8. Ask a rhetorical question.

By ending your speech with a rhetorical question, you leave in the minds of your listeners a thought that directs their attention to the response you seek. Rhetorical questions in effect challenge the audience, as if you were asking them, "Can you do this task?" or "Will you do what needs to be done to deal with this problem?"

Asking thought-provoking questions at the end of your talk can change apathetic audiences into lively ones. You stir them into thinking actively about the answers you want them to find by themselves.

A classic example of closing a speech by asking rhetorical questions is the concluding paragraph in a speech delivered over 200 years ago which keeps alive the name of Patrick Henry. Addressing the delegates of the Second Virginia Convention, he ended his speech as follows:

> "Gentlemen may cry peace, peace—but there is no peace. The war is actually begun! The next gale that sweeps from the north will bring to our ears the clash of resounding arms! Our brethren are already in the field! Why stand we here idle? What is it that gentlemen wish? What would they have? Is life so dear, or peace so sweet, as to be purchased at the price of chains and slavery? Forbid it, Almighty God! I know not what course others may take; but as for me, give me liberty, or give me death!"

Note the four rhetorical questions in that conclusion. We can imagine the sledgehammer impact on the delegates of Henry's passionate, vehement and fiery closing words. We know that the convention voted to commit the state of Virginia to prepare for war. The power of Patrick Henry's eloquence had moved the delegates to action.

Modern speakers also use rhetorical questions in closing their speeches, but more sparingly than Patrick Henry did.

In a speech to the American people, Ronald Reagan spoke of launching a nationwide effort to encourage them to participate in volunteer programs for needy persons. He ended his speech with these two sentences: "As Tom Paine said 200 years ago, 'We have it within our power to begin the world over again.' What are we waiting for?"

Another present-day speaker, deploring the bigness of government, ended his speech by first quoting from Ecclesiastes that there's "a time to keep silent and a time to speak" and then rhetorically asking "Is this not a time to speak?"

Discussing American coal exports, a speaker said, "We cannot afford to renounce a policy of free trade . . ." and ended his talk as follows:

"In *Julius Caesar*, Shakespeare writes: 'There is a tide in the affairs of men, which taken at the flood leads on to fortune.' A new energy tide—a coal tide—can lead us to a greater fortune. But, as Shakespeare went on to say, 'On such a full sea we are not afloat, and we must take the current when it serves or lose our ventures.' The time to decide is now. Will we take the tide at the flood?"

Addressing the Water Pollution Control Federation, a speaker concluded his speech with these words: "I suggest that on the issue of water quality control, you can be the most informed—and, if you choose, the most effective—mediators we have. Ask yourself two very simple questions about all of this. The first is: If not *us*, who? The second is: If not *now*, when?"

Another speaker ended his talk, "There is truly nothing for nothing any longer. Can we cope with that fact? Will we?"

In a college commencement address, a speaker concluded as follows:

"Wise choices are the distinguishing mark of an educated man. You, too, can be on the side of the angels. Can you afford to be anywhere else? With what greater wisdom can you be wise?"

In asking rhetorical questions at the end of a speech, as the above examples show, none of the speakers seeks information from the audience but wants to emphasize a point. Questions impress more than mere statements. Besides, the questions bring the listener in as an active partner with the speaker, creating a sense of dialogue between them even though no voiced answer is expected. But the speaker does expect the listener to think about the answer to the question.

9. Illustrate

To illustrate you may use examples, stories, anecdotes, incidents or any happenings, as all of these classifications mean something that is described or narrated. An appropriate illustration is suitable for a speech ending because it dramatizes the speaker's point and makes it more compelling. An illustration may be real or fictitious, but it must relate to the speaker's purpose. Used as a wind-up device in a speech, an illustration has to tie in with your subject or with what you want your audience to do or believe.

Harvey C. Jacobs in his speech "Freedom to Know" emphasized the individual responsibility of each person but recognized the temptation to abdicate responsibility because people wonder how one person can make a difference. So he ended his speech with a brief story that tied in with his central theme and drove home his point. Here's his closing:

> "There is the story that in a tiny French village, the peasants decided to honor their parish priest by each one bringing to the parish house the next Sunday a bottle of wine for the pastor's empty wine barrel. The pastor was delighted, and he asked all to join him in a glass of wine from the now full barrel. But when the tap was opened, only water came out. You see, each peasant had brought water instead of wine—thinking that all the others would bring wine and that one bottle of water would never be noticed."

A. L. Jones in his speech "A Question of Ecology: The Cries of Wolf" claimed that ecology is not on the verge of disaster, despite "cries of wolf." So he closed his speech by drawing a moral lesson from an Aesop fable. He began his conclusion, "We are all familiar with the Aesop fable about the shepherd boy and the wolf." Jones told how the boy twice fooled villagers by falsely shouting "Wolf! Wolf!" and then when a wolf did appear, the villagers didn't believe the boy's shouts. After Jones finished telling the details of the fable, he tied Aesop's story to his theme and clinched his point with these final sentences:

> "The moral is: those who are found to misrepresent facts are not believed even when they speak the truth. In recent months, we have heard cries of wolf with respect to our oxygen supply, the build-up of carbon monoxide, the disappearance of species, phosphates in the lake, thermal pollution, radiation effects on health from nuclear power plants, the Amchitka nuclear tests, lead in gasoline, and mercury in fish, to name a few. For the most part, these cries have not been malicious but have been based largely on fear, ignorance or misinformation. The people have listened to these cries and have come running to the rescue but they are not finding many wolves.
>
> "Let us not cry wolf until we are reasonably certain that we have done enough homework to know what a wolf looks like. Otherwise we may undermine our credibility and not be believed by the people when we warn them of the real wolves that do exist."

Aesop's fables can help you end your speeches eloquently because his stories have a moral which you can tie in with your theme. If you'd rather end more quickly than the time it takes to relate the details of a story, use a much briefer incident or anecdote. For example, a speaker emphasized in his speech the importance and usefulness of education that leads people to practical results. He ended his talk by telling a short anecdote and adding a final sentence to tie the anecdote to his subject. Here's how he closed:

"When Theodore Roosevelt had read the book of Jacob Riis, *How the Other Half Lives*, his fighting spirit—as great in peace as in war—was aroused. He went down to lower Manhattan, climbed the creaking stair in the tenement and knocked at the door. Mr. Riis was not at home. Then the caller took out his visiting card and wrote: 'Have read your book and came to help—Theodore Roosevelt.' Such reading, such study, is the sort of education America needs today."

10. Refer to historical or current event.

This technique, used more often in the introduction of a speech where it can serve as a text or lead-in to the body, is also serviceable in the conclusion. By referring to a specific historical or current event, you can clinch the main point of your speech or compare the past with the present as a closing observation.

For example, Helen B. Wolfe of the American Association of University Women gave a speech in which she saw a historical parallel between the 19th Amendment (women's right to vote) and the Equal Rights Amendment (ERA). Referring to ERA, she attributed its failure to the "backlash phenomenon." In the conclusion of her speech she again compared ERA with the earlier women's movement by referring to a specific historical event. From this reference she drew a comparison with ERA's fate and a challenge to recover quickly from defeat. Here's her conclusion:

> "November 2, 1915, was a memorable date in New York State history. That was the vote on the Suffrage Amendment to the state constitution. It was a long hard-fought battle, and that night as the returns came in, it was apparent that suffrage had lost. At the suffrage headquarters in New York City, the women were discouraged and defeated. Suddenly, the chairwoman of the Manhattan women, Mrs. Laidlow, jumped up and said they must start their new campaign that very night. At midnight, the night suffrage was defeated, she led a parade through midtown Manhattan proclaiming the start of the 1917 campaign for state suffrage. And in 1917 it carried.
>
> "That was the indomitable spirit that bounced back from defeat after defeat to give us the vote in the first place. Now, though in the midst of a backlash, we must start the campaign anew. We must vigilantly guard the rights we have already won and secure the promise that lies ahead of us. Together we will emerge from the temporary darkness of the backlash and walk again in the season of light."

11. Refer to yourself.

Using personal reference as a technique in closing a speech can be as effective as in beginning a speech. In both cases, referring to yourself serves to personalize your talk by establishing a relationship of mutual trust or emotional affinity between you and your audience.

Douglas MacArthur, for example, went to West Point at age 82 to accept an award for services to his nation. He gave an eloquent farewell speech in which he reinforced the cadets' commitment to the values of "duty, honor, and country," the motto inscribed on the academy coat of arms. Here's how he ended his speech:

> "The shadows are lengthening for me. The twilight is here. My days of old have vanished—tone and tints. They have gone glimmering through the dreams of things that were. Their memory is one of wondrous beauty watered by tears and coaxed and caressed by the smiles of yesterday. I listen vainly, but with thirsty ear, for the witching melody of faint bugles blowing reveille, of far drums beating the long roll.
>
> "In my dreams I hear again the crash of guns, the rattle of musketry, the strange, mournful mutter of the battlefield. But in the evening of my memory always I come back to West Point. Always there echoes and re-echoes: duty, honor, country.
>
> "Today marks my final roll call with you. But I want you to know that when I cross the river, my last conscious thoughts will be of the Corps, and the Corps, and the Corps.
>
> "I bid you farewell."

William Pitt the Elder, English statesman and topnotch orator of his day, in his speech "On an Address to the Throne," tried to use his influence on behalf of the American colonies in opposition to King George III. Pitt was then old and ill and had less than a year to live. He ended his speech in the House of Lords as follows:

> "My Lords, I am old and weak, and at present unable to say more; but my feelings and indignation were too strong to have said less. I could not have slept this night in my bed, nor reposed my head on my pillow, without giving this vent to my eternal abhorrence of such preposterous and enormous principles."

Even reading his words today, you can almost hear him tell, in glowing and rhythmic terms, how profoundly outraged he felt. The acoustic effect that results from the harmonious succession of his words pleases the ear, while the words themselves reveal his righteous anger and passionate conviction.

12. Use humor.

Because humor is a powerful tool for public speakers, a separate chapter is devoted to it in this book (see Chapter 14, "Enhance Your Eloquence with Wit and Humor").

More often used in opening remarks and in the body of a speech, straight humor doesn't lend itself as effectively in closing a speech unless the purpose of your talk is solely to entertain. Leaving the audience laughing is, of course, the best way to end a speech to entertain.

But in other types of speeches, the audience may be in no mood for sheer fun at the end of the speech with a serious purpose. In such speeches, the use of humor as a concluding technique tends to work better when combined with other elements, such as a brief story or quotation that evokes a chuckle or a smile while strengthening the speaker's sincere and heartfelt proposition.

When Adlai Stevenson of Illinois made his concession speech in his first presidential campaign, he ended as follows:

> "Someone asked me, as I came in, down on the street, how I felt, and I was reminded of a story that a fellow townsman of ours used to tell—Abraham Lincoln. They asked him how he felt once after an unsuccessful election. He said he felt like a little boy who had stubbed his toe in the dark. He said that he was too old to cry but it hurt too much to laugh."

Note how Stevenson mixed his humor with a bit of pathos.

John F. Kennedy, then a U.S. senator, concluded his eloquent commencement speech at Harvard University as follows:

> "I would urge that our political parties and our universities recognize the need for greater cooperation and understanding between politicians and intellectuals. We do not need scholars or politicians like Lord John Russell, of whom Queen Victoria remarked, he would be a better man if he knew a third subject—but he was interested in nothing but the Constitution of 1688 and himself. What we need are men who can ride easily over broad fields of knowledge and recognize the mutual dependence of our two worlds.
>
> "'Don't teach my boy poetry,' an English mother recently wrote the Provost of Harrow. 'Don't teach my boy poetry; he is going to

stand for Parliament.' Well, perhaps she was right—but if more politicians knew poetry, and more poets knew politics, I am convinced the world would be a little better place to live on this Commencement Day of 1956."

Although Kennedy was wholly serious in pleading for a better understanding of politicians by intellectuals, he avoided a heavy-handed closing that might have sounded unduly severe to his audience of intellectuals. Instead, by using a couple of amusing brief stories that were to the point, he highlighted his proposition and pleasantly got his message across to the audience.

POINTS TO REMEMBER

The functions of a speech conclusion are to:

1. Satisfy the audience, leaving them in the proper mood or frame of mind.
2. Restate briefly in different words what you said in the body of the speech.
3. Emphasize your main points and central idea, helping the audience to remember them.
4. Crystallize your thoughts, pointing out what it all means or adds up to.
5. Secure a favorable reaction from the audience, motivating them to respond to your request or suggestion.

One or more of the following techniques for closing a speech can achieve those functions.

1. Appeal for action or belief.
2. Use a quotation.
3. Summarize.
4. Relate conclusion to introduction.
5. Build up to a climax.
6. Emotionalize.
7. Visualize the future.
8. Ask a rhetorical question.
9. Illustrate.
10. Refer to a historical or current event.
11. Refer to yourself.
12. Use humor.

CHAPTER 7

Strengthen Your Eloquence with Transitions

THE LAST THREE CHAPTERS FOCUSED ON ORGANIZING the parts of a speech to the extent of structuring a framework and fleshing it out with ideas, facts and examples. At this point of development the framework may seem disconnected, with the parts of the speech related only in subject matter.

You now must join together these various parts to form a speech with unbroken continuity. This you do by using transitions. You may naturally insert transitions while you're developing the basic structure of your ideas, but that's a time when you have many other things to think about. To concern yourself then with transitions may interrupt the flow of your thoughts. For that reason, write most of the transitions after you've constructed the framework when you can see more easily where transitions are needed.

Unlike readers who can see indented paragraphs on the printed page, your listeners cannot see the scheme of indentation in your speech. They may get cues from your pauses when you deliver it, but they depend mostly on your words for signals that you've finished the introduction and you're starting the body of your speech, that you've completed one point and you're going on to another, and similar changes in direction.

Because your audience cannot turn back as readers can to reread the pages of a book, your listeners cannot check back on what you've said once it has been spoken, or know when you're moving from one idea to another, or understand the relationship between them—unless you provide them with transitions.

To summarize the preceding thought and forecast the one that follows, you need more than the simple mechanical use of transitional conjunctions. These help, of course, but to be eloquent the connections should also grow out of the ideas of the speech. Such transitions connect the thoughts, just as the string in a necklace links together each bead.

IMPORTANCE OF TRANSITIONS

Lack of suitable and sufficient transitions makes a speech sound choppy, jumpy, blurs distinctions between its parts, and may fail to differentiate between major and minor ideas or points. When transitions are missing, your audience might say of your speech, as the Duke of Athens said of Peter Quince in Shakespeare's *A Midsummer-Night's Dream*, "His speech was like a tangled chain; nothing impaired, but all disordered."

Transitions enable you to move smoothly from idea to idea and from one sentence to another and to hold all parts of your speech together to keep it whole. By preventing your speech materials from becoming a twisted mass, transitions save your speech from sounding "like a tangled chain."

Transitions are to speeches what rivets are to assembling parts of an automobile, what welding is to shipbuilding, or what the couplings between the cars are to a moving train. Transitions in speeches are like signals for changing lanes or making turns when driving a car. As highway signs guide motorists along the route to their destination, so do speech transitions guide audiences as speakers develop their ideas.

Just as road signs sometimes read on one side, "Entering Oshkosh" and on the other, "Leaving Oshkosh" so do speech transitions look both ways—look back over the material already covered and look forward to new material. That is, the transitions tell listeners what the speaker has just finished saying and what he or she is going to say next.

Now that we have seen why a transition in a speech is important, you might ask, "Just what is a transition?"

That last sentence is itself a transition, as it shifts from a discussion of the importance of a transition to its meaning. The dictionary defines a transition as the process or an instance of changing or passing from one thing to another. In music, a transition is a shifting from one key to another or a passage connecting two sections of the musical composition. In speaking a transition is a word, phrase, sentence or a group of sentences that relates a preceding idea to a succeeding one, or that connects parts of the speech.

Like a train conductor making station announcements, you use transitions in a speech to flash messages which in effect say to your audience, "I'm leaving this part of my talk and going on to the next." A transition is an in-between statement in which you say, "Now let's move on to another fact," "Here's a new angle to consider," or "Here's another example of what I mean."

You can turn such transitions into a more distinctive style of expression, such as "And now I come to the evidence that should tie a knot in your mind." That phrasing is different enough from ordinary transitions to perk up the listener's ears.

FUNCTIONS OF TRANSITIONS

By definition, then, transitions are words, phrases or sentences which accomplish a shift from one part or point in a speech to another. That statement expresses the essential nature of a transition as well as its general function. Transitions perform, however, a variety of specific functions, namely:

1. *To summarize the ideas just completed before beginning the next phase of the subject.* You may say something like this: "Before we start determining the causes of this problem, let's go over what we have already covered. We have found . . . We have shown . . . We have further discovered . . ."

2. *To pinpoint a certain idea to let the audience know the speaker means to highlight it.* This use is illustrated by the following transitional sentence from Edmund Burke's eloquent speech on "Conciliation with America": "Adhering, as I do, to this policy, as well as for the reasons I have just given, I think this new project of hedging in population to be neither prudent nor practicable."

3. *To introduce one or more examples of a point already made.* You might say, "The point I've been making is admittedly theoretical and hard to understand. So let me give you some specific instances."

4. *To show the speaker is moving from one part of the speech or from one idea to another.* This function is illustrated by two excerpts

from Ralph Y. McGinnis' speech, "What Did Abraham Lincoln Stand For?" The first one shows transition from the introduction to the body of the speech: "What did Abraham Lincoln stand for? To answer this question we might adopt the classical Aristotelian approach of analyzing Lincoln's personal character, his intellectual capacities, and his emotional nature. What DID Abraham Lincoln stand for? Representing his personal character . . ." The second excerpt shows transition from one idea to another: "Closely akin to Lincoln's quality of honoring truth was his high regard for ethical conduct."

5. *To indicate the relationship between the ideas involved.* Ralph Y. McGinnis used this function in his speech on Lincoln: "Those were the qualities of the mind and thinking of Abraham Lincoln. And now, what qualities compose the heart and soul of Lincoln?"

6. *To introduce evidence.* Say something like this: "Now, you might agree with these things that I've been saying and yet you wonder what can be done about them without losing values that we all cherish. I can appreciate why you may be doubtful or skeptical, so I'll now provide you with conclusive evidence to assure you that my plan is safe from all risks."

7. *To serve beyond the function of transition and as a notable thought in itself.* Using this function may require a longer transition. Adlai Stevenson in his speech "The American City—A Cause for Statesmanship" used three short paragraphs as transition from one main point (need for funds) to his next main point (need for long-range planning). The first sentence of each paragraph is a connecting link between the two main points but within each paragraph Stevenson eloquently inserted analytical observations and questions on the urban renewal problem. Here are the three transitional paragraphs:

> "Money is not enough. Indeed the wrong amount of money at the wrong time and in the wrong place may hinder rather than help our efforts to construct the city of the future. We Americans have a penchant for believing that sufficient inputs of energy and dollars can solve any problem. We rush in where angels fear to tread and frequently we profit, but sometimes we learn why the angels, in their greater wisdom, have not joined us and preferred to stay aloft. Urban reconstruction is a case in point.
>
> "Despite the laudable efforts we have been making to deal with various aspects of the problem in the generation since the New Deal began, does the sum of these parts add up to a meaningful whole? Instead of developing a comprehensive program, are we in danger

of creating a patchwork, a conglomeration of temporary and short-sighted solutions to pieces of a problem which cannot be handled piecemeal? Even in that haven of generalities—a preamble to a federal law—we look in vain for a comprehensive statement of what we are after.

"What do we want our downtown centers to become? What, in the long run, are the proper uses of the land in the 'gray belt'? What kind of transportation system will best meet our needs? How do we want to use the remaining open space around our cities—for parks, for wild-life reservations, for industries or for the next wave of developments?"

TECHNIQUES FOR TRANSITIONS

So much for the varied functions of transitions. Equally varied are the techniques for achieving those functions, including the following:

1. *Guidewords*. These serve the same purpose in speeches as catchwords in printing and guideposts in traveling. Intended to catch attention, a catchword is the first or last entry word printed as a guide at the top of pages in dictionaries, encyclopedias and telephone directories. Guideposts are signs placed at roadsides and crossroads to direct travelers to their destinations. Similarly, guidewords command attention because they provide signals which imply to your audience that a certain kind of idea is coming or that you will develop it in a particular way. For example, if you begin a transition with the guideword "Unlike," you signal your audience that you'll contrast one point with another.

Here's a list of some typical guidewords:

To add a point or introduce similar points: besides; also; and; moreover; furthermore; in addition.

To compare: similarly; likewise; in like manner; in the same way; in the same vein.

To contrast: unlike; on the other hand; contrary to; in contrast; conversely.

To enumerate or show sequence: first; second; third; next; lastly; finally.

To show result: therefore; thus; hence; consequently; accordingly.

To emphasize: indeed; in fact; in truth; to be sure.

To indicate time: now; then; eventually; frequently; infrequently; occasionally; rarely; meanwhile; meantime; immediately; afterward; before; later; after.

To indicate place: here; nearby; opposite to; beyond; adjacent to.

To show purpose: to this end; for this purpose; with this object; with this goal; toward this objective.

To summarize: to sum up; in brief; in short; in sum; all in all.

To introduce examples or evidence: for example; for instance; to illustrate.

To show concession: notwithstanding; nevertheless; however; true; acknowledging; admitting; conceding; in spite of; despite; though; although; granted; assuming.

Because guidewords are short, easy to understand, and point up ideas, they help you smooth the way from one sentence to another or between parts of your speech.

Lincoln used such guidewords frequently in his speeches. His long speech at Cooper Union, for example, is divided into two parts. The first part deals with the question of whether the founding fathers believed that the control of slavery rested with Congress or with the territories. In preparing for this speech Lincoln had researched chronicles and letters of the founding fathers to determine the historical facts, which he discussed in the first part of his speech.

When Lincoln was finished with the first part, he moved on to the second part to make a plea directly to the Southern people for a better understanding. Starting his transition from the first to the second part of his speech with the guideword, "But," Lincoln said: "But enough! . . . This is all Republicans ask—all Republicans desire—in relation to slavery . . . And now, if they would listen—as I suppose they will not—I would address a few words to the Southern people."

Thomas H. Huxley, English biologist and teacher who gave lectures and speeches popularizing science, was once described by the American journalist and critic H. L. Mencken as "perhaps the greatest virtuoso of plain English who has ever lived." Huxley often used guidewords for transitions in his speeches, as he did in "The Method of Scientific Investigation." Here are some examples from that speech:

"You will understand this better, perhaps, if I give you some familiar example."

"In the same way, I trust that you . . ."

"In the first place . . ."

"True, it is a very small basis, but still it is enough to make an induction from . . ."

2. *Questions*. Questions in transitions catch the attention of your listeners and help them to follow you in your answers.

Henry W. Grady, whose speech "The New South" gave him national fame, made the transitions to each new section of that talk by asking one or more questions and then answering them. Note in the following excerpts Grady's use of the guideword "but" and how the questions are eloquently phrased to grab attention and sustain interest:

"What does he do—this hero in gray with a heart of gold? Does he sit down in sullenness and despair? Not for a day . . ."

"But in all this what have we accomplished? What is the sum of our works? We have found out that . . ."

"But what of the negro? Have we solved the problem he presents or progressed in honor and equity toward solution? Let the record speak to the point . . ."

"But have we kept faith with you? In the fullest sense, yes . . ."

3. *Echoes*. Make a transition from one point to another by echoing a few words from the previous sentence or paragraph to the next. Bruce Lockerbie in his speech "Teaching Who We Are" said, "I encourage you to commit yourself totally to teaching and to learning; but most important, we need teachers willing to make a total commitment to people." He began the next paragraph, "How do we go about making a commitment to people?" Echoing the words "commitment to people" from a preceding paragraph to the one following effectively connects the two paragraphs and highlights ideas in both.

4. *Enumeration*. By enumerating your points as you specify them one after another, you not only avoid confusion in the minds of your listeners, but also make your points stand out, giving emphasis to each. The following passages from Edmund Burke's speech on "Conciliation with America" enumerate his reasons for urging conciliation with the American colonies instead of using force against them:

> "First, permit me to observe, that the use of force alone is but temporary. It may subdue for a moment, but it does not remove the necessity of subduing again; and a nation is not governed which is perpetually to be conquered.
>
> "My next objection is its uncertainty. Terror is not always the effect of force; and an armament is not a victory. If you do not succeed, you are without resource; for, conciliation failing, force remains; but, force failing, no further hope of reconciliation is left. Power and authority are sometimes bought by kindness, but they can never be begged as alms by an impoverished and defeated violence.
>
> "A further objection to force is that you impair the object of your

> very endeavors to preserve it. The thing you fought for is not the thing which you recover; but depreciated, sunk, wasted, and consumed in the contest. Nothing less will content me than *whole* America. I do not choose to consume its strength along with our own . . .
>
> "Lastly, we have no sort of experience in favor of force as an instrument in the rule of our colonies. Their growth and their utility have been owing to methods altogether different . . ."

Note that Burke achieves the advantages of enumeration without labeling them numerically, after "First," substituting "Next . . . Further . . . Lastly," thus avoiding the monotony of similar expressions. Recognizing the importance of transitions, he always carefully constructed even minor ones.

In the transitions quoted above also notice that they go beyond the function of transition and evolve into notable thoughts in themselves. His striking thoughts are rendered doubly striking by his well-turned phrases: "perpetually to be conquered," "armament is not a victory," "bought by kindness," "begged as alms," "consumed in the contest."

Houston Peterson, who compiled *A Treasury of the World's Great Speeches*, writes in that anthology, "In the entire history of eloquence, the mind of Edmund Burke stands out supreme."

5. *Repetition.* The transitional techniques of guidewords, questions, echoes, and enumeration are all useful ways of tying thoughts together, although those methods may seem obvious or simple. But repetition of key words, restatement, synonyms and other substitute words or phrases are more subtle techniques, yet equally effective.

Speakers often repeat key words because when main words are repeated the central theme is stressed. But restatement with synonyms and other substitutes can produce the same impressive effects as repetition of key words. For example, Thomas H. Huxley skillfully weaves restatements, among other transitional devices, in the following two excerpts from his speech "The Method of Scientific Investigation":

> "You have all heard it repeated, I dare say, that men of science work by means of induction and deduction, and that by the help of these operations, they, in a sort of sense, wring from Nature certain other things, which are called natural laws, and causes, and that out of these, by some cunning skill of their own, they build up hypotheses and theories . . . To hear all these large words, you would think that the mind of a man of science must be constituted differently from that of his fellow men; but if you will not be frightened by

terms, you will discover that you are quite wrong, and that all these terrible apparatus are being used by yourselves every day and every hour of your lives.

"There is a well-known incident in one of Moliere's plays, where the author makes the hero express unbounded delight on being told that he had been talking prose during the whole of his life. In the same way, I trust that you will take comfort, and be delighted with yourselves, on the discovery that you have been acting on the principles of inductive and deductive philosophy during the same period."

Huxley's varied connective devices work together to produce tightly unified and smooth flowing sentences and paragraphs. Note the several uses in the first paragraph of the personal pronoun "they" and demonstrative pronoun "these" which provide links by referring to something previously mentioned as well as the use of the transitional phrase "in the same way," which explicitly refers to the preceding sentence. These help to draw the sentences and paragraphs together.

But in addition to the devices of transitional words and phrases, the factor that also works strongly to connect Huxley's sentences and paragraphs is the technique of repetition in the form of restatements by use of different words. Here's a tabulated comparison of how Huxley repeats the same idea in different words:

every day and every hour of your lives (first paragraph, last phrase)	during the whole of his life (second paragraph, end of first sentence) during the same period (second paragraph, last phrase)
express unbounded delight (second paragraph, first sentence)	take comfort, and be delighted (second paragraph, last sentence)
on being told (second paragraph, first sentence)	on the discovery (second paragraph, last sentence)

In those paragraphs Huxley makes the restatements in different words hardly noticeable, but they achieve coherence and emphasis which reinforce each other.

6. *Pronouns and Demonstratives.* Unlike guidewords such as those described and illustrated above, personal and demonstrative pronouns are not ordinarily thought of as being transitional because they connect differently. They refer the audience back to the same persons or things mentioned in the same or preceeding sentences.

The dictionary defines a personal pronoun as a substitute word for a noun which refers to persons or things: I, you, he, she, it, we, they, their, them, his, her, himself, herself. By definition, a demonstrative pronoun points out the persons or things referred to: this, that, these, those.

Here's an excerpt from John F. Kennedy's inaugural address:

> "To those new *states* whom we welcome to the ranks of the free, we pledge our word that one form of colonial control shall not have passed away merely to be replaced by a far more iron tyranny. We shall not always expect to find *them* supporting our view. But we shall always hope to find *them* strongly supporting *their* own freedom—and to remember that, in the past, those who foolishly sought power by riding the back of the tiger ended up inside." (Italics added.)

Note how Kennedy achieves transitions between the sentences. He links them by means of pronouns that refer to logical antecedents. The italicized words "them" and "their" clearly and unmistakably refer back to "states" in the first sentence. True, several nouns come between "states" and the first "them." But "states" is the only noun to which "them" and "their" can plausibly refer because the others are singular.

If there's any chance of confusion, you should either repeat the antecedent or use a synonym for it. And if repetition proves awkward, recast your sentence.

Other kinds of transitional pronouns are demonstratives, which connect by pointing to something previously mentioned. Demonstratives frequently used are *this, that, these*, and *those*. By replacing "the" in many sentences, demonstratives strengthen the coherence between loosely connected sentences.

Notice how Theodore Roosevelt achieves a smooth transition from the introduction to the body of his speech dedicating the laying of the cornerstone for a new House of Representatives office building:

> "Over a century ago Washington laid the cornerstone of the Capitol in what was then little more than a tract of wooded wilderness here beside the Potomac. We now find it necessary to provide by great additional buildings for the business of the government . . . but the underlying facts of human nature are the same as they were then. Under altered external form we war with *the same tendencies toward evil* that were evident in Washington's time, and are helped by *the same tendencies for good*. It is about some of *these* that I wish to say a word today." (Italics added.)

The demonstrative pronoun "these" in the last sentence definitely refers to "the same tendencies toward evil" and "the same tendencies for good" in the preceding sentence. The word "these" not only shows Roosevelt's transition from introduction to body but also indicates what he will talk about.

7. *Parallel Structure.* This puts similar or contrasting thoughts in the same grammatical construction. You link sentences together by repeating the sentence pattern. Parallel construction connects similar or contrasting ideas tightly and makes them easier to understand and remember because they line up as clearly as items in a list. This technique is illustrated in the following quotation from former United States senator J. William Fulbright:

> "There are two Americas. One is the America of Lincoln and Adlai Stevenson; the other is the America of Teddy Roosevelt and General MacArthur. One is generous and humane, the other narrowly egotistical; one is modest and self-critical, the other arrogant and self-righteous; one is sensible, the other romantic; one is good-humored, the other solemn; one is inquiring, the other pontificating; one is moderate and restrained, the other filled with passionate intensity."

All the parallel phrases in the above quotation develop Fulbright's central theme that there are two Americas. Note that the contrasting characteristics between the two Americas line up as paired elements in a series. The contrast is eloquently pointed up by the parallel construction.

Sometimes parallel items are introduced by these pairs of words: either/or; both/and; neither/nor; not/but; not only/but also. Such naturally related words or expressions typically result in parallel construction. Parallelism is also related to balance. Both can work in the same sentence, though parallelism has to do with structure and balance with the importance of the sentence parts. Both parallelism and balance create rhythm and emphasis, and both help make sentences easy to remember.

Parallel construction, though structural in nature, can also fill the need for an emotional transition. A transition with parallel sentences or parallel phrases can produce an emotional appeal or a dramatic effect, as shown in the following passage from Douglas MacArthur's speech, "Farewell to the Cadets":

> "Always for them: duty, honor, country. Always their blood, and sweat, and tears, as we sought the way and the light and the truth . . . Their resolute and determined defense, their swift and sure attack, their indomitable purpose, their complete and decisive vic-

tory—always victory, always through the bloody haze of their last reverberating shot, the vision of gaunt, ghastly men, reverently following your password of duty, honor, country."

Notice the use of "always" as the beginning of parallel phrases and the double repetition of "duty, honor, country," the cadets' motto. Preceding the transitional passage quoted above, MacArthur talked about the sort of soldiers the West Point graduates would one day lead; his long experience with them in military campaigns, on the battlefields, around campfires; his personal knowledge of their courage and patriotism. Immediately following the transition quoted above, MacArthur picked up the last words of the transition—"duty, honor, country"—and connected them with the first sentence of the next passage, beginning "The code which those words perpetuate . . ." and continuing with an explanation of what the code embraces.

Another speaker, Bruce Lockerbie, in his speech "Teaching Who We Are," used parallel structure to make a transition between a preceding passage starting, "We teach best by example" and a succeeding one beginning "Which brings me to a point of issue." The transition statement, consisting of three parallel sentences, follows:

> "We show by example that we care about people, but we must also show by example that we believe in what we teach; that it's worthwhile to be a teacher of music by participating in music making outside of school, singing in a local choir or playing in a community orchestra. We show that learning and teaching history is valid by being a historian, or at least by belonging to the local historical association. We show that learning and teaching health is important by demonstrating good health habits ourselves."

8. *Humor*. A transition is especially effective in moving from humorous into serious material. Since this situation involves combining fun with facts, you want to be sure the audience not only laughs but also focuses on your serious information. As a change of pace, the wit or humor can lead up to a transition or serve as a transition itself.

Here's how Bruce Lockerbie, in his speech "Teaching Who We Are," uses a humorous quotation to lay the groundwork for his serious message:

> "W. C. Fields is alleged to have answered the question, 'How do you like children?' with these words: 'Well cooked.' No one, no matter how humane, can stand to be in the presence of adolescents 24 hours a day, but if you propose to be a teacher, it helps to like kids.
>
> "Ask that 8th grade girl how she's doing in school. If she responds

> positively, it's a sure bet that her eagerness isn't just because of the content of her courses; she'll go on to say, 'I really like Miss So-'n-so. She's nice.' Ask that 11th grade boy why he's considering dropping out of school. He'll probably tell you that, in addition to his sense of purposelessness academically, his teachers don't like him very well, and the feeling is mutual. Ask almost any middleaged or elderly person to tell you about schooldays. He won't remember the textbooks, she won't recall the dates and battles; but you'll hear the names of specific teachers whose personal traits and evident concern are stamped upon the memory."

(For more on humor, see Chapter 14, "Enhance Your Eloquence with Wit and Humor.)

9. *Maxims*. By definition a maxim is a saying of a general truth, principle or rule of conduct. That means, of course, maxims include proverbs, mottoes, epigrams and similar sayings. All have not only the wisdom of the years stored up in them but also are eloquent in expression. So they can help to create eloquent transitions.

In his speech "The American City—A Cause for Statesmanship" (quoted earlier in this chapter), Adlai Stevenson referred to the proverb, "Fools rush in where angels fear to tread" in a transition from one point to the next. He said, "We rush in where angels fear to tread and frequently we profit but sometimes we learn why the angels, in their greater wisdom, have not joined us and preferred to stay aloft."

Douglas MacArthur, in his speech to the West Point cadets (also previously quoted in this chapter), spoke about their commitment to their motto, "duty, honor, country". Throughout his speech he eloquently used the motto as a transitional device to move from one aspect of his subject to another and, in so doing, he unified all parts of his talk.

Here are examples of his transitions:

> "Duty, honor, country: those three hallowed words reverently dictate what you want to be, what you can be, what you will be . . . The unbelievers will say they are but words, but a slogan, but a flamboyant phrase . . . But these are some of the things they do . . ."

Speaking of the soldiers on the battlefields, he said they followed "your password of duty, honor, country. The code which those words perpetuate embraces the highest moral law."

10. *Internal Summaries*. Transitional summaries are called internal to differentiate them from the concluding summary at the end of

a speech. You can make an internal summary of the introduction of your speech to serve as a transition into the body. You can have internal summaries elsewhere in your speech—wherever you believe they will help your audience to follow you. Especially useful in longer speeches, internal summaries review what you have already covered and point ahead to what you're going to say next.

So internal summaries are intermediate statements that hook something preceding with something following and interrelate the two. This technique is illustrated by Thomas H. Huxley's brief internal summary in his speech, "The Method of Scientific Investigation" (quoted earlier in this chapter for other purposes):

> "So much, then, by way of proof that the method of establishing laws in science is exactly the same as that pursued in common life. Let us now turn to another matter (though really it is but another phase of the same question), and that is, the method by which, from the relations of certain phenomena, we prove that some stand in the position of causes towards the others."

Huxley's first sentence directly and decisively summarizes all that he had been saying before. Throughout his speech up to the point of his internal summary, he asserted and proved with examples that the method of scientific investigation is like the working of the human mind, that is, scientists think just like other people. In the other sentence of his internal summary he tells both what's coming up next and the connection between his preceding idea and the one that follows.

A SHORT WRAP-UP

Transitions help significantly in creating a smooth-sounding and unified speech. They tie everything together both for you and your audience.

By making it possible to connect different thoughts and to move from one idea to another without sudden and unexpected changes in subject matter, transitions clarify your message and hold the interest of your audience.

You owe it to your listeners to provide them with a sufficient number of well-chosen signs and signals in your speech when you shift from one part or point to the next.

If you pay attention to your transitions, they will be of tremendous benefit to you in the making of an eloquent speech.

CHAPTER 8

Use Rhetorical Devices for Eloquence

RHETORICAL DEVICES ARE LANGUAGE TECHNIQUES that arrange words into distinctive phrases and sentences for greater force and fluency. By conveying your thoughts and feelings more clearly and impressively, rhetorical devices brighten flat and colorless speech material and lift it out of the ordinary category to the level of eloquence.

Robert Frost, who won four Pulitzer Prizes for poetry, once talked to an audience about rhetorical devices, which he called "technical tricks." As he finished, a woman rose from her seat and asked, "Mr. Frost, when you're writing one of your beautiful poems, surely you're not thinking of technical tricks!" Frost said, "I revel in them."

Public speakers, like poets and prose writers, use rhetorical devices or technical tricks just as workers in any skilled occupation use "tricks of the trade." From an overall standpoint, the difference between an ordinary speech and an eloquent one is that the eloquent speech has rhythm. Basically, speech rhythm is the flow or movement of language through patterns created by rhetorical devices.

Audiences respond to rhythm. As Louis Untermeyer, poet and anthologist, put it: "We grow up in rhythm. We feel it physically in the breath, the pulse and the heartbeat; we measure it in our walking stride; we quicken to it in the sway of the dance. We feel it psychologically—we are lulled by the swing of a hammock; we are excited by the beat of a drum." S. I. Hayakawa, in *Language in Thought and Action*, writes: "From the boom-boom of a childish drum to the subtle nuances of cultivated poetry and music, there is a continuous development and refinement of man's responsiveness to rhythm."

Rhythm appears in all the arts, though it shows itself in different ways. In painting, it's associated with regular or harmonious patterns created by design and color but also, as in sculpture, with geometric forms and lines. In music and speeches, rhythm manifests itself as sound. Even reading silently can make you aware of the unuttered sound as well as of the sense.

RHYTHM IN PROSE

You may say, "Rhythm is all right for poetry, but not for prose." Yet the Bible contains some of the most eloquent prose rhythm ever written. So do Shakespeare's plays, which contain thousands of rhythmic speeches composed entirely in prose.

H. W. Fowler, in *Modern English Usage*, writes: ". . . live speech, said or written, is rhythmic, and rhythmless speech is at the best dead . . . while rhythm does not mean counting syllables and measuring accent-intervals, it does mean so arranging the parts of your whole that each shall enhance, or at the least not detract from the general effect upon the ear; and what is that but seeing to it sentences sound right?"

How does a public speaker see to it that sentences sound right? By using rhetorical devices. The rest of this chapter will consist of an account of rhetorical devices that make sentences sound right—and eloquent.

Judging by its frequency and variety in speeches, repetition is probably the most popular and versatile of all rhetorical devices. Napoleon Bonaparte is said to have remarked that the eloquent orator needs only one tool—repetition. This highly effective rhetorical device is applied in many different ways to attract attention, emphasize thoughts and generate emotions.

It's natural and usual in speaking to repeat things for emphasis or emotional effect. Repetition of words may not look good in print but it sounds mighty good to the ear. That's one reason this technique is especially effective in public speaking. Another reason is that it grabs attention. Most important of all, the repetition eloquently gets the message across to the audience.

Words vanish into the air when spoken and listeners can't go back to reread or ask the speaker to repeat. So it's important to repeat the idea if you want them to understand—and remember—what you say.

In a study by market researchers, 80 percent of the consumers questioned correctly answered "Alka-Seltzer" when they were asked to give the name of the product they associated with the words, "Plop, plop, fizz, fizz . . ." The repetition of these words certainly helped them to remember the product.

Repetition takes many forms. You can repeat a single word, a phrase, or an entire idea. You can repeat any of these items two or more times. You can put the repeated words at the beginning, in the middle or at the end of a phrase, clause or sentence. You can say a single word more than once anywhere in the same or nearby sentences. You can repeat a central idea again and again by sprinkling it throughout your speech.

1. Repetition at the beginning

The rhetorical device of repeating a word or phrase at the beginning of consecutive clauses or sentences achieves several eloquent effects: forms a rhythmic pattern; reinforces the speaker's deeply felt and strongly held beliefs; stirs the listener's emotions; and forcefully drives the message home. Following are examples from actual speeches:

Abby Kelley Foster, an eloquent pioneer woman orator in America, in a speech against slavery and referring to America as the land of the free, said: "Free to snatch the babe from the arms of its father or mother—free to drag the husband and wife asunder! Free to scatter families to the four winds!" Notice the effect of repeating "free" at the beginning of each clause in arousing emotions as Foster emphasizes how members of slave families became separated from one another. Her example is short but speakers have used such repetition in extended passages with as much eloquence.

Robert G. Ingersoll, American lawyer, was a popular and highly paid orator who dazzled audiences for some thirty years in the last century. In an eloquent speech nominating James G. Blaine for president, Ingersoll started with, "The Republicans of the United States demand as their leader in the great contest of 1876 a man of intelligence, a man of integrity, a man of well-known and approved political opinions." He immediately followed this sentence with seven succeeding sentences each beginning with the words, "They demand . . ." Here are the sentences:

> "They demand a statesman; they demand a reformer after, as well as before, the election. They demand a politician in the highest, the broadest, and best sense—a man of superb moral courage. They demand a man acquainted with public affairs . . . They demand a man broad enough to comprehend the relations of this government to the other nations . . . They demand a man well versed in the powers, duties, and prerogatives of each and every department of this government. They demand a man who will sacredly preserve the financial honor of the United States . . ."

Ingersoll, who became known as "the eloquent agnostic," concluded his speech by using the same technique of repeating identical words at the beginning of successive clauses: "Gentlemen of the convention, in the name of the great Republic . . .; in the name of all her defenders . . .; in the name of all her soldiers living; in the name of all her soldiers dead upon the field of battle; and in the name of those . . . whose sufferings he so vividly remembers . . . Illinois nominates for the next President of this country that prince of parliamentarians, that leader of leaders, James G. Blaine."

Here's an example from a 1932 campaign speech by Franklin D. Roosevelt which illustrates repetition of the same words at the beginning of consecutive sentences for both clarification and emphasis:

> "We cannot go back to the old prisons, the old systems of mere punishment under which when a man came out of prison he was not fitted to live in our community alongside of us. We cannot go back to the old system of asylums. We cannot go back to the old lack of hospitals, the lack of public health. We cannot go back to the sweatshops of America. We cannot go back to children working in factories."

THE ECHO EFFECT OF REPETITION

Martin Luther King's "I Have a Dream" speech demonstrates how the same words at the beginning of successive sentences can result in haunting refrains. That speech was delivered in 1963 at the Lincoln Memorial in Washington, D.C. to over 200,000 people in his audience at the site and countless more who heard it on national radio and watched it on television.

King spoke with intense passion and the listeners could feel his emotions flowing not only from his ideas but also from his repetition of language that made them clear and emphatic. The repetition had the effect of an echo that connected one sentence with the next. After citing the signing of the Emancipation Proclamation he continued:

> "But one hundred years later, we must face the tragic fact that the Negro is still not free. One hundred years later, the life of a Negro is still sadly crippled by the manacles of segregation and the chains of discrimination. One hundred years later, the Negro lives on a lonely island of poverty in the midst of a vast ocean of material prosperity. One hundred years later the Negro is still languishing in the corners of American society and finds himself an exile in his own land."

Repeated four times, "one hundred years later" sounds like a refrain. Toward the end of his speech King visualized a brighter and happier day when justice would triumph. He started eight consecutive sentences with "I have a dream . . ." Then, with a refrain of "Let freedom ring," he built up toward a high emotional climax that culminated with the words, "Free at last! free at last! thank God Almighty, we are free at last!"

By using repetition at the beginning of successive sentences with a variety of phrases to avoid monotony and with a uniformity of structure to sustain a constant meaning, King eloquently produced a powerful cumulative effect.

This technique of repeating one or more words at the beginning of consecutive sentences is sometimes called the "I see" construction when the speaker portrays a vision or forecasts the future. Adlai Stevenson in the 1952 campaign for president described his vision of America using the "I see" technique:

> "I see an America where no man fears to think as he pleases, or say what he thinks. I see an America where slums and tenements have vanished and children are raised in decency and self-respect. I see an America where men and women have leisure from toil . . . I see an America where no man is another's master . . . I see an America at peace with the world. I see an America as the horizon of human hopes."

Sometimes speakers use the "I see" repetition in a reportorial instead of a visionary sense. When Adolf Hitler ordered his armies to invade Russia during the Second World War, Winston Churchill delivered one of his most eloquent speeches, saying in part:

> "I see the Russian soldiers . . . guarding the fields . . . I see them guarding their homes . . . I see the 10,000 villages of Russia . . . I

> see advancing upon all this, in hideous onslaught, the Nazi war machine . . . I see also the dull, drilled, docile, brutish masses of the Hun soldiery, plodding on like a swarm of crawling locusts . . . I see the German bombers and fighters in the sky . . . I see that small group of villainous men . . ."

Some speakers have substituted "I look forward to" as a variation of the "I see" phrase in the visionary sense. Here's an excerpt from a speech by John F. Kennedy in 1963:

> "I look forward to a great future for America, a future in which our country will match its military strength with our moral restraint, its wealth with our wisdom, its power with our purpose. I look forward to an America which will not be afraid of grace and beauty . . . I look forward to an America which commands respect throughout the world . . . I look forward to a world which will be safe not only for democracy and diversity but also for personal distinction."

The possibilities for variety in repeating words or phrases at the beginning of clauses or sentences are endless. Lincoln said: "I particularly object to . . . slavery . . . I object to it because it assumes that there can be moral right in the enslaving of one man by another. I object to it as a dangerous dalliance . . . I object to it because the fathers of the republic eschewed and rejected it . . ."

Franklin D. Roosevelt said: "Whoever seeks to set one nationality against another, seeks to degrade all nationalities. Whoever seeks to set one race against another, seeks to enslave all races. Whoever seeks to set one religion against another, seeks to destroy all religion."

2. Repetition in the middle

You can also harness the power of repetition to command attention and emphasize meaning by repeating a word in the middle rather than at the beginning of a sentence, as these examples show:

"Man is not the creature of circumstances; circumstances are the creatures of men." (Benjamin Disraeli)

"If a man owns land, the land owns him." (Ralph Waldo Emerson)

"Our ultimate good is a world without war, a world made safe for diversity . . ." (Lyndon B. Johnson)

"We stand today on the edge of a new frontier, a frontier of unknown opportunities and perils, a frontier of unfulfilled hopes and threats." (John F. Kennedy)

3. Repetition at the end

Repetition of the same word at the end of the clauses or phrases also increases the likelihood that your thought will be understood and remembered by your audience. Here are some examples:

"I was born an American; I live an American; I shall die as an American." (Daniel Webster)

"Let our object be our country, our whole country, and nothing but our country." (Daniel Webster)

"When I was a child, I spoke as a child, I understood as a child, I thought as a child." (The Bible)

"The government was created by the States, is amenable to the States, is preserved by the States, and may be destroyed by the States." (John Tyler)

4. Repetition of a single word anywhere

The rhetorical device of repetition can result in eloquent expressions even when a single word is said more than once anywhere in the same or nearby sentences. Some language purists frown on this practice and invoke the rule of thumb against such repetition, preferring to substitute synonyms.

On the other hand, H. W. Fowler, in *Modern English Usage*, says this: "The fatal influence is the advice given . . . never to use the same word in a sentence—or within 20 lines or other limit . . ." Daniel Webster endorsed what he called "the true use of repetition." He said, "There is something which may be called augmentative repetition that is capable sometimes of producing great effect."

Here is an example from a John F. Kennedy speech of "augmentative repetition" that reveals a stronger statement than would have been possible without the repetition of "neglect": "We will neglect our cities to our peril, for in neglecting them we neglect the nation."

Listen to the eloquence generated by Churchill in his use of augmentative repetition in his first speech as Prime Minister before Parliament in 1940:

> "You ask, what is our policy? I say it is to wage war by land, sea and air. War with all our might and with all the strength God has given us, and to wage war against a monstrous tyranny never surpassed in the dark and lamentable catalogue of human crime. That is our policy.
>
> "You ask, what is our aim? I can answer in one word. Victory.

> Victory at all costs—victory in spite of all terrors—victory, however long and hard the road may be, for without victory there is no survival. Let that be realized. No survival for the British Empire, no survival for all that the British Empire has stood for, no survival for the urge, the impulse of the ages, that mankind shall move forward toward its goal."

Read Churchill's words aloud and note the effect of the echo in his repetition of "war," "victory" and "survival."

Ernestine Rose, an eloquent pioneer woman orator in America who became known as the "Queen of the Platform," spoke on temperance, slavery and women's rights. Here's an excerpt from one of her speeches:

> "The slave groans in his chains; woman groans in her supposed inferiority and in her oppression; man groans in his ignorance; men and women groan in poverty; society groans in dishonesty, in falsehood, in dissipation, in vice, in crime, in misery."

If Rose had substituted synonyms for "groans" to avoid repeating it five times, this passage would have lost its impact. Repetition of the same word increases its intensity. Listeners' ears respond to repetition of sound, which also reinforces their memory.

William Faulkner, in his eloquent speech accepting the Nobel Prize for literature, achieved strong emphasis by repeating single words:

> "It is easy enough to say that man is immortal simply because he will endure . . . I believe that any man will not merely endure: he will prevail . . . It is his (the poet's) privilege to help man endure by lifting his heart . . . the poet's voice need not merely be the record of man, it can be one of the props, the pillars to help him endure and prevail."

In those few sentences Faulkner repeats "endure" four times, "merely" and "prevail" twice and uses words beginning with the letter "p" half a dozen times. His regular repetition of "endure" produces an emotional weight as it gathers great emphasis. Reinforcing his purpose with the other repetitions, he creates the effect of rhythm and enriches his total meaning.

REPEATING KEY WORDS

Woodrow Wilson often repeated key words. Here's a single sentence from a speech where he repeats the same word four times: "Compared with the importance of America, the importance of the Democratic party, the importance of the Republican party, the importance of every other party, is absolutely negligible."

Abraham Lincoln's use of repetition in the Gettysburg Address generates powerful rhythm. Repeatedly he uses the words "nation," "conceived," "dedicate," "consecrate," "devotion" and "people." These words, echoed multiple times in his short speech, sound like the chanting of rhythmic incantations. With each recurrence, he arouses sharper and deeper emotional effects.

These effects are achieved by blending rhythm with meaning. Rhythm itself in speeches means little unless it brings out the thought more strongly. When Lincoln repeated "dedicate" six times he wasn't trying to create a rhythmic effect for its own sake. Each time he uses "dedicate" the word points up the thought. That's also true of his three-time use of "people" at the end as he creates a succession of rhythmic strokes sounding like drumbeats, leaving a lasting impression.

5. Repetition of central idea

Another way to make effective use of the repetition technique is to repeat your central idea over and over again throughout your speech. Such repetition, like the theme song recurring in a musical play, creates a singleness of impression which keeps the central idea in the minds of your listeners and thus emphasizes it. This effect is admirably illustrated in Theodore Roosevelt's eloquent speech "The Man with the Muckrake," a model of meaningful repetition.

Roosevelt's central idea is that dishonest politicians and businessmen admittedly should be exposed but indiscriminate mudslinging makes the public conscience insensitive and finally benefits the scoundrels. He said:

> "The men with the muckrakes are often indispensable to the well-being of society; but only if they know when to stop raking the muck, and to look upward to the celestial crown above them, to the crown of worthy endeavor."

Dramatizing his theme, Roosevelt linked it with the story in John Bunyan's *The Pilgrim's Progress* of the Man with the Muckrake, "who could look no way but downward, with the muckrake in his hand; who was offered a celestial crown for his muckrake, but who would neither look up nor regard the crown he was offered, but continued to rake to himself the filth of the floor."

Again and again Roosevelt repeated his central idea but in different words and each time he stressed its relationship to Bunyan's character who lost his sensitivity because he became preoccupied with muck.

6. Antithesis

Another highly sensitive rhetorical device for eloquence is antithesis. This technique balances contrasting ideas by using parallel arrangements of words, phrases or clauses that make the contrasted ideas stand out. Here are examples from John F. Kennedy's Inaugural Address:

> "If a free society cannot help the many who are poor, it cannot save the few who are rich."
>
> "And so, my fellow Americans: ask not what your country can do for you—ask what you can do for your country."

Kennedy's words convey meaning briefly, emphatically and eloquently. Yet all are plain words heard every day. But by using antithesis, that is, balancing contrasted expressions, he creates striking effects. With almost exact parallels on both sides of each equation, he sharpens the contrast of ideas and gives them emphasis that heightens their impact.

Antithesis greatly contributes to the strong rhythm of Lincoln's Gettysburg Address, in which he emphasizes ideas by placing them in clear and direct contrast in a pair of words or phrases, as in these examples:

"... a final resting place for those who here gave their lives that that nation might live ..."

"The brave men, living and dead ... have consecrated it far above our poor power to add or detract."

"The world will little note, nor long remember what we say here, but it can never forget what they did here."

7. Rhetorical question

A rhetorical question assumes its own answer. The question is not asked to get information but to emphasize a point—to make more of an impression than a mere statement could. With the answer already implied, the rhetorical question is both a question and a statement, thus having a double impact on the audience. That's why the rhetorical question is one of the most effective rhetorical devices in speeches.

The eloquent and powerful orator Patrick Henry, called "the tongue of the Revolution," frequently used rhetorical questions. As he was nearing the conclusion of his "Call to Arms" speech, he asked several rhetorical questions: "Why stand we here idle? What is it that gentlemen wish? What would they have? Is life so dear, or peace so sweet, as to be purchased at the price of chains and slavery?" These questions led dramatically to Henry's concluding words, "I know not what course others may take; but as for me, give me liberty, or give me death!"

Speeches in Shakespeare's plays have many rhetorical questions. Shylock in *The Merchant of Venice* asks six rhetorical questions in one speech: "Hath not a Jew eyes? Hath not a Jew hands, organs, dimensions, senses, affections, passions? . . . If you prick us, do we not bleed? If you tickle us, do we not laugh? If you poison us, do we not die? And, if you wrong us, shall we not revenge?"

Shylock expects no direct reply to those questions. But Shakespeare has him ask them because questions stimulate listeners, reach out and grab their attention, and sharpen the message. By posing his questions Shylock focuses attention on his point that Jews are no different from other people. His questions make listeners weigh in their minds the details he presents.

Angelina Grimke, one of America's first women orators, while delivering a speech was constantly interrupted by an angry, shouting and stone-throwing crowd that had gathered outside the building to protest against her speaking. In her day it was shocking and scandalous for a woman to speak on a public platform. As if she were grouping artillery pieces for tactical purposes, she stopped in the middle of her speech and asked a battery of rhetorical questions:

> "What is a mob? What would the breaking of every window be? What would the leveling of this hall be? Any evidence that we are wrong, or that slavery is a good and wholesome institution? What if the mob should now burst in upon us, break up our meeting, and commit violence upon our persons, would that be anything compared with what the slaves endure?"

By asking such vivid and sharply pointed rhetorical questions, Grimke projected her points eloquently. She could have simply stated her thoughts in straight declarative sentences, but not with the same effect. They would have lost their vigor. Asking rhetorical questions is like putting words into the listener's mouth. And the obvious answers are the same for almost everyone in the audience.

8. Alliteration

Alliteration is using two or more successive words each beginning with the same letter. Dr. Lynn Harold Hough, former president of Northwestern University, once said that alliteration gives a speech "the gracious loveliness of finely wrought phrases." The Bible says, "Speech finely framed delighteth the ears" (note the alliterated second and third words).

By repeating the sound of the same letters and slowing down the tempo, alliteration creates attention and emphasizes meaning. One of the oldest rhetorical devices, alliteration has never lost its fascination for both speakers and listeners. It's a simple technique, easy to apply, as in these examples: "Practice produces polished speeches," "Weeping willows wave in the wind," and "Wage war against poverty, privilege and pillage."

Now listen to examples from masters of alliteration:

"The majestic, the magnificent Mississippi." (Mark Twain)

"The deadly, drilled, docile, brutish masses of the Hun soldiery . . ." (Winston Churchill)

"With bloody, blameful blade, he bravely broached his boiling, bloody breast . . ." (William Shakespeare)

Alliteration doesn't have to consist of consecutive words as in the above examples. You can still achieve similar results by using alliteration of nearby words, as shown in the following example from a speech on securing world peace through the law: "What we lawyers want to do is to substitute courts for carnage, dockets for rockets, briefs for bombs, warrants for warheads, mandates for missiles."

The great Roman orator Cicero alliterated by skipping a beat or scattering the words here and there, as in this example: "The short period of life is long enough for living well and honorably."

Lincoln so sprinkled alliteration in the Gettysburg Address that you're hardly aware of the repeated letters unless you look for them: "Four score and seven years ago our fathers brought forth on this continent a new nation, conceived in liberty and dedicated to the proposition that all men are created equal."

Theodore Roosevelt, in his speech "The Man with the Muck-rake," said: "No good whatever will come from that warped and mock morality which denounces the misdeeds of men of wealth . . . which denounces bribery, but binds itself to blackmail."

Here are some modern examples of sprinkled alliteration: "It is easy enough to say . . . that when the last ding-dong of doom has clanged . . . even then there will be one more sound." (William Faulkner); "You must emerge, bright and bubbling with wisdom and well-being . . ." (Adlai Stevenson); "Finally, whether you are citizens of America or citizens of the world, ask of us here the same high standards of strength and sacrifice which we ask of you . . ." (John F. Kennedy); "It is time . . . to climb down off the buckboards of bigotry." (LeRoy Collins); "My record is one of progress, not platitudes; performance, not promises." (Gerald Ford).

9. Simile

A simile is a rhetorical device that compares one thing with something else, using "like" or "as" to show the comparison. The things compared may be essentially different yet strikingly similar in one or more points of resemblance or in the effect produced.

By suggesting pictures or images in the listener's mind, a simile makes speaking more vivid and conveys the speaker's meaning more clearly, as in these examples: "Exciting as a ride on a stone camel" or "Love is like a rose." By pairing up love and a rose, you let the audience think of them together and attribute to love the flower-like characteristics of a rose, an easily recognized object familiar to all.

Here are examples of the simile from some eloquent public speakers:

"This idea that you can merchandise candidates for office like breakfast cereal—that you can gather votes like box tops—is, I think, the ultimate indignity to the democratic process." (Adlai Stevenson)

"We will not be satisfied until justice rolls down like waters and righteousness like a mighty stream." (Martin Luther King)

"Suddenly, true reality appears like the brightness of lightning in a formerly dark place. Or, slowly, true reality appears like a landscape when the fog becomes thinner and thinner and finally disappears." (Paul Tillich)

"Durable as the stars." (Daniel Webster)

"*Squatter Sovereignty* squatted out of existence, tumbled down like a temporary scaffolding." (Lincoln)

"Energy in a nation is like sap in a tree; it rises from the bottom up; it does not come from the top down." (Woodrow Wilson)

10. Metaphor

A metaphor, like a simile, is a rhetorical device that identifies one thing by another. So the purpose of a metaphor is the same as that of a simile. But the difference between these two techniques is that a metaphor makes an implied comparison while a simile makes a direct comparison. "All the world's a stage" is a metaphor but "All the world is like a stage" is a simile. "A heart of stone" is a metaphor because it links the heart with associations attached to a stone.

Martin Luther King eloquently used these metaphors in his speech "I Have a Dream":

"The life of the Negro is still sadly crippled by the manacles of segregation and the chains of discrimination."

"Let us not seek to satisfy our thirst for freedom by drinking from the cup of bitterness and hatred."

11. Analogy

The analogy is another rhetorical device whose function is to make something clear by comparing it with something else. Compared with a simile and a metaphor, both usually brief, the analogy stretches out the comparison to a fuller extent. Speakers use the analogy to bring out the meaning of an idea that's hard to understand or to express clearly in just a few words. The analogy, therefore, involves a comparison more complex or extensive than a simile or a metaphor.

People understand things more easily when what is being explained is properly connected with what they already know. So speakers in using analogies compare the idea they're trying to get across with what the audience is likely to be familiar with. C. S. Lewis, who taught literature at Cambridge University, said in a speech:

> "There are two ways in which the human machine goes wrong. One is when human individuals drift apart from one another, or else collide with one another and do one another damage, by cheating or bullying. The other is when things go wrong inside the individual—when the different parts of him (his different faculties and desires and so on) either drift apart or interfere with one another. You can get the idea plain if you think of us as a fleet of ships sailing in formation. The voyage will be a success only, in the first place, if the ships do not collide and get in one another's way; and secondly, if each ship is seaworthy and has her engines in good order."

CONCLUDING THOUGHTS

Rhetorical devices catch the quality of what you're saying much more clearly, vividly, forcefully and gracefully than ordinary statements can. For these reasons rhetorical devices result in eloquent expressions.

Remember, however, that rhetorical devices are not ornamental afterthoughts obviously added on, but dictated by the whole tone of your speech, like rhythm in poetry or music. Rhetorical devices are a means, not an end in themselves. They should not call attention to themselves as techniques consciously used, but should naturally and inconspicuously contribute their share to the clarity, vigor and beauty of your expression.

Nor should any rhetorical device be overused. If applied too often in the same speech, it might become tiresome to listeners and defeat its purpose. When used at suitable intervals it will interest them and make it easier for them to understand and remember what you say.

CHAPTER 9

Shape Your Eloquence with the Rule of Three

ONE OF THE EASIEST AND MOST EFFECTIVE TECHNIQUES you can use for eloquence is the rule of three. This rule is also known as the triad. Although it's a rhetorical device, the rule of three or triad was not covered in the preceding chapter because this device is so important that it deserves an entire chapter.

Intended to achieve clarity, force and grace, the rule of three enables you to say things in threes in any unit of language: words, phrases, clauses, sentences, paragraphs, even entire speeches. Basically, the rule of three calls for a speaker to say something in groups of three: three items, three points, three whatever.

The eloquence of saying something in threes can be judged by well-known examples such as the following:

"For thine is the kingdom, and the power, and the glory." (The Lord's Prayer)

"We hold these truths to be self-evident, that all men are created equal, that they are endowed by their Creator with certain unalienable rights, that among these are life, liberty and the pursuit of happiness . . . we mutually pledge to each other our lives, our fortunes, and our sacred honor." (The Declaration of Independence)

"Unwept, unhonored, unsung." (Sir Walter Scott)

"Never in the field of human conflict was so much owed by so many to so few." (Winston Churchill)

"I see one-third of a nation ill-housed, ill-clad, ill-nourished." (Franklin D. Roosevelt)

"With malice toward none; with charity for all; with firmness in the right." (Abraham Lincoln)

The rule of three helps public speakers to achieve eloquence in five ways:

1. As a pattern of expression for rhetorical effects.
2. As a process for thinking and developing ideas.
3. As a formula for organizing speeches.
4. As a device for constructing wit and humor.
5. As a method for creating speech titles.

PATTERN OF EXPRESSION FOR RHETORICAL EFFECTS

How do the eloquent quotations cited above stir up people's emotions? The words and the compelling way they're arranged in groups of three make it almost impossible for listeners or readers to say them without emotion. See for yourself. Try saying those words aloud without putting some feeling into them.

By grouping the thoughts in threefold sequence, those quotations attract attention by creating rhythm, accomplishing understanding, and facilitating remembrance. They sound like the musical triad, a chord of three tones, all agreeably related and pleasing to the ear. By its cumulative rhetorical effect, the triple recurrence strengthens the ideas expressed and makes them eloquent.

Words used in series of three often have the same meaning but when so arranged they add eloquence to what you say because they provide the power of repetition, as in shame, dishonor, disgrace; destroy, demolish, annihilate; frauds, myths, shams.

As a vitalizing technique, repetition strengthens an impression and creates a rhythm. Repetition emphasizes an assertion by making it intense and solid through persistence. Listeners deeply feel its significance when you say something three times. Saying it once, then again and yet again compels them to understand and to remember. Carrying them along with the build-up of the repetition, you impress a telling image on their senses.

Describing a theory as "nonsense, drivel and bunk," a speaker used words that all meant the same thing to the audience, that is, the theory was senseless or absurd. But to say "nonsense" wasn't strong enough. Adding "drivel" and "bunk" to "nonsense" increased the impact of his meaning threefold.

Sometimes the three words, though synonyms, have differences in meaning but you fortify your thought by first using a strong word, then a stronger word, and finally the strongest word. Based on a "good, better, best" hypothesis, one word, phrase or clause may be sufficient to generate a little interest; two would be stronger; but three would allow you to reach the highest point of rhetorical intensity. Three in a series, arranged in order of increasing importance, show a gradual progression. This interpretation may explain, for example, why plays and operas generally require three acts for the highest drama.

In the Gettysburg Address, Lincoln said, "we cannot dedicate—we cannot consecrate—we cannot hallow—this ground." He used the words dedicate, consecrate and hallow as precisely as a mathematician uses numbers. Although all three words mean to set something apart for a particular purpose, they don't express exactly the same thing. An added implication differentiates them from one another.

"Dedicate" means solemn and exclusive devotion to a sacred or serious use. "Consecrate" even more strongly than "dedicate" implies endowing something with a richer quality. And "hallow" is still stronger, implying inherent holiness as in the Lord's Prayer.

Lincoln confirms these meanings in subsequent sentences. While honoring the heroic dead, he acknowledges the need for "the living to be dedicated here to the unfinished work . . . that from these honored dead we take increased devotion to that cause . . ." If he had said in the preceding sentence only "dedicate," he would have implied exclusive devotion to the battlefield's use as a burial ground. But by adding the stronger "consecrate" and yet stronger "hallow" and by pausing between the three groups of words, he gave special prominence to each synonym and greater significance to the solemn occasion at Gettysburg—and made those words unforgettable.

Interestingly enough, a famous quotation from another eloquent speaker, Winston Churchill, is misstated by almost everybody because he used a fourfold instead of a threefold pattern. Although he actually said, "I have nothing to offer but blood, toil, tears and sweat," most people know the quotation as "blood, sweat and tears."

Not only have people transferred his original four-part series into three parts by dropping "toil" but they've also transposed "tears" and "sweat." The fact that the quotation was changed from four parts to three attests to the triad's powerful appeal. "Toil" is unnecessary because it conveys the same idea as "sweat." The acoustic effect produced by "blood, sweat and tears" pleases the ear better than "blood, tears and sweat." Say both combinations aloud and compare for yourself.

OMIT CONNECTIVES FOR GREATER IMPACT

Although Churchill's speeches include other four-part sequences, he certainly knew about the triad and used it often. Many times he even intensified the impact of the three-part series by omitting conjunctions, as he did eloquently in these examples:

"The heroes of modern war lie out in the cratered fields, mangled, stifled, scarred . . . It is mass suffering, mass sacrifice, mass victory."

"Civilization will not last, freedom will not survive, peace will not be kept, unless a very large majority of mankind unite to defend them . . ."

Note how in the above examples all the three-part groupings flow evenly, uninterruptedly, harmoniously. Add to or remove from them and see what happens. Chances are the meaning changes or the cadence vanishes. Certainly the total impact is diminished.

Many threefold expressions consist of single words or words combined into phrases and clauses. Woodrow Wilson, one of the few eloquent speakers among American presidents, said in a speech that peace forced upon the loser ". . . would be accepted in humiliation, under duress, at an intolerable sacrifice, and would leave a sting, a resentment, a bitter memory . . ." Note the two triads, each containing single words and phrases.

In his eloquent address to the cadets of the U.S. Military Academy at West Point, Douglas MacArthur effectively combined single words, phrases or clauses into several three-part groups in a short passage:

> "Duty—Honor—Country. Those three hallowed words reverently dictate what you ought to be, what you can be, what you will be. They are your rallying points: to build courage when courage seems to fail; to regain faith when there seems to be little cause for faith; to create hope when hope becomes forlorn."

Listen to Hubert H. Humphrey eloquently repeating "not enough" in three groups of words to amplify and emphasize his point: "There are not enough jails, not enough policemen, not enough courts to enforce a law not supported by the people."

USING FULL SENTENCE TRIADS

But you can also use the same technique with a series of three complete sentences building up to an eloquent conclusion. Here's an example from a Woodrow Wilson speech: "Valor is self-respecting. Valor is circumspect. Valor strikes only when it is right to strike." Notice also the triple repetition of the word "valor."

Today's public speakers also use the threefold pattern. They say: "First, let us discuss . . . Next, let us take up the second point . . . And finally, in the third place, let us consider . . ." Sometimes the speaker puts it this way: "My approach is threefold."

In a speech delivered to the Parent Teacher Association, a speaker scattered at intervals a dozen triads, including: ". . . you grow with strength, with power, with your traditional high purpose . . . Education should move our children in the realms of competency, capability, and cope-ability . . . Teachers, parents, students—working together with a positive attitude—can turn education around. . ."

Referring to over-regulation of banks, a speaker said it leaves them "hamstrung:

—unable to expand into natural markets;

—unable to offer competitive interest rates;

—unable to cope with high inflation . . ."

This series of three phrases and the repetition of "unable to" with each phrase strengthen the thought expressed and can be spoken with rhythm. The triple repetition of "unable to" in a written piece would be considered repetitious, that is, unnecessary, slovenly and tiresome to the eyes. One "unable to" would have been enough. But in a speech the triple use of "unable to" is deliberately repetitive to achieve greater impact and create rhythm that's easy on the ears.

Here are excerpts from other speeches:

"Persistence, determination, and courage have a lot to do with the qualities of leadership."

"We have wastefully frittered away resources, opportunities and time with divided counsel, faint hearts and ineffective leadership."

"We are simply recognizing, redefining, and restoring the old historical link which bound us in the past."

". . . intellectual, cultural, and material development free of strife, conflict, and confusion."

"stuffed with gossip, nonsense, vain talk."

"claims of sincerity, pledges of peace, and expressions of goodwill."

"Contradictions, paradoxes and dilemmas will be constant realities."

"The high technology innovations coming on line today offer . . . the potential for heightened employee boredom, frustration and alienation."

"Ideas, words and symbols have consequences."

"It is a tribute to the capacity of modern labor to respond, to adapt and to move with the times into new areas of service and growth."

"Rhetoric won't do it, but hard work, common sense, and self-discipline *will* do it."

"Never before in history or in any other land has a people accomplished so much, given so much, and asked so little."

"Reward/subsidize/support—yes, but the winners and not the losers!"

"Watch for efforts to block, detour and derail regulation in the field of energy."

COMMON WORDS SUFFICE

Each of those expressions gets the speaker's point across effectively with commonly used words. So your own stock of words is generally sufficient to draw from to say things in groups of three words, phrases or clauses. A large vocabulary by itself doesn't make you eloquent. Basically, you speak only as well as you think. What's necessary, then, is to first think of ways to fit your meaning into the best possible expression.

Sometimes you run into problems. For example, you search your mind for a word and it somehow gets away from you. It's the kind of word that's on the tip of your tongue but that you can't say. And yet it eloquently reflects exactly what you mean and properly fits in the mold of your three-way expression.

Another problem could be that a word which flashes into your mind expresses your idea but isn't eloquent. You know there are more ways than one to say something and some ways are more powerful than others.

So what's the next step? Turn to *Roget's International Thesaurus* or a book of synonyms. Such reference sources present you with various possibilities from which you can choose the one that strikes you as the best.

Roget's thesaurus groups words according to categories of ideas. It lists broad topics, followed by subtopics, with each divided into even more specific categories under which synonyms are shown. You look up your idea word in Roget's alphabetical index and find under it the closest synonym, which refers you to a numbered section in the text. When you turn to that section, if what you find there doesn't satisfy you, scan nearby categories of similar, contrasting or opposite words. Sometimes you can say thoughts more eloquently in a negative way than in a positive way. Seeing a procession of words in one direction or another may stimulate your thinking and expression in ways that hadn't previously suggested themselves. As Roget points out, once you see all the words, "an instinctive tact will rarely fail to lead you to the proper choice."

If you want to confine your search only to synonyms, you'll locate them easier and faster in books of synonyms which arrange them alphabetically. In either *Roget's International Thesaurus* or a synonym book you'll likely find suggestions for eloquent phrasing. So either book is useful to turn to when your mind fails to summon up the right word and needs to be jogged. Neither book, however, gives definitions. If you're not sure of the exact meaning of the synonyms you located, check out their definitions in a dictionary. Otherwise your threefold expressions could mean something entirely different from what you intended.

PROCESS FOR THINKING AND DEVELOPING IDEAS

Here's how the rule of three helps you think and develop ideas. Suppose you were to prepare a speech about a problem in your community. Thinking the problem through requires you to identify it, diagnose it and find a way to solve it. So you ask yourself three questions:

1. What are the facts?
2. Why do they create a problem?
3. How can the problem be solved?

The problem must be something that greatly concerns you. The eloquent philosopher Ralph Waldo Emerson said, "The hardest task in the world is to think." So if you're not really troubled by the problem, you may try to solve it merely by rule of thumb rather than think it through.

Before you think about any problem, you must of course know what it is. Remember, a problem well defined is half solved. Start the thinking process by getting the relevant facts. That answers the "What" question. Then you analyze the facts so that they may yield clues to what's wrong. This involves looking at the information closely. Guided by this knowledge, you determine what relationships exist among the facts that create the problem. All this answers the "Why" question.

Finally, you tackle the third question, which is about the solution. As you think about the problem, your mind will naturally come up with some tentative solutions. You weigh the pros and cons of each, considering its advantages and disadvantages. This allows you to eliminate all except what you consider your best answer. And that clears up the "How" question.

In addition to these three basic "What," "Why," and "How" questions which lead to your main points, you can ask yourself during your process of thinking three related questions which provide secondary points: "What else," "Why else" and "How else."

With such self-interrogating questions, you can prime your mental pump and pile up your speech material as the answers to them stimulate your thinking and crystallize your ideas. The three basic and the three related questions that help you think and develop ideas for your speeches can be applied to almost any problem or subject.

FORMULA FOR ORGANIZING SPEECHES

The rule of three can help to organize your speech. Here's how:

"A whole is that which has beginning, middle and end." So said Aristotle, the Greek philosopher and master of the theory of public speaking. And he was right. Although there are many ways to organize speech material, every speech must have three principal parts: introduction, body, conclusion.

The three questions you asked yourself in the above example of the community problem become the framework around which you build the introduction, body and conclusion of the problem-cause-solution type of speech.

The three-part pattern works just as well in other types of

speeches. In the "tell-tell-tell" type, first, tell them what you're going to say; second, tell them; and third, tell them what you said.

You start the speech by telling your audience, "I'm going to talk about inflation and how it affects everybody." Next, tell them what you want to say about inflation and show how it affects our lives. Finally, you tell them, "I hope I've given you a few ideas about inflation and shown you how it hurts everybody" and briefly summarize what you told them.

In the "past-present-future" type of speech, first say, "Looking back . . ."; second, "Now, let's consider the present situation . . ."; and third, "As we look ahead. . ."

Lincoln's ten-sentence Gettysburg Address is a fine example of this type of speech. He starts off in his first sentence by citing a past event and in the second sentence speaks of the present, revealing his theme. Those two sentences complete the introductory part of his address. In the second part, which has seven sentences, he develops his theme. In the third part, consisting of a final sentence, he concludes with a look to the future: ". . . that this nation under God shall have a new birth of freedom—and that government of the people, by the people, for the people shall not perish from the earth."

Note how Lincoln ends with threefold patterns, using three prepositional phrases and repeating the word "people" three times.

DEVICE FOR CONSTRUCTING WIT AND HUMOR

The triad also works well in constructing humorous and witty expressions. Here's how Ambrose Bierce, author of *The Devil's Dictionary*, used three phrases to define a lecturer: "One with his hand in your pocket, his tongue in your ear and his faith in your patience."

Here's an example consisting of three single words: "This man doesn't chase after women because he's moral, modest, and old."

The humorist Mark Twain used three clauses to say: "The only way to keep your health is to eat what you don't want, drink what you don't like and do what you'd rather not." Lincoln, too, used three clauses in humorously defining an orator as one "who throws back his head, shines his eyes, and leaves the consequences to God."

Wit or humor in the three-unit series also can be expressed in numerical order, designating first, second, and third. Somerset Maugham, the English writer, once said: "The first duty of a woman is to be pretty, the second is to be well-dressed and the third is never to contradict." Sometimes the numerical order takes the one-two-three form," as in these words of historian Henry Adams: "One friend in a lifetime is much, two are many, three are hardly possible."

These and many similar examples of how the triad is used in humor follow a formula. The first item in the group of three establishes a pattern; the second repeats it, thus fixing it more firmly in the mind of the listeners who now know what to anticipate; and the third surprises them with an unexpected twist.

This threefold construction can be used in jokes, where the punch line comes after two brief build-up lines, or in comic stories, which follow the same three-part arrangement but involve fuller development of incidents, ideas or characters.

METHOD FOR CREATING SPEECH TITLES

Further proof of the powerful appeal of the rule of three is the fact that writers as well as public speakers often use it to create titles. Here's how:

An advertisement on cruises to the Mediterranean and Greek islands was titled "Mosques, Myths and Monuments." Note how alliteration lends itself eloquently in triad titles, both in this advertisement title and in actual titles shown below:

Books

Manias, Panics and Crashes
God, Church, and Flag
Stress, Sanity and Survival
Men, Beasts, and Gods
Gentlemen, Scholars and Scoundrels

Magazine Articles

Of Risks, Hazards and Culprits
Noah, the Flood, the Facts
Of Yankees, Cabbages, and Kings
Love, Marriage and Crime

Speeches

Liberty, Leadership, License
News, Good News and Better News
People, Productivity and Profits

Hard Work, Common Sense and Self-Discipline
You Can't Fool *Any* of the People *Any* of the Time *Any* More
Priests, Prophets, and Politicians
Competition, Controls and Catastrophe
The American Collectivist Myth: Its Roots, Its Results, Its Downfall

A MAGICAL NUMBER

Like magic, the number three seems irresistible. Think about it. Note how frequently it appears in our culture. Remember the old saying, "All good things come in threes." The Greek philosopher and mathematician Pythagoras regarded "three" as the perfect number.

The ancient Greeks who believed the world was ruled by three gods revered beauty, laughter, and love. The ancient Chinese worshipped gentleness, frugality, and humility. In Scandinavian mythology the "Mysterious Three" sat on three thrones above the rainbow. The Hindu Trimurti consists of three gods: Creator, Preserver, and Destroyer. Christians believe in the Trinity by which God exists in three persons. Faith, Hope, and Charity are the three Christian graces. Three wise men paid homage to the newborn Jesus and brought three gifts: gold, frankincense, and myrrh.

Three dimensions form the physical world—earth, sea, and air. Man himself has three dimensions: body, mind, and spirit. Nature is threefold: mineral, vegetable, and animal. Time has three aspects: past, present, and future. Government is divided into three levels: national, state, and local. To mark the boundary line of a state's territorial waters, the "three-mile limit" is prescribed.

Society has three economic classes of people—upper class, middle class, and lower class—and three cultural classes: highbrow, middlebrow, and lowbrow. United States citizens shout three cheers for the red, white, and blue.

The charm of the number three starts in childhood with nursery rhymes and fairy tales: "Baa, baa, black sheep/Have you any wool?/ Yes sir, yes sir/Three bags full." You remember this one—"Three blind mice, see how they run!" Children also learn the three R's and enjoy the three-ring circus.

Fascination with the number three continues into adulthood. Tom, Dick, and Harry are tall, dark and handsome. Some people see no evil, hear no evil, speak no evil. Benjamin Franklin said, "What I tell you three times is true." Psychoanalysts divide the human personality into three functional parts: id (instincts); ego (consciousness); and superego (conscience).

The principles of composition are three: unity, coherence, and emphasis. Authors write from three points of view: first, second, or third person. Drama has three divisions: tragedy, comedy, and satire. The three classical principles of dramatic construction are unity of time, unity of place, and unity of action.

Sports lingo shows the power of "three." Track and field events feature a "triple jump" in which contestants make three consecutive jumps. In baseball a batter is out after three strikes and a "triple play" puts out three players. A "triple threat" is a football player who excels in running, kicking, and passing.

The number three often appears in the titles of books, plays, movies, songs, and speeches. Here are a few examples: Three Lives; Three Soldiers; Three Men in a Boat; The Three Musketeers; The Three Sisters; Three Smart Girls; Three Coins in the Fountain; The Unholy Three; Three Nightmares; Three Faces of Eve; Three Lights in the Tower.

As you have seen, the number three has always had a strong psychological appeal. And the rule of three is a handy tool for speakers. It helps you to think and organize your material in an orderly fashion and to express yourself eloquently in a symmetrical and rhythmic manner.

CHAPTER 10

Move Your Audience with Eloquent Delivery

NO MATTER HOW GOOD YOUR CONTENT or how effective your words, your speech is not a speech until you deliver it. A song must be sung. A play must be performed. A speech must be spoken. Delivery makes your speech come alive.

"Eloquence," said the French writer Francois de la Rochefoucauld, "lies as much in the tone of the voice, in the eyes, and in the speaker's manner, as in his choice of words." Aristotle, the Greek philosopher and rhetorician, observed that speakers can "heighten the effect of their words with suitable gestures, tones, dress, and dramatic action."

Demosthenes, Greece's greatest orator, believed that delivery is the secret of successful public speaking. When asked what was the first ingredient of oratory, he answered, "Action"; and what was the second, he replied, "Action"; and what was the third; he still answered, "Action." Cicero, Rome's greatest orator, said, "Delivery is a sort of language of the body—the management, with grace, of voice, countenance and gestures."

The elements of physical delivery—voice and bodily action—work best when coordinated with your mind and emotions. If your thoughts and feelings emerge from a complete understanding of your subject and real interest in it, your delivery will look and sound spontaneous because it will clearly reflect your sincerity. If you must force enthusiasm, your delivery will appear artificial.

SYNCHRONIZE YOUR VOICE WITH ACTION

Using voice and bodily action effectively requires engaging both the mind and the emotions and synchronizing them. This is similar to making sound exactly simultaneous with the action in films or radio and television productions. Your mind, emotions, voice and body all should work together to get your message across to your audience.

Your voice reflects your thoughts and feelings while your gestures reinforce them. Voice and gestures directly relate to the content of your speech.

Just as you cannot deliver a speech without a voice, so you cannot deliver it without bodily action. A speech may be thought of as words set to music with some accompanying action. Words say what we think; vocal tones provide the "music" and reveal how we feel about what we think; gestures reinforce our thoughts and sometimes convey them even without words.

When talking with friends or acquaintances, both children and adults use hands, arms, facial gestures or other bodily action to get their message across. As in breathing, that's a natural, instinctive thing to do. That's why we use gestures even when our listeners cannot see us, as when talking on the telephone. Likewise, speakers on the public platform must give vent to the same impulse.

True enough, ideas can be conveyed from one person to others by actions alone, as in the old silent movies. The expressive body and facial movements of the silent actors told the story. But the "talkies" clearly proved to be superior entertainment and the "silents" disappeared. Will Rogers, whose humor wasn't successful in the silent movies, became a leading box-office star in talking pictures. His oral delivery made the difference. His humor was much funnier to movie audiences when they heard him speak.

Words, voice, gestures and visual aids are components of speech that express your thoughts and feelings. A speech can stand all by itself because it has substance. For example, a speech can be effectively heard on radio without gestures or visual aids. But gestures and visual aids, by themselves, on radio would be like an empty bag. As Benjamin Franklin said, "'Tis hard for an empty bag to stand upright."

Nevertheless, both gestures and visual aids can make your speech a better one because they reinforce what you say. Audiences receive impressions from what they see as well as from what they hear.

You may hear on the radio a speaker who makes no vivid impression on you. When you hear the same speaker on television and see his or her appearance, posture, facial expressions and gestures, you may be more favorably impressed. The speaker's personality comes through by the use of both oral and visual means instead of only oral.

But the purpose of gestures or visual aids is to promote, not overshadow the content of your speech. So they should not outweigh the thoughts you carefully formulated in your speech. A speech is primarily ideas expressed in words and the visual aspects assist in the process of getting your message across to the audience. By simultaneously using all the elements—words, voice, gestures and visual aids—you can deliver your speech eloquently. Here are specific suggestions for accomplishing that objective:

1. Control nervousness and put it to constructive use.

Like almost everybody else, you'll feel some degree of nervousness or stage fright when you face an audience. This is as true of actors, singers and other stage performers as it is of public speakers. An opera singer once said, "The person who doesn't get the least bit nervous at the prospect of stepping on a stage will never move an audience to wild ecstasy. When I stop getting nervous before I sing, that's when I'll retire."

Many eloquent speakers—Abraham Lincoln, Henry W. Grady, Winston Churchill, Adlai Stevenson, to name a few—testified to stage fright.

Lincoln suffered from stage fright every time he began a speech. His face seemed lifeless, his body powerless to move. But as he got into his subject he became more at ease. Before long, his body moved in harmony with his ideas. Grady said, "Every nerve in my body was strung tight as a fiddle-string." Churchill said he felt "a nine-inch square block of ice in the pit of my stomach." Always nervous when beginning a speech, Stevenson ran his hand down his lapel and started in a high-pitched voice. But soon he became absorbed in his thoughts and spoke with eloquent passion.

Maybe such experiences can be explained by Cicero's observation centuries ago that "The better the speaker, the more profoundly is he frightened of the difficulty of speaking, and of the doubtful fate of a speech, and of the anticipations of an audience."

Nevertheless, experience in public speaking does reduce the degree of tensions, even if you never completely lose the feeling. More important, a reasonable amount of nervousness makes you a better speaker if you control it and put it to constructive use. Thorough and careful preparation of everything connected with your speech is probably the best direct control of stage fright. When you're well-prepared, you're in control. That prevents any fear of failure.

To fortify yourself with still more self-confidence, while you're waiting to be introduced, put yourself in the proper mental attitude. Adopt a success attitude by saying to yourself something like this: "I'm glad I'm here to talk with this wonderful audience about this subject. I know that I know it. What I have to say is important for this audience. I'll make them understand what I say and how I feel about it."

Those few sentences will let you speak out of love rather than fear of your audience. You'll feel confident and reveal the look of authority, just as a singer once psyched himself up for his operatic debut by reading about the early experience of superstar Enrico Caruso.

When you actually face the audience to speak, you'll naturally feel keyed up and tense. This should cause you no anxiety, however, since your foolproof preparation avoided any chance of failure. Realize that your tension at this point is like a racehorse's champing at the bit as the race begins. Energized by its nervousness, the racehorse sets off in a burst of activity. In the same way, use the extra energy and heightened emotion of your initial tension to strengthen the delivery of your speech. Your audience will soon respond positively. Then you'll forget all about yourself and concentrate on what you say.

2. Use the extemporaneous method of delivery.

"Extemporaneous" delivery is often confused with "impromptu" delivery. In the extemporaneous method your speech is thought out in advance, planned with great care, usually written down, rehearsed orally and delivered from the outline or notes prepared beforehand. The impromptu method requires no preparation of any kind until a few minutes before delivery.

You may prefer to read your speech manuscript aloud, if you can read it so well that it doesn't sound like reading. Or you may want to memorize your whole speech, if you can deliver it so that your audience never knows you memorized it. Otherwise a speech read from manuscript or delivered from memory may sound like a monotonous, singsong recitation and the audience will surely tune you out. Usually, only a professionally trained and experienced actor or actress can effectively read or memorize entire speeches.

3. Remember the audience judges you even before you speak.

Before you even start to speak, your audience will subconsciously judge you. The first impression your audience takes in of you is entirely visual. If they like what they see, you've started off well. As the wise philosopher Publilius Syrus said a long time ago, "A fair exterior is a silent recommendation." Your audience will eagerly look forward to what you'll say and will be inclined to accept your ideas. But if your audience doesn't like what they see, you've created obstacles in your path.

What does the audience see? They see all that appears—a visual impression based on how you look, how you stand, and how you move. Are you thinking that you can't judge a book by its cover? Maybe so. But a person is not a book. Anyway, audiences do form an opinion of a speaker by his or her external looks.

So after you're introduced by the chairman or toastmaster, remember you're on display. In the few seconds that follow, how you look and whatever you do can help or hurt you in the eyes of your audience.

Walk confidently and briskly to the speaker's stand. Don't slouch. Hold your head and shoulders up. Smile at the audience. Rest your hands at your sides, or lightly on the lectern. Don't suddenly grasp the lectern and hold on to it tightly as though you were using it as a crutch. That action might be effective if used during your speech to accompany an emotional moment but clutching the lectern before you begin to talk would be seen by the audience as an outlet for your nervousness.

The speaker's posture at the lectern is as important as the stance from which an athlete starts or operates. A proper stance at the lectern helps you to begin speaking effectively because your stance affects breathing and shows your mental attitude to the audience. Don't let your body sag like a tired horse's. Don't stand like a soldier at attention—that's too stiff a posture for a public speaker and will turn off your audience. Stand straight with an equal distribution of your weight on both feet, one foot advanced slightly beyond the other. In that way your posture has balance and symmetry, with the shoulders on the same level.

All this discussion on posture and bodily movement is to show their importance in displaying self-confidence on your part and creating a favorable impression on the part of the audience toward you. A poor stance and awkward movements will reveal to the audience your indifference or fear. Either sign will indicate that you're not going to speak with enthusiasm, confidence and authority.

Regarding your physical looks, you may not be able to do much with your face and body, but you certainly can choose clothing that enhances your looks. Ask yourself, "How will the audience be dressed?" and "How does the audience expect me to dress?"

Answers to those questions will help you avoid wearing anything that would offend the audience and distract their attention from what you'll say. For safety's sake follow conventional lines in the matter of clothing. Neither overdress nor be too casual. Dress neatly, cleanly and conservatively, if you want to impress your audience favorably.

How you look at the audience also helps form their opinion of you. "Eye contact" doesn't mean a vague look in the general direction of your audience. That's not the way to make good first impressions. Eye contact is actually the first source of rapport with your listeners. It's the first time you're meeting them and the first time they're meeting you. Look them in the eye! That's what people do in private conversation. They look at each other's face and focus on the eyes because eye contact deepens the meaning of what they're communicating.

The eyes are eloquent communicators not only before you speak but also throughout your speech. Whether the size of your audience is small, medium or large, catch the eye of each member for a few seconds. That helps relax you and makes each person feel you're speaking directly to him or her. As your eyes contact listener after listener, you also see their facial expressions and know whether your message is getting through to them. Their nods of approval show smooth sailing. If they seem bewildered or distracted, you're in for stormy weather and you need to get them back on board your ship or lose them.

4. Use a microphone.

If the audience and room are small, you may not need a microphone. But if it's a large audience and auditorium, a microphone will considerably help both you and your audience—unless you're like William Jennings Bryan or Wendell Phillips whose powerful voices penetrated to every part of any huge indoor or outdoor meeting place where thousands of people could hear them without the aid of today's loud-speaker systems.

A microphone enables you to speak better and easier. You'll be more relaxed, avoid straining your voice, and achieve inflections that would be impossible before a large audience without using a microphone. You can produce effective tone shadings by lowering the volume of your voice and compensating for it by getting a little closer to the microphone while simultaneously slowing down your words. This way you can eloquently nail down significant points.

A few don'ts about the stationary microphone: don't stand too close to it; don't stick your face or mouth against it; and don't speak into it. Instead of speaking directly into the microphone, speak across it. If you're using visual aids or moving on the platform, use a lapel microphone.

5. Speak the way you do in conversation.

Your voice is the basic link between you and your listeners and should be easily heard by them. Everything in your speech is lost if they can't hear you. If they can't hear you, they disregard you, daydream, doze off, or talk with persons next to them. From the standpoint of the audience, your voice should be heard without conscious effort or strain. Nor should it be so loud that it disturbs listeners.

The volume of your voice depends on the size of the room and the size of the audience. If the size of both is small, your normal volume should be loud enough for people in the last row to hear comfortably. If you're not sure whether you're being heard, ask, "If you can hear me in the last row, will you please raise your hand?"

Just as music swells and softens, so your voice should vary in volume. Speak some words louder than normal for emphasis and some softly for variation. If you maintain the same normal volume throughout your speech, it will sound boring and monotonous. Your volume will change automatically, however, if you speak with sincerity.

The more closely your manner of speaking in public resembles the way you speak in private conversation, the more eloquent you will be. That's because you're speaking naturally, you're concentrating on the substance of whatever you're saying, and you're expressing your thoughts convincingly.

Speaking conversationally doesn't mean talking monotonously. On the contrary, when people engage in conversation, their talk is lively. Their voices sparkle with change—change of pitch, change of volume, change of pace. Their voices move up and down, never stay at the same tone. Their voices range all the way from whispers to shouts. They speak fast, slowly and at an in-between pace. Like changing the tempo of a musical piece, changing the rate of speaking provides their conversation with rhythmic animation.

VOICE REFLECTS ATTITUDES

If that's the way people normally speak in private conversation, why not speak the same way in public? The people who speak in conversation are the same people who sit in audiences and the same people who talk on the public platform. Your voice is what your audiences hear and it's your voice that reflects your attitudes and reactions. So your normal changes in pitch, volume and pace serve as techniques of interpretation in communicating your thoughts and feelings.

Franklin Roosevelt's direct speaking manner in public speeches undoubtedly accounted in large measure for his eloquence in convincing most of his audiences in four presidential campaigns. In fact, some of his opponents maintained that his speech delivery was the only reason for his effectiveness.

In a friendly and reassuring voice, Roosevelt spoke directly, clearly and forcefully. All this was reflected almost entirely in his voice, since his physical condition restricted bodily action to head movement and facial expression. He needed both hands and both arms to support his weight and steady himself at the speaker's stand.

Winston Churchill was another master in the use of his voice. Though not an outstanding voice, it served him well. With varying inflections he emphasized words and showed his feelings. He spoke distinctly and slowly, even haltingly. A biographer wrote, "Something seemed to make him chew every word several times before allowing it to escape from his lips. It was as if he wanted to suck all the juice out of it and savor its taste to the fullest."

What distinguished Abraham Lincoln's ordinary voice was its intensity, which stemmed from his convictions and a burning desire to express them. He felt deeply about what he said, so he spoke from his heart. "Great speeches," observed author E. B. White, "are as much a part of a man as his eyeballs or his intestines." Poet William Butler Yeats put it this way, "He that sings a lasting song thinks in a marrow bone." And according to poet Frederick Goddard Tuckerman, "What is drawn from the heart alone bears the impress of immortality."

Speaking intensely made it also possible for Lincoln to be heard. An eyewitness report of the delivery of his second inaugural address stated: "Every word was clear and audible as the somewhat shrill and ringing tones of Lincoln's voice sounded over the vast concourse." His slow rate of speaking enabled him to emphasize his important words and helped his listeners to understand his points. He once said,

"I am compelled by nature to speak slowly, but when I throw off a thought it seems to me, though it comes with some effort, it has force enough to cut its own way and travel at a greater distance."

Most of us have an adequate voice for effective speaking. Yes, some voices sound better than others and a few are good enough for singing grand opera. Some public speakers, like Franklin Roosevelt and William Jennings Bryan, are golden-voiced or silver-tongued. But Lincoln and Churchill were not. And most of us have average voices. That's all you need to speak in conversation or on the public platform.

Shakespeare advised actors to "Speak the speech . . . trippingly on the tongue." His advice also applies to public speakers. To speak "trippingly" is to speak naturally, effortlessly, clearly. If you speak with sincerity, you won't even have to give conscious attention to variety in your voice because sincerity causes the appropriate changes in pitch, volume and pace.

6. Fit your gestures to your words.

"Suit the action to the word," said Shakespeare to actors. That's excellent advice for public speakers, too. Gestures and words go hand in hand.

Some speakers believe in practicing and rehearsing gestures as well as in marking the places in their notes or speech manuscript. Other speakers say such "canned" gestures look mechanical and stiff.

Using gestures can eloquently strengthen your words. But if you fully understand your ideas and truly feel the emotion when you're speaking on the public platform, you'll gesture naturally, as you do in conversation.

Although professional actors rehearse gestures, they follow the playwright's words and stage directions. All bodily action by public speakers, however, must start from within themselves because they're revealing their own thoughts and feelings. During the actual delivery, the speaker should concentrate on communicating ideas and let gestures come spontaneously.

Even so, gestures depend not only on the content of your speech but on the occasion and the size of the room as well as the size of the audience. For example, a member of Congress giving a college commencement speech would act more like a statesman than a politician. As a statesman, he'd be more restrained in gesturing on that occasion than he would at a political rally. He'd also choose a subject that would require only a modest use of moderate gestures compared to the fist-pounding and wild arm-swinging freely used at a political rally.

Speaking to a small audience in a small meeting room, you'd use gestures similar to the quantity and type normally used in conversation. On the other hand, speaking to a large audience in an auditorium, you'd use gestures with a broad sweep so that they could be seen by members of the audience at a distance from you.

THOUGHTS COMPEL GESTURES

In any case, gestures should grow out of the substance of your speech. Gestures and speech ideas go together. You'll feel compelled to gesture when and where your thought requires such an action.

William Jennings Bryan, speaking at a national political convention, said, "You shall not press down upon the brow of labor this crown of thorns, you shall not crucify mankind on a cross of gold." As he said "crown of thorns," he raised his hands to his head, dug his fingers in his temples as if he were being pierced by sharp-pointed thorns. When he said "cross of gold," he held out his arms like a cross giving the effect of being bound to the cross and crucified in the flesh, stood in that posture for a few seconds, then lowered his arms to his sides, concluding his speech.

When Patrick Henry was nearing the end of his "call to arms" speech before the convention of delegates in Richmond, Virginia, he asked, "Is life so dear or peace so sweet as to be purchased at the price of chains and slavery?" As he said "chains and slavery" he bowed his head, locked his hands together as if he were a slave in chains, and raised his "chained" hands over his head. Continuing with "I know not what course others may take, but as for me, give me liberty, or give me death!" he lowered his arms, threw back his body and strained against his imaginary chains as if to break them; and when he said, "or give me death!" he pretended to stab himself, holding in his right hand an ivory letter opener as if it were a knife.

Your gestures certainly don't have to be as dramatic as Bryan's or Henry's to be effective. Norman Thomas, social reformer and political leader, was a brilliant speaker and constantly in demand, speaking several times a week. Part of his eloquence were his simple gestures, such as pointing his finger, flinging out his arm, shaking his head. John Kennedy used few gestures, mostly a short straight jab in the air with his hand to emphasize his points.

Other great speakers who favored simple gestures include Daniel Webster, using the pointing finger and the open palm of the hand;

Henry Clay who shrugged his shoulders; Wendell Phillips who used the open palm, first with one hand, then the other and sometimes the index finger, palm or fist of one hand into the palm of the other; Lincoln, before he became president, extended his index finger of the right hand or raised both arms with clenched fists for emphasis, but as president, no bodily action accompanied his speeches, probably because he then delivered them from manuscript.

7. Use visual aids to reinforce your ideas.

Use visual aids only when you determine you need them to get your message across. They should not be used merely as crutches, gimmicks or props, no matter how attractive, cute, ingenious or novel they may be. Nor should they be used to the extent that the speaker's talk becomes a spoken aid to a visual display. That's not public speaking. And you don't have to illustrate with a visual aid every point in your speech.

Why use visual aids? To reinforce ideas. If you present an idea simultaneously with talk and visual aid, chances are you double the audience's understanding and retention of that idea. This is especially true if the idea is complicated or difficult to put into words. Charts and graphs, for example, are particularly useful in establishing trends.

Here are some suggestions for using visual aids effectively:

—Choose aids which reinforce exactly those points you want to emphasize.

—Show the aid while you're talking about it in the speech.

—Make sure the aids are large enough for all members of the audience to see easily.

—Keep the aids simple and clear, free from distracting or too many details.

—Use different types of aids for different points to heighten audience interest.

—Maintain eye contact with your audience while they're looking at the aid.

8. Use the pause technique for a variety of purposes.

As in music and acting, the pause is a powerful technique in public speaking. Mark Twain, a frequent user of the pause, described it as "that impressive silence . . . which often achieves a desired effect where no combination of words, however felicitous, could accomplish it."

Yet many speakers shudder as they imagine that pauses suggest they've lost their train of thought. So they rush through their words or use distracting sounds like "ah" or "er." Instead, they could help both themselves and the audience by pausing. If the speaker continues to look at the audience during a pause, they will appreciate it as part of the speech.

Here are several ways you can use the pause technique:

To punctuate a speech. A printed piece that lacks punctuation confuses or frustrates readers. Audiences react the same way to speeches without pauses. Just as punctuation marks denote stops of varying degrees, so do pauses range from a split second to several seconds. Because punctuation is for the eyes and pausing for the ear, punctuation and pauses don't always coincide, as in this sentence from one of Churchill's speeches (slant lines show pauses):

> "Let us, therefore, / brace ourselves to our duties, / and so bear ourselves / that, if the British Empire and its Commonwealth / last for a thousand years, / men will still say, / 'This / was their finest hour.'"

By pausing after "This" where there's no comma, Churchill made sure the audience wouldn't miss the words that followed.

To control breathing. That's why some speakers phrase their thoughts to allow themselves places to pause and inhale. These pauses not only enable them to refill their lungs but also give audiences a breather. The pause as a moment of refreshment was the basis of the Coca-Cola Company's advertising slogan, "The Pause That Refreshes."

To sharpen humor. In telling a humorous story, pause just before you come to the punch line. This alerts the audience to listen expectantly for your next words. Then deliver the punch line. Pause again to let the listeners get your point and laugh. This is important because laughter is catching and spreads fast. First one laughs, then another and then others. In a few seconds all are laughing.

To strengthen questions. Questions in speeches should be followed by pauses. If you want the audience to reply aloud, you have no choice but to pause. If you answer the question yourself or it implies its own answer, pausing after the question allows the listeners time to think about the response. This draws them in as unspoken but absorbed participants. In any case, the pause after a question or a series of questions results in closer communication with the audience.

To quiet down the audience. After you're introduced to speak, there's automatic applause. When it stops, before you begin talking, wait for the audience to settle in the seats. After you say "Mr. Chairman," pause again slightly and continue with "Ladies and Gentlemen." Pausing before you start speaking and between the salutation and introduction gives you poise and rivets the audience's attention as you make the first impressions.

To emphasize your main points. The body of your speech, containing most of your material, provides many opportunities for using pauses to point up thoughts. Silence signals the listeners as if you were telling them, "Now hear this" or "Let this sink in."

Franklin Roosevelt often paused between phrases for emphasis. In his first inaugural address, speaking about "the unscrupulous money changers," he said:

> "They know only the rules of a generation of self-seekers. They have no vision, / and when there is no vision / the people perish. The money changers have fled from their high seats in the temple of our civilization. We may now restore that temple / to the ancient truths. The measure of the restoration lies in the extent to which we apply social values / more noble than mere monetary profit."

Notice how Roosevelt arranged words into short phrases for pauses and for a change of pace mingled them with longer phrases or entire sentences without pauses.

To dramatize your conclusion. Just before you come to the end of any speech, signal ahead to your audience that you're reaching your conclusion. Step forward on the podium or lean forward if you're behind a lectern. Then pause. Now every eye is focused on you and every ear is tuned in to you as your audience looks forward to what's coming next.

Pauses at appropriate points during your closing statements will create a cumulative effect and make your last words stand out compellingly. When you finish talking, remain standing as you pause for a second to let your words register a final impression. Then bow slightly and return to your seat.

By dramatizing the contrast between sound and silence, the pause compels attention. There's more to communication than words; pauses can make silence more eloquent than words. When a speaker on the public platform pauses, the stillness that fills the room tells the story eloquently. You can hear the proverbial pin drop. Everyone fixes his or her eyes on the speaker with complete attention.

Giving a speech with pauses draws out the fullest meaning from language in expressing thoughts and feelings. That's why eloquent speakers have used the pause to add power to their speeches. And the potent pause will work for you, too.

A WORD OF SUMMARY

Immediately following the delivery of a speech, some members of the audience go up to the speaker to say some complimentary things similar to the following:

1. You looked wonderful on that platform.
2. You sounded great.
3. I liked your charts and graphs, especially the colors.
4. Your ideas convinced me I had the wrong slant on the subject.

If you were the speaker, which one of those four statements would you appreciate the most?

The first three comments would show your delivery techniques called attention to themselves and away from the content of your speech. The fourth comment would indicate you focused the listener's attention on what you said, not how you said it. By persuading the listener you communicated your message and achieved the purpose of your speech. That should give you the deepest pride.

When an actor plays a role, the audience applauds him not for his techniques but for his realistic re-creation of a character in a play or novel. Being immersed in the character he's representing, the actor is so completely occupied in making the imaginary character come alive as to lose his own identity as a person.

Similarly, a public speaker should be so wholly absorbed in communicating his thoughts to the audience that he is free from the conscious use of techniques.

"Art," says the Latin proverb, "lies in concealing art." The American painter James Whistler echoed the same observation when he said, "Industry in art is a necessity—not a virtue—and any evidence of the same in the production is a blemish, not a quality; a proof not of achievement but of absolutely insufficient work, for work alone will efface the footsteps of work."

Although techniques are used by both the actor and speaker, their success depends on how vividly and convincingly they communicate to their audiences without showing any traces of their painstaking work beforehand. Whistler put it this way, "To say of a picture, as is often said in its praise, that it shows great and earnest labor, is to say that it is incomplete and unfit for view."

Speech delivery, then, should communciate without calling attention to its techniques.

CHAPTER 11

Enrich Your Speech with Eloquent Quotations

"I HATE QUOTATIONS."

That's what Ralph Waldo Emerson said. But he changed his mind ten years later when he said, "Next to the originator of a good sentence is the first quoter of it."

More than a century after his death, Emerson is often quoted today and many of his phrases have become household words. Early dubbed the "Sage of Concord" and later "The Wisest American," he said our knowledge is the accumulated thought and experience of countless minds. He kept a journal which he called his "savings bank" for depositing ideas and quotations to use in speeches and writings. He used over 3,000 quotations from nearly 900 authors, poets and philosophers. Emerson, you see, certainly believed in quotations.

So do eloquent public speakers. From ancient to modern times they have used the quotation as a most important speech technique. Using quotations opens the door to an immense treasure house of choice morsels of wisdom and experience on any subject. Books of quotations glow like chests of jewels. Tolstoy, the Russian novelist and philosopher, said, "The short sayings of wise and good men are of great value. They are like the dust of gold or the sparkle of the diamond."

Views of great persons or experts are usually impressive and lend justification to what the speaker says. Because quotations command authority, using them reinforces ideas and makes them more powerful.

Successful public speakers, therefore, often use quotations. The

19th century reformer Wendell Phillips, who electrified audiences, quoted or cited the opinions of others 29 times in a speech that glitters even in cold print. Winston Churchill's speeches show he frequently turned to Bartlett's *Familiar Quotations*, which he said "is an admirable work, and I studied it intently." Adlai Stevenson typically quoted half a dozen times in a 20-minute speech. John F. Kennedy loved quotations and used them freely in making speeches.

Kennedy quoted others 21 times in a political campaign speech. All the quotations were short, many only phrases. Theodore C. Sorensen, Kennedy's speech collaborator, writes in his book *Kennedy*: "While I learned to keep a *Bartlett's* and similar works handy . . . (Kennedy) was the chief source of his own best quotations. Some were in the black notebooks he had kept since college—some were in favorite reference books on his desk . . . most were in his head. He would not always be certain of the exact wording or even the author of a quotation he wanted, but he could suggest enough for his staff or the Library of Congress to find it."

This chapter will deal with the speech techniques involved in the use of quotations, including:

1. Why Use Quotations?
2. Ways to Use Quotations.
3. Where to Find Quotations.
4. How to Select Quotations.
5. How to Deliver Quotations.

WHY USE QUOTATIONS?

Why should you use quotations in speeches? Doesn't the audience expect you to give your ideas and your views on the subject? No matter how good the quotation, it's still not you. It doesn't replace your own thinking, nor are the words yours.

All that is true. But here are reasons why quotations improve your speeches:

1. Quotations strengthen your point.

Your audience will be impressed if you show that prominent experts, honored persons, well-known personalities or famous historical figures agree with what you say. The persons you quote strengthen your point and help you sell it.

You say, for example, "A long time ago Socrates said this. . . . Later, Thomas Jefferson said the same thing in these words . . . Then John F. Kennedy expressed the same thought this way . . ." By citing the three quotations, you produce a cumulative effect. Then you tie them all together with your own thought as you say, "And the idea is just as valid now as it has been down through the ages."

2. Quotations add authority.

Merely mentioning a famous person's name pricks up listeners' ears, intensifies interest and arouses curiosity. So they listen with eager anticipation. This helps you to achieve greater impact in sharing thoughts with them. Because a speech becomes linked in memory with its quotations, they will remember what you say as long as they associate it with the quotes.

When suitably chosen and properly used, the quotation is a public speaker's best friend. "Quotations have great service for speeches," said Aristotle, "because people are pleased when a speaker hits on a wide general statement of opinions that they hold in some partial or fragmentary form."

By quoting, you show you're not the only person with the same opinion or attitude. This tends to sway audiences toward accepting what you say as right or reasonable. Here's how Emerson made the same point: "Another's thoughts have a certain advantage with us simply because they are another's."

3. Quotations make speeches sparkle.

Quotations are usually expressed eloquently. They add a touch of class to speeches. They offer clarity, vividness, beauty or wit which ordinary speakers would find hard to match. "A great man quotes bravely," said Emerson, "and will not draw on his invention when his memory serves him with a word as good." And some speakers agree with the French essayist Michel de Montaigne, who said "I quote others only in order the better to express myself."

4. Quotations provide humor.

This doesn't mean using quotations to get the audience merely to laugh, but to further your thought or emphasize it. For example, in a political campaign speech John F. Kennedy was saying that the President had not faced up to a number of problems. Then he added, "Much has been said—but I am reminded of the old Chinese proverb: 'There is a great deal of noise on the stairs but nobody comes into the room.' The President's State of the Union Message reminded me of the exhortation from King Lear that goes: 'I will do such things . . . what they are I know not . . . but they shall be the wonders of the earth'."

With those two quotations Kennedy poked fun at his political opponent. Later, injecting homespun humor in the same speech, he presented another quotation, "It is not enough merely to represent prevailing sentiment—to follow McKinley's practice, as described by Joe Cannon, of 'keeping his ear so close to the ground he got it full of grasshoppers'."

WAYS TO USE QUOTATIONS

1. As a speech opener.

Audiences seem to give their best attention during a quotation. That's probably why many speakers use a quotation when they must first arouse the audience's interest.

Here's a remarkably effective introduction by John F. Kennedy who uses with his first words a quotation that emphatically thrusts itself into instant attention:

> "'Our Constitution is color blind,' wrote Mr. Justice Harlan before the turn of the century, 'and neither knows nor tolerates classes among citizens.' But the practices of the country do not always conform to the principles of the Constitution. This message is intended to examine how far we have come in achieving first-class citizenship for all citizens regardless of color, how far we have yet to go, and what further tasks remain to be carried out."

That introduction stands out conspicuously because the striking quotation not only creates attention but also because it's short with clear and decisive application to Kennedy's subject.

Another speaker also used a short, apt and well-expressed quotation at the start of his speech on education and public policy:

> "George Bernard Shaw wrote that 'we have no more right to consume happiness without producing it than to consume wealth without producing it.'

"In our affluent society we are blessed with both continually rising production and continually rising consumption of material wealth. At the same time, we are not keeping pace in the production of those human resources that make for quality and creativity in our lives. In these areas—the vital areas of the public happiness—we have begun to live off our intellectual capital, trying to consume more happiness than our efforts are producing."

Short quotations are preferred over long ones. Even two or three short quotes are better than one long quotation. Quotes from several persons who agree carry far greater influence than one quote. You're also more likely to sustain the audience's attention with brief selections. Sometimes, however, short quotes may fail to achieve your purpose. Then you may use a long quotation if it's eloquently phrased and not complicated. Here's an example of a speaker who included a long, yet eloquent and fitting, quotation in the introduction of his speech on the function of books in civilization:

"Books are not dull, inanimate, unimportant sheets of paper attached to cardboard bindings. Without the written recordings of man's thoughts and emotions civilization would be impossible. Clarence Day has expressed well the importance of books in these words:

'The world of books is the most remarkable creation of man. Nothing else that he builds ever lasts. Monuments fall. Nations perish. Civilizations grow old and die out—and after an era of darkness—new races build others, but—in the world of books are volumes that have seen this happen again and again—and yet live on—still young—still as fresh as the day they were written—still telling men's hearts of the hearts of men—centuries dead!'"

2. In the body of a speech.

Quotations in the body of a speech support general statements, back you up and add substance to your points. Such strengthening makes your ideas more believable than if you merely state them. Your audience is less likely to accept an idea with only your say-so. By using quotations you muster support for your views from famous persons standing behind you. Your listeners will recognize their prestige and authority which will influence them to agree with you.

The keynote speaker at an annual convention of the Maryland School Food Service Association quoted in the body of his speech the following words from Rudyard Kipling:

"I keep six honest serving men
They taught me all I knew
Their names are What and Why and When
And How and Where and Who."

Commenting on each of Kipling's six serving men, the speaker supported with quotations his central idea that challenges are opportunities in disguise. Under each of the six men he made his comments and used quotations from famous people to heighten the effect of his message.

Under "Who," for instance, the speaker said that opportunities are made available for every one and a second look at even trouble will show it's an opportunity in disguise. To shore up his views he quoted brief observations of five persons. In the same way the speaker took up each of Kipling's other serving men, using quotations from different authorities or experts.

In a speech delivered at the Illinois State Legislature during a Lincoln memorial observance, the speaker used 32 quotations in the body of his talk. That's a lot, yet none was superfluous. All the quotes came from Lincoln, the speaker's subject; all but two had only one or two sentences; and each was appropriate to the speech topic.

Skillfully weaving the quotes throughout the body of his speech, the speaker dealt with his central theme, "What did Abraham Lincoln stand for?" He identified ten qualities of Lincoln and used the quotations to substantiate or illustrate each. For example, in describing Lincoln's sense of responsibility, the speaker said, "Lincoln always assumed that every person had the personal responsibility, indeed a personal obligation, to improve himself and to respect the government of his country which granted him opportunity to improve himself."

To sustain this view, the speaker offered evidence in Lincoln's own words. From Lincoln's speech to the Young Men's Lyceum of Springfield, the speaker quoted: "Let every American, every lover of liberty, swear by the blood of the (American) Revolution, never to violate the laws of the country; and never to tolerate their violation by others . . . Let every man remember that to violate the law is to trample on the blood of his father." In the same way the speaker covered each of the other nine Lincoln qualities.

In a commencement address delivered at the Mississippi University for Women, a speaker eloquently used in the body of her speech six brief Biblical verses to hang her thoughts on. In addition the verses helped her thread her ideas into a continuous strand and relate them to her theme that the future is purchased by the present.

For instance, she quoted one of the verses, "There is a time to weep and a time to laugh—a time to mourn and a time to dance." She followed this quotation with her own points: "If in the present we can remove the thorn of discrimination against women, which has caused us to mourn and weep, then we will purchase a future of equal partnership for men and women which will enable us to laugh and dance together." This pattern was maintained by the speaker for each of the quotations she used from the Bible.

3. To end a speech.

The last words in a speech are what your audience remembers the longest. That's why a quotation at the end of a speech can drive home your message in one powerful or clinching blow. In a speech delivered to the Canton Lions Club in Ohio, the speaker emphasized as his theme the need to sustain and strengthen America's free enterprise. His closing words were as follows:

> "And if all Americans who love this country and wish to sustain it will do what is necessary to renew our national sense of self-confidence, there can then be no doubt that America, this new world, will remain—in the words of the American poet, Edgar Lee Masters—'Forever new to the hands that keep it new'."

Another speaker, talking to the Public Affairs Council in Washington, D.C. about the federal government, ended his speech as follows: "I know how it can be changed—how we can realize the opportunities of the new age. And the surprising thing is that we are on the right track. Let me leave you and the President with one more quote from Will Rogers. He said, 'Even those who are on the right track will get hit if they just sit there'."

Those two examples both show how a brief quotation can end your speech on a note of finality with a minimum of words. This doesn't mean you must restrict yourself to equally short quotations in ending a speech. A long quotation enabled one speaker, whose theme was preserving America's freedom, to conclude eloquently as follows:

> "We must continue to work as leaders of American business to preserve our free enterprise system and its Siamese twin—personal liberty. There is no greater inspiration to do so than that contained in the words of Winston Churchill as he spoke of another compelling challenge at the onset of World War II:
>
> 'Still if you will not fight when you can easily win without

bloodshed, if you will not fight when your victory can be sure and not too costly, you may come to the moment when you will HAVE to fight with all the odds against you and you have only a precarious chance of survival. There may even be a worse case; you may have to fight when there is no hope of victory because it is better to perish than to live as slaves.'"

Or you can use two short quotations and work them into some final words of your own that bear directly on your theme or strongly suggest what you want your audience to think or do. A lawyer used this technique eloquently in a speech on "A Profile in Courage" delivered to the St. Thomas More Society of America in Washington, D.C. Here's his conclusion:

> "Let me say a final word about what St. Thomas More—who *was* and *is* great by conforming to conscience rather than convenience and consensus—can mean for you and me in our practice of the law.
>
> "Theodore Roosevelt once said: 'The most timid rabbit alive is not afraid of a dead issue.' Adlai Stevenson added that, 'We are all brave enough to be against George III or Negro slavery.' It is also easy enough to applaud the action of St. Thomas More.
>
> "But what about . . . the decision you know is the right decision . . . but which the majority feel is the wrong opinion? . . . Will we join if only in spirit the exalted ranks of St. Thomas More?"

Sometimes you need to set up a scene before ending a speech with a strong and satisfying quotation, whether short or long. A Lincoln quotation provided John F. Kennedy with a forceful and solemn ending in a speech to the National Press Club in Washington, D.C. Framing the quotation with dramatic impact, he set the scene, showing what Lincoln had been doing just before the momentous occasion. Then came the Lincoln quote, which he followed with a short series of sharp sentences of his own to intensify the feelings of his audience. Listen to his conclusion:

> "When Lincoln went to sign the Emancipation Proclamation after several hours of exhausting handshaking that had left his arm weak, he said to those present: 'If my name goes down in history, it will be for this act. My whole soul is in it. If my hand trembles when I sign this Proclamation, all who examine the document hereafter will say: 'He hesitated.'
>
> "But Lincoln's hand did not tremble. He did not hesitate. He did not equivocate. For he was the President of the United States. It is in this spirit that we must go forth in the coming months and years."

A few days after Kennedy was assassinated, Lyndon B. Johnson addressed a joint session of Congress and concluded by using a well-known quotation as the last words. But first Johnson set the scene to foster the right mood and reiterate his theme. Here's what he said:

> "We meet in grief; but let us also meet in renewed dedication and renewed vigor. Let us meet in action, in tolerance, and in mutual understanding.
>
> "John Kennedy's death commands what his life conveyed—that America must move forward. The time has come for Americans of all races and creeds and political beliefs to understand and to respect one another . . .
>
> "I profoundly hope that the tragedy and the torment of these terrible days will bind us together in new fellowship, making us one people in our hour of sorrow. Let us here highly resolve that John Fitzgerald Kennedy did not live—or die—in vain. And on this Thanksgiving Eve, as we gather to ask the Lord's blessing, and give Him our thanks let us unite in those familiar and cherished words:
>
> 'America, America,
> God shed His grace on thee,
> And crown thy good
> With brotherhood
> From sea to shining sea.'"

4. As a framework for an entire speech.

You may consider the quotation as something that enhances a speech but is not an essential part of it. Instead of an accessory, however, the quotation can be the actual framework of a speech. Interestingly enough, quotations can provide you with probably the simplest and easiest techniques for constructing an entire speech.

For example, suppose your subject is "Courage." Look it up in a book of quotations and see what's been said about it. You find Churchill's words, "Courage is the first of human qualities because it is the quality which guarantees all others."

As you read on, you arrive at other quotations that reflect the same idea in different ways. Then you keep going under "Courage" to see what else you can discover. You come to these words of the British author Charles Caleb Colton: "To constitute a great man both physical courage and moral courage are necessary." This statement adds to your information by showing the need for at least two kinds of courage.

As you continue searching you find that view corroborated by Theodore Roosevelt who said, "No man is worth much . . . if he is not capable of feeling righteous wrath and just indignation, if he is not stirred to hot anger by misdoing, if he is not impelled to see justice meted out to the wrongdoers . . . if he does not possess both moral and physical courage."

Those quotations trigger your own thinking. They're useful not only for what they say but also for what they suggest. They're seed thoughts that provide you with an outline for your speech. Your theme might be, "Courage is the most important human quality and necessary to do anything truly worthwhile." Churchill's words could be your introduction, you might weave Colton's into the body, and Roosevelt's could serve as your conclusion because they summarize the whole speech.

Of course you need to flesh out your outline with expanded thoughts and examples of people who have shown courage. Among the great masters of courage Roosevelt and Churchill shine with particular brilliance. Undaunted by fear, danger, pain or ridicule, they demonstrated both physical and moral courage dozens of times. A few examples from their lives would round out your speech.

The illustration on "Courage" presented above is only one sample of how quotations can help you build up an entire speech. You can apply the same technique to almost any subject.

WHERE TO FIND QUOTATIONS

Scores of quotation books are available. Many have indexes of author and subject. Others show the quotations under topics arranged alphabetically. General quotation books are John Bartlett's *Familiar Quotations* and Burton Stevenson's *The Home Book of Quotations*. These two authoritative and popular books are often referred to as simply "Bartlett's" or "Stevenson's."

Another general anthology is the *Oxford Dictionary of Quotations*. The *International Thesaurus of Quotations*, which gives you the same service with quotations that *Roget's International Thesaurus* gives you with words and phrases, has three indexes: author, key words and categories. George Seldes' *The Great Quotations* includes less familiar and more provocative entries.

Among the specialized collections are *Quotations from Shakespeare, Quotations from Lincoln*, and *The Quotable Woman*, which devotes itself exclusively to quotes from notable women. Some collections specialize in recent quotations, such as *The Penguin Dictionary of Modern Quotations* and *Contemporary Quotations*.

You can also obtain suitable quotations from reading books, plays, poems, newspapers and magazines as well as from listening to speeches and radio or watching television. Poems provide an effective change of pace in the use of quotations, since your speech is in prose. Use only parts of poems unless they're short and preferably lines that rhyme. Rhymes appeal to the ear. Light verses you find in newspapers and magazines can help you inject touches of humor in your speeches while making your points.

So that you don't forget them, you should write down quotations you find in your current reading or listening and file them on cards or in notebooks for later use. Such quotations will sound fresher than those found in anthologies and the most recent ones will update your speeches.

HOW TO SELECT QUOTATIONS

1. Make sure the quotation is easy to understand.

Any quotation you use in a speech should explain itself. If it's not easily understood or you need to describe the conditions of bygone times to make it apply to your point, it's not worth using no matter how famous the person you're quoting. "There's a way to do it better—find it" said Thomas Edison. And he was right. He was talking about laboratory experiments but his advice also applies to selecting quotations. Among the thousands of quotations readily available you'll find enough that don't require translation or explanation.

2. Use different authorities.

One quotation from a person of ancient times may be sufficient. Then one from modern times. Another from a recent year. Also vary the types of authorities: philosopher, poet, novelist, statesman, scientist, lawyer, educator, industrialist. Using quotations from persons differing in national origin or type of work can add interest to what you say.

3. See that the quotation fits.

The quotation should apply to today's conditions and match the thought you're trying to express. The quotation should also fit the audience. A quotation that will be understood and appreciated by one audience may not be as well received by another. For example, an audience of corporation executives and a group of labor union members are likely to have different reactions.

Consider not only the type of audience but also the opinion it may have of those you quote. Audiences won't be receptive to quotations from persons they don't admire or trust.

HOW TO DELIVER QUOTATIONS

If direct quotations contain more than 50 words or so, paraphrase them—for example, "Thomas Jefferson said, in essence . . ." Or quote only part of it and summarize the rest. A note of warning—beware of twisting the quotation out of its true meaning.

To give weight to your quotations, provide names instead of "Someone" or "A college professor." If the name isn't readily recognizable, further identify the quote's author. You might say, "Mr. Donald Jones, Chairman of the Oshkosh Bank" or "Ms. Jane Gorman, professor of economics at the State University."

Here's how President Ronald Reagan handled the matter of further identifying the author of a quotation. In his Inaugural Address, Reagan quoted Dr. Joseph Warren. Before Reagan cited the quotation he identified Dr. Warren as president of the Massachusetts Congress and a man who might have become one of the greatest Founding Fathers if he hadn't been killed in the battle of Bunker Hill. This recognition of Dr. Warren as a historical figure strengthened the authority of the quotation. Showing him as a hero gave his words emotional impact and fitted the patriotic theme of Reagan's address.

Avoid quoting unimportant or irrelevant information such as the title, date and page of your source. That clutters up the quotation and draws the audience's attention away from what was said by the person quoted.

So does using the words "quote" and "unquote." Some speakers say "I'll now read you a quotation" or "I have a quote here." Then they continue, "Albert Einstein said, and I quote," winding up with "end of quote" or "unquote." And hardly elegant is the practice of other speakers who raise and crook two fingers of each hand to signal the quotation's beginning and ending.

To deliver quotations more smoothly, you might want to try another way. Use pauses and a change of pace and pitch. Begin with "George Washington said." Pause. Then give the quotation rather slowly and in a different tone to make it sound extra important. At the end, pause again. After that, resume with your own words in normal delivery.

POINTS TO REMEMBER

Although quotations are effective in any part of a speech, they're usually found in the introduction to grab instant attention or in the conclusion to drive home the message. Quotations in the body of a speech support the speaker's points that clarify and amplify his or her central idea.

The rule of moderation applies to the use of quotations as it does to anything else. No speech should be a miniature book of quotations. The purpose of quotes is to bolster your ideas, not replace or substitute for them.

Two or three short quotes are preferred to a single long one. They give you the advantage of multiple opinions and hold your audience's attention. But occasionally you may find a long quotation better serves your purpose.

Make sure the quotation is easy to understand. Use different authorities. See to it that the quotation applies to the present time and matches the thought you have in mind. See that the quotation also fits the audience.

Above all, keep in mind what the British author Isaac D'Israeli (father of the statesman, Benjamin Disraeli) observed. In his *Curiosities of Literature* he wrote, "Those who never quote in return are seldom quoted."

CHAPTER 12

Choose the Right Words for Eloquence

EVEN THOUGH YOUR SUBJECT IS GOOD, your material well-organized and your delivery skillful, chances are your speech won't be eloquent if it doesn't have the right words. The right choice of words is the very source of eloquence.

The English language provides many words with similar meanings but only one is the right word—the one that expresses your exact meaning. If you think exact meanings don't matter, remember Mark Twain's advice: "Use the right word, not its second cousin. The difference between the almost-right word and the right word is really a large matter—it's the difference between the lightning bug and lightning. A powerful agent is the right word."

When Confucius, the Chinese philosopher and would-be reformer, was asked what his first deed would be if he became Emperor, he replied, "I would re-establish the precise meaning of words." When Franklin D. Roosevelt prepared his speeches he "took a keen pleasure in the precise selection of words," his secretary said. John F. Kennedy, according to his speech collaborator, looked at words "as tools of precision to be chosen and applied with a craftsman's care to whatever the situation required. He liked to be exact."

Other eloquent public speakers—Abraham Lincoln, Woodrow Wilson, Winston Churchill, Adlai Stevenson, Martin Luther King, to name a few, also eagerly searched for the right word.

The French people have a perfect expression for the right word. They call it "le mot juste," meaning the word that fits exactly. When your words fit exactly, they glow with eloquence. The right words—

the eloquent words—fit exactly when they fulfill the demands of the audience, the occasion and the speaker.

DETERMINE AUDIENCE LEVELS

As audiences vary according to their educational and occupational backgrounds as well as social and economic levels, so will your vocabulary and choice of words differ in addressing them. Knowing your audience's level of education, for example, can cue you as to how sophisticated your language should be.

Speaking at a meeting of college professors, you'll use a more extensive vocabulary than if you were talking to a group of high school students. Similarly, if you're addressing top management executives, your language will differ from your words to an assembly of Boy Scouts. And the different audiences will know by your choice of words whether you're talking down to them, over their heads or at their level.

You also want to select words that fit the occasion. At ceremonies, such as dedications, national holidays or commencements, the language should be formal. At other occasions, such as banquets, local community affairs or civic club meetings, the language may be informal.

The difference between formal and informal speech may be compared to the difference between formal and informal clothes: formal is dressy and elegant; informal, casual and ordinary. Formal speech is dignified and serious; informal, less lofty and more relaxed.

Lincoln's right words elevated his Gettysburg address high above the ordinary and gave it a dignified tone. He sprinkled in his speech such words as "dedicate," "consecrate," "hallow" and "devotion." These words not only sound eloquent but also convey noble thoughts concerning dedication.

On the other hand, American lawyer and orator Joseph H. Choate wisely used a lighthearted tone and chose informal language in after-dinner speeches. Whether pleading a case in court, addressing a public meeting or speaking on an after-dinner occasion, he was noted for his eloquence in both form and expression. Here's an excerpt from his after-dinner speech at the New York State Chamber of Commerce:

> "When I compare your appearance at this moment with what it was when you entered this room, when I look around upon these swollen girths and these expanded countenances, when I see that each individual of the Chamber has increased his avoirdupois at least

ten pounds since he took his seat at this table, why, the total weight of the aggregate body must be startling . . . I should be the last person to add a feather's weight to what has been so heavily heaped upon you."

FEEL COMFORTABLE WITH WORDS

Besides selecting words that fit your audience and the occasion, you need to choose words that fit you, the speaker. To fit you means more than you think. It means you must feel comfortable with your words. It means you're accustomed to using them. It means you can pronounce them without stumbling. It means they must sound like you.

When Edward Everett and Lincoln, both eloquent speakers in different styles, spoke to the same audience on the same occasion at Gettysburg, they used words that sounded like them. Everett had earned a doctor of philosophy degree, had been a professor at Harvard University and later its president. Lincoln had less than a year of schooling. So Everett could and did use many long and scholarly words like "obsequies," "effusion," "adjurations," "strategical" and "egregious." In sharp contrast, Lincoln spoke mostly short and simple words still in common use today—over 70 percent of his words are only one syllable.

If Lincoln had tried to speak Everett's language, the audience would have been shocked and would have wondered, "What's happened to Honest Abe? That's not the way he talks." By the same token, if Everett had tried to use Lincoln's words, the audience would have wondered, "What's come over Old Everett? That doesn't sound like him."

Your words must not only sound like you, but also must clearly express your exact meaning. Remember, the purpose of language is to reveal thought, not to hide it. If you don't say exactly what you mean, you can't expect your audience to understand what you're trying to communicate.

Anatole France, the French novelist and Nobel prize winner, once said, "The finest words in the world are only vain sounds if you cannot comprehend them." And the German poet Goethe put it this way, "Everyone hears only what he understands."

How does a child react when you say, "Look up and down before you cross the street"? Perhaps the child thinks you mean look up at the sky and down at the pavement. Of course, your meaning is obvious to you, but is it clear to the child?

You may have wondered why you think easily and clearly about a subject, yet find it difficult to make the audience understand you when you give a speech. In a person-to-person conversation, the "That's what I heard you say—But that's not what I meant" exchange can and often does take place. Listen to this discussion, for example, between Humpty Dumpty and Alice in Lewis Carroll's *Through the Looking Glass:*

"When *I* use a word," said Humpty, "it means just what I choose it to mean—neither more nor less." To which Alice remarked, "The question is whether you *can* make words mean so many different things." Humpty said, "The question is, which is to be master—that's all." Next, Humpty used a seven-syllable word, "impenetrability." Puzzled, Alice said, "Would you tell me please what that means?"

The trouble with Humpty's English, as Alice found out, is that you can't understand what he says unless he explains it. Words should mean the same to the audience as they mean to the speaker. But the exchange between Humpty and Alice usually isn't possible between speaker and audience.

SAME WORDS CAN DIFFER IN MEANING

We don't always say what we mean, and sometimes even the same words can mean different things to different people. Many words have more than one meaning, even opposite meanings. Take the word "tough." Among its many meanings is the sense of a *tough* character—rowdy, crude and vicious. But another meaning is that of a *tough* soldier—manly, sturdy and hardy.

"Cheap" means a lot of different things: low-priced; shoddy workmanship; stingy; miserly; vile; worthless; contemptible. "Streamlined" refers to something designed or organized for maximum efficiency, including simplifying and modernizing. In addition to its positive meaning, streamlined has negative connotations: corner-cutting and skimpiness.

Because such words can be used in different senses, they're called ambiguous or equivocal words. So in using them you need to think not only of what they mean to you, but of what they will mean to those in your audience. To be sure you're understood, give special attention to them. This you do by specifying and illustrating exactly what you mean.

The fault isn't so much in the language as in the users. Plumbers, carpenters, engineers or surgeons can't do their jobs properly if they don't know their tools and how to use them. The same is true of the speaker, whose tools are ideas and words. As such the speaker must have something to say, and must know how to say it.

Words are to a speaker what colors are to a painter. The painter carefully chooses his colors, applies them on the canvas and creates shadings, lights and shadows to correctly convey certain impressions to viewers. Similarly, to make listeners understand, the speakers should choose the right words, taking into consideration both their denotative and connotative meanings. A word's denotative meaning is how it's defined in the dictionary; the connotative meaning consists of what's associated with the word. For example, the word "home" *denotes* the place where people live but *connotes* comforts, intimacy and privacy.

Lincoln, a master of words, gave close attention to the quality of his words as determined by their definitions and associations. Referring to his expression of an idea, he once said, "I was not satisfied until I had put it in language plain enough, as I thought, for any boy I knew to comprehend. This was a kind of passion with me, and it has stuck by me; for I am never easy now, when I am handling a thought, till I have bounded it north and bounded it south, and bounded it east and bounded it west."

Unlike Lincoln, however, some speakers use words carelessly and with complacent familiarity—failing to give them the attention and respect they deserve. Anyone who has tried to answer a child's recurring question, "What does that mean?" knows that even common words are often hard to explain. Sometimes, we don't even know the meaning of a word. Other times, our listeners derive one meaning when we have another in mind.

More than anything else, clarity in language is what audiences demand. They have the absolute right to expect every speaker to say clearly and exactly what he or she is talking about. And the speaker should make it easy for the audience not only to understand, but also impossible to misunderstand.

The familiar words "slender" and "skinny" have the same basic meaning, no excess fat, yet each suggests other meanings. Being slender connotes gracefulness and good proportions. Being skinny implies an extreme leanness that suggests lack of proper nutrition.

Likewise, "stout," "portly," "plump" and "obese" all denote superfluous body weight; yet "stout" connotes a thickset build; "portly" suggests impressive size and dignity; "plump" implies a pleasing fullness of figure; and "obese" calls to mind a body marred by fat.

MAKE SURE IT'S THE EXACT WORD

So what can you do? To determine the exact word, note the shades of meaning of synonyms or similar words. See that the connotations of your words cast the right shadows, as the painter does to depict his impressions. Check the dictionary and choose the word that carries your exact meaning.

Besides their denotative and connotative meanings, words have other characteristics that can influence your choice. Words are general or specific; abstract or concrete; long or short; emotive; slang; and jargon.

A general word is an all-inclusive word that identifies a group of persons or things; a specific word points to a particular item or detail. The difference between "general" and "specific" is a matter of degree. "Criminal" is general; "thief" is less general; "pickpocket" is specific. "Food" is general; "dessert" is specific; "pie" is even more specific.

The more general words are, the harder it is for an audience to know precisely what you intend them to mean. You should therefore seek the most specific word possible for your context.

Abstract words are vague because they represent no tangible image—words like courage, liberty, oppression, justice, democracy. All are familiar abstract words, yet if you ask a dozen persons what each word means, chances are you'll get twelve different answers. That's because we interpret them in terms of our own ideas and emotions, often the result of personal background and experience.

Concrete words refer to what we can see, hear, touch, taste and smell, as in these examples: smudge, siren, smooth, bitter, musty. Some concrete words are so expressive that they sound like what they mean. Instead of using the ordinary word "cry," for example, use the more expressive words that echo or directly imitate the natural sound: bawl, yelp, sob, whine, wail, yowl, snivel, whimper.

Other concrete words simulate the action they describe as well as suggest the associated sound. The opening consonants "bl" in "blast" and "blare" compel the lips to move forcefully and suggest the sounds. "Flare," "flame," and "flicker" imitate the sound with the flapping of the tongue.

Such words when spoken make the sounds and meanings they represent come alive. The same applies to many other words. Examples abound, but these may suffice: whistle, shimmer, shiver, shudder, crunch, sputter, hush, sizzle, gurgle, crash, splash, roar. They're words with verve and dash. Being vivid, they create pictures and trigger the imagination; being simple and familiar, they strike quick meanings and immediately stick in listeners' minds.

Socrates, the Greek philosopher, once said, "When anyone speaks of iron and silver, the same thing is present in the minds of all. But when anyone speaks of justice and goodness, we part company and are at odds with one another and with ourselves."

EXPLAIN ABSTRACT WORDS

We see, then, how use of abstract words can block communication. But what can we do about it? What can we say in our speeches to make sure abstract words mean the same to our listeners as they do to us?

The problem of abstract words can't be solved by merely replacing them with concrete synonyms. Usually there aren't any. And if you say to an audience, "Let me give you an idea of what I mean," you naturally can't present them with a thought the way you would hand them an apple. But you can make your abstract thought tangible so they can grasp it as though their minds had hands.

How? Compare your idea with a real, specific object. You might say, "Love is like a rose and blooms with affection." By identifying love with the rose, you ascribe to love the qualities of a flower and invest it with the beauty, freshness and vigor everyone associates with blossoming flowers.

You can also pinpoint your abstraction by defining or explaining it and giving examples. Here's how Lincoln talked about liberty in one of his speeches: "We all declare for liberty; but in using the same word, we do not all mean the same thing. With some, the word liberty may mean for each man to do as he pleases with himself and the product of his labor. While with others, the same words may mean for some men to do as they please with other men and the product of other men's labor. Here are two, not only different, but incompatible things, called by the same name—liberty. And it follows that each of the things is, by the respective parties, called by two different and incompatible names—liberty and tyranny."

DRAW PICTURES WITH WORDS

Still another way to deal with abstract words is to make your thoughts visible so your listeners can see them as pictures in their heads. Listen to these words from a speech by Franklin D. Roosevelt: "A radical is a man with both feet firmly planted in the air. A conservative is a man with two perfectly good legs who, however, has never learned how to walk forward. A reactionary is a somnambulist walking backward." Whether or not his listeners agreed with what he was saying, Roosevelt drew such simple, clear pictures that it's doubtful anyone failed to understand exactly what he meant.

Specific and concrete terms invigorate and brighten speeches and help make them eloquent. That's why speakers are repeatedly advised to "Be more specific" and "Be concrete."

Stressing the value of specific and concrete words is not to say, however, that you should never use general and abstract words. You need abstract language to discuss theories, beliefs and values. In handling certain subjects, you will find it virtually impossible to avoid general or abstract words. Subjects such as economics and philosophy demand them. The same is true of less academic but still theoretical and generalized topics like honesty, loyalty, morality.

Nor does talking on abstract subjects have to be vague and dull. Use abstract statements to express your main points and support them with details and examples dressed in specific and concrete language. That combination clarifies and reinforces your generalities with substance and conveys your meaning interestingly and exactly.

The eloquent Declaration of Independence is a case in point. Dealing with an abstract subject—freedom from tyranny—the Declaration combines general and specific words:

> "We hold these truths to be self evident: that all men are created equal; that they are endowed by their Creator with *certain* unalienable rights; that among these are life, liberty, and the pursuit of happiness . . . But when a long train of abuses and usurpations . . . evinces a design to reduce them (the people) under absolute despotism, it is their right, it is their duty to throw off such government . . Such has been the patient sufferance of these colonies; and such is now the necessity which constrains them to *alter* their former systems of government. The history of the present king of Great Britain is a history of *repeated* injuries and usurpations . . ." (Italics added.)

The three words in italics are not the words Thomas Jefferson used in his original draft. His words were: "inherent and unalienable rights") (changed by Congress to "certain unalienable rights"); "expunge" (changed to "alter"); and "unremitting" (changed to "repeated"). Which are the right words?

Viewed in Jefferson's context, his phrase "inherent and unalienable rights," is actually more precise, since *inherent* refers to what's so deeply implanted that it's part of one's nature, while *unalienable* means can't be surrendered or transferred; *expunge*, meaning to wipe out of existence, is more specific than *alter*, which means merely to change; and *unremitting* signifies unceasing activity without slackening or halting and is more precise than *repeated*, which implies only a few or many times.

In each of those instances Jefferson apparently considered his choice closer to his meaning than the one used by Congress. After expressing his general points in abstract language, he presented concrete supporting details in the next eighteen paragraphs which describe each oppressive act that the king had committed against the colonies. That's how Jefferson used abstract language, combining it eloquently with specific information.

THE POWER OF SHORT WORDS

Now let's see how the size of words affects your speeches. Short words are powerful. Churchill's "blood, toil, tears and sweat" and many other eloquent phrases helped win a war. As John Kennedy said, "Churchill mobilized the English language and sent it into battle." William Gladstone, English statesman and orator, closed his eloquent speech on the Irish Question by saying, "Ring out the notes and the memory of discord; ring in the blessed reign and time of peace." Observe that fifteen of those eighteen words are monosyllables.

Of sixty-six words in one of Shylock's speeches in *The Merchant of Venice*, fifty-seven have only one syllable. Believing that Jews and Christians are alike as people and should be treated the same, Shylock says he's a Jew who is "fed with the same food, hurt with the same weapons, subject to the same diseases, healed by the same means, warmed and cooled by the same winter and summer, as a Christian is. If you prick us, do we not bleed? If you tickle us, do we not laugh? If you poison us, do we not die? And if you wrong us, shall we not revenge?"

Shylock's short words make his message eloquent. Compelling attention and conviction, they also arouse strong emotions.

Do those examples suggest that you should use only short words? No. Many long words are in common use—communication, consideration, achievement, cooperation, environment, preparation, disappointment, to cite a few. Besides, all short words can make a speech staccato, abrupt, disjointed. The speech would sound monotonous and boring.

Experienced speakers don't ask themselves, "Should I use a short or a long word?" Instead, they ask, "Is this the *right* word to say what I mean?" "What we need is a mixed diction," Aristotle said over 23 centuries ago. His point remains valid today. A mixture of short and long words is best, as Shakespeare proved.

Like many other speeches in Shakespeare's plays, Portia's "quality of mercy" speech in *The Merchant of Venice* shows patterns of short and long words interspersed here and there, as in this excerpt: "His scepter shows the force of temporal power, the attribute to awe and majesty . . ." Mixing short and long words gains the advantages of both. Short words provide punch—they command attention. Long words allow a more rhythmic flow because of their extra syllables. By using both short and long words Portia adds force and beauty to what she says about mercy. At the same time she achieves a dignified tone in her language.

DIGNITY OF LANGUAGE STANDS OUT

Dignity of language stands out in the speeches of many distinguished speakers, past and present. Daniel Webster, one of America's most eloquent orators, once said, "I never use a big word when I can find a short one." But the texts of his printed speeches contain many long words. Here are some of them: destitution, palpable, solicitous, veracity, interrogatory, obtuseness, veneration, transcendent, ignominiously, exigencies.

Even Wendell Phillips, another eloquent American speaker, who delivered his speeches in a conversational and colloquial style in sharp contrast to the bombastic oratory then popular, didn't always shun long words. Looking at some of his speeches, we find about 10 percent of the words in them have three or more syllables such as: prerogative, usurpation, presumptuous, inevitable, solemnity, proportionately.

In addition to the charm, color and variety that long words add to a speech, their sound commands attention and enriches the speaker's meaning. Listen to William Pitt the Elder, using these concluding words in an eloquent speech on the proper relationship between England and the American colonists: "I could not have slept this night in my bed, nor reposed my head on my pillow, without giving vent to my eternal abhorrence of such preposterous and enormous principles."

Pitt's eloquent long words show their superiority over any short words he might have used in their place. Even in cold print his words express fervent personal emotion and deeply-felt righteous anger and sound clear-toned, forceful, lyrical.

But do our present-day speakers use big words? Yes, indeed! Scan any current issue of *Vital Speeches*, a semi-monthly collection of today's noteworthy speeches, and you'll find a number of long words. Here's a sampling: presumptuous, resurgence, microcosm, immutable, promulgation, disputatiousness, exhilarating, preponderance, vindictiveness, attributable, prognostications, contentiousness.

Although in his book *Modern English Usage*, H. W. Fowler says that short words are generally better than long ones, he also writes: "There are many good reasons, however, against any attempt to avoid a polysyllable if it is the word that will give our meaning best; moreover, the occasional polysyllable will have added effect from being set among short words."

DEALING WITH EMOTIVE WORDS

Emotive words are those whose sense may be distorted by preconceived adverse reactions, unreasonable or unfair attitudes of hostility, and feelings rooted in suspicion, fear or intolerance. Words such as agitator, demagogue, dictator, communist, huckster, lobbyist, brat, flunky, jalopy and hick have feelings associated with their meanings, and express or appeal to emotion. They have tones, overtones and subtones derived from temperament, background or experience of the persons hearing them.

Emotive words create problems because they can easily misrepresent ideas and thus prevent straight communication. This is not to suggest that emotive words are necessarily taboo. But if you use them, it may be well to bear in mind what Rudyard Kipling, the English author, said: "Words are the most powerful drug used by mankind. Not only do words infect, egotize, narcotize and paralyze, but they enter into and color the minutest cells of the brain."

So if your aim is to color the attitudes of your listeners or propagandize them, emotive words will help you. But if you want to express reality as it is, apart from personal feelings or prejudices, you'll avoid emotive words and be purely factual. Even mere facts can speak eloquently for themselves.

ASK ABOUT SLANG

Trying to decide whether or not to use slang? If so, ask yourself these questions: "Does it convey my meaning? Will my listeners understand clearly what I mean? Will they be offended? Would standard English be as effective, or even better?"

You might say, "If I must ask myself all those questions, wouldn't it be wiser to skip slang and stick to standard language?" And you'd be right. We all speak to be understood and to earn respect as we speak. Slang doesn't give quality to speeches. Many words and phrases in standard language express thoughts better and with more dignity. So slang is neither necessary nor desirable.

Bergen Evans and Cornelia Evans, in *A Dictionary of Contemporary American Usage*, wrote: "Slang is language regarded as unsuitable for standard cultivated speech . . . much slang is vivid and clever and forceful. Much more of it, however, is merely faddish and infantile and its consistent use does not display the fullness of expression that the user thinks it does."

This doesn't mean we should be snobbish, only cautious about slang. Slang may be obscure or cover more than one meaning. What does "let him have it" mean? Does it mean literally what it says, or does everyone know its slang meaning? What is "the bottom line"? Is it the last line or the final result?

Agreed, some slang may be useful in giving your speech folksy touches or bristling phrases. Listen to Ralph Waldo Emerson as he eloquently talks to his audience about slang: "I confess to some pleasure from the stinging rhetoric of a rattling oath in the mouths of truckmen and teamsters . . . Cut these words of the street and they bleed; they are vascular and alive; they walk and they run."

But even when slang is picturesque, it isn't worth the risk if it might baffle or offend the audience. If you use slang in your public speeches, it should be in the proper setting with the right audience and in its latest context, as slang changes fast and often.

JARGON'S A PROBLEM

Jargon, according to H. W. Fowler's *Modern English Usage*, is "talk that is considered both ugly-sounding and hard to understand." Edwin Newman, in *Strictly Speaking*, writes it is used because "it sounds weighty, important." He believes, however, "it may be better to grunt unintelligibly than to use such language, for it is so impersonal and manufactured as to be almost inhuman."

Newspaper columnist James Kilpatrick, after attending a meeting of professional urbanologists, said, "Every word they uttered was an English word; their every sentence had a definable subject and verb. But after 45 minutes, I realized I had not understood a thing they were saying. One expert spoke earnestly of prioritizing the ongoing input. Another asserted the need to redefine and restructure the corollary mechanisms."

Ernest Boyer, the former United States Commissioner of Education, in a speech delivered at a national convention of the Speech Communication Association, said, "Signs point to a decline in our ability to express ourselves clearly and precisely. Every day in my own world of education, bureaucratic jargon seems incessantly to clutter up the day. Regulations and guidelines are gnarled and contorted and warped by legalese . . . We have target groups, rifleshot policies, thrusts, impacts and zeroings."

Just what is jargon? Originally an old French word meaning "warbling of birds," jargon has evolved to mean mainly shop talk or technical language used by professionals, tradespeople, athletes or other specialists. This definition takes in a lot of territory because jargon breeds abundantly in today's society as new industries and occupations spring up.

Since all professions, occupations, hobbies, sports and other groups have special ideas, techniques, tools and materials, each needs a specialized vocabulary to designate these things. So jargon is certainly a useful tool of communication among people in the same group.

Speaking the same language, people in specialized groups can understand each other easily, quickly, exactly and effectively. Dentists know "caries" is tooth decay. Physicians know "conjunctivitis" means eye inflammation. Government leaders know "overkill" means to destroy a target with more force than is required. Lawyers know "testator" is a person who leaves a will in force at his death. And computer personnel know "software" means computer programs.

But when you use jargon in a speech to an audience outside of the specialized group, your listeners will probably find themselves puzzled over your meaning, become annoyed and stop listening. Obviously they won't understand what you say. And using jargon on such an occasion may even make you seem foolish. If you must use jargon in speeches to lay audiences, explain it by simple definitions and examples, or put the specialized words in a context of familiar ideas.

CONCLUDING WORD

Novelist Joseph Conrad, a distinguished stylist in the English language, once said, "Give me the right word and I'll move the world." Even though you may not want to move the world, if you choose the right words for eloquence, you'll experience a new sense of self-confidence and you'll command the respect of your audience the next time you give a speech.

One man did want to move the world. All his life he aspired to glory and leadership. He achieved his goal with eloquent speeches. In fact, his speeches became models of eloquence in his own lifetime.

For his books and "brilliant oratory," he was awarded the Nobel Prize for literature. He is the only person ever honored with a Nobel Prize citation for oratory. His name is Winston Churchill. The next chapter draws seven lessons in eloquent speechmaking from an analysis of his life and speeches.

CHAPTER 13

The Anatomy of a Master of Eloquence

WHAT CAN YOU LEARN FROM WINSTON CHURCHILL to help you become an eloquent speaker? He wasn't a natural orator, not at all. His voice was raspy. A stammer and a lisp marred many of his speeches. Nor was his appearance attractive. A snub nose and a jutting lower lip made him look like a bulldog. Short and fat, he was also stoop-shouldered.

Yet Churchill became probably the most eloquent orator of the twentieth century. How did he do it?

In each of several schools he attended, young Winston was consistently a poor student. When he was 12, he entered his last school, Harrow, where he again soon reached the bottom of his class.

Was he stupid or lazy? Neither. He later explained, "Where my reason, imagination or interest were not engaged, I would not or I could not learn." One subject fascinated him, however. That was the English language.

Of all his teachers he believed only one—Robert Somervell—was successful. Somervell, who taught English, inspired him to acquire a feeling for words and develop a knack for using them. "I do not believe," said Somervell, "that I have ever seen in a boy of 14 such a veneration for the English language."

Churchill's debt to Somervell as a teacher of English is recorded in his autobiography: "Mr. Somervell was a man who knew how to do it and thus I got into my bones the essential structure of the ordinary English sentence—which is a noble thing. The only thing I would whip boys for is not knowing English. I would whip them hard for that."

As a schoolboy Churchill enjoyed learning poetry by heart and demonstrated a remarkable ability to memorize. He won a prize for reciting perfectly 1,200 lines from *Lays of Ancient Rome*, a poem by Thomas Babington Macaulay, English historian, author and statesman. Macaulay and the English historian Edward Gibbon dazzled him with their styles, especially their flair for phrasing. The impact they made on his mind stayed with him for life and helped form his style, as his speeches show.

Even as a teenager he was already addicted to grandiose phrases—the kind he was to savor and roll on the tongue in his speeches. In a school essay, for example, he wrote "hoary time," "boundless eternity" and "the apex of glory."

FEELING FOR WORDS

Reading Macaulay and Gibbon gave young Churchill, as he later said, "the feel for words fitting and falling into their places like pennies in the slot." He found Macaulay's style "crisp and forcible" and Gibbon's "stately and impressive." Because their styles were markedly different and yet both charmed him, this showed, he said, "What a fine language English is." Both in his books and speeches, he used a blend of Macaulay's and Gibbon's styles and, as he once said, "I stuck in a bit of my own from time to time."

Lord Moran, Churchill's physician and intimate friend, wrote in his book about him, "Without that feeling for words he might have made little enough of life. For in judgment, in skill in administration, in knowledge of human nature, he does not at all excel."

Lesson number one for public speakers from Churchill: Know, respect and love the English language.

The greatest influence in Churchill's early life was his father, Lord Randolph Churchill who at 37 became Leader of the House of Commons where he was a powerful but stormy figure. The son visited Parliament and, enraptured, heard the debates. Sitting, watching and listening, he absorbed the oratory as if by osmosis.

In his autobiography, Winston wrote, "From where I crouched on the floor of the Gallery peering through the balustrade I could see the effect" the speeches produced on the audience. Referring to the eloquent William Gladstone, he recalled, "The Grand Old Man looked like a great white eagle at once fierce and splendid. His sentences rolled forth majestically and everyone hung upon his lips and gestures."

Young Winston admired his father and imagined that one glorious day he'd stand side by side with him in the House of Commons and fight the great battles that swirled around him. This dream persisted, though his father spent little time with his son and had concluded he was unfit for a career in law or politics because of his poor scholastic record.

When his father died at 45, Winston was 21 and his dream of comradeship with him and entering Parliament at his side was over. He vowed, however, to pursue his father's goals alone and "vindicate his memory." Devotedly, he read and re-read all his father's speeches and memorized many of them.

Winston also read and studied the eloquent speeches of the great orators in British history: Oliver Cromwell, Edmund Burke, the Earl of Chatham, William Pitt the Younger, John Bright, Benjamin Disraeli, and Gladstone. In analyzing their speeches, which he often read aloud, he would compare their styles and note the features that distinguished them.

CHURCHILL'S MODEL

Adlai Stevenson, himself an eloquent speaker, once asked Churchill who or what had helped create his oratorical style. Churchill replied, "It was an American statesman who inspired me and taught me how to use every note of the human voice like an organ. He was my model. I learned from him how to hold thousands in thrall." Then Churchill quoted long excerpts from Bourke Cockran's speeches.

Bourke Cockran, lawyer, Congressman from New York and noted national orator of his time, was indeed a major influence in Churchill's speechmaking. When they first met, Churchill was 21 and Cockran 41. Churchill described him as "a remarkable man . . . with an enormous head, gleaming eyes and flexible countenance."

Witnesses testify to Cockran's wide-ranging voice, which could rumble like thunder or be as sweet as a lute. Whether speaking in the House of Representatives or before immense crowds, he entranced his audiences. In 1892 he gave a nominating speech at the Democratic national convention in Chicago. The audience consisted of a thousand delegates and 20,000 spectators. When Cockran began to speak, it was two o'clock in the morning and the audience had already listened to ten hours of speeches. Yet he spoke with such glowing eloquence that his audience listened spellbound in wonder and admiration.

Churchill and Bourke Cockran became acquainted when Churchill visited the United States in 1895. On his way to Cuba as a military observer of the war between that country and Spain, Churchill stopped in New York City and was Cockran's guest for a week.

This was Churchill's first visit to the States, so there was much to see and do and Cockran arranged a full itinerary. Yet day and night they talked at length. Young Winston, himself a talker, was held spellbound by his older host. In a letter to his mother, Churchill wrote, "I have great discussions with Mr. Cockran on every conceivable subject from economics to yacht racing. He is a clever man from whose conversation much is to be learned."

Churchill and Cockran also talked a great deal about speechmaking. When Churchill asked his advice on how to spellbind an audience of thousands, Cockran told him to speak as if he were an organ, use strong words and enunciate clearly in wave-like rhythm.

SINCERITY, THE NAME OF ELOQUENCE

"Only a speaker who is sincere can be eloquent," Cockran said to Churchill, "because sincerity is the name of eloquence." "What people really want to hear," continued Cockran, "is the truth—it is the exciting thing—speak the truth." Cockran explained what he did to prepare himself for speeches: learned everything he could about his subject; stored in his mind the material he gathered from his reading and study; simplified the most difficult issues with everyday examples and illustrations; concentrated on the strongest point or argument and built it up to an irrefutable conclusion.

Churchill and Cockran also talked about their mutual admiration for Edmund Burke's oratory. "How I should have loved to have heard him," Cockran said. At Churchill's request, Cockran read aloud some of his own speeches. As he listened to Cockran's fine phrases and eloquent delivery, young Churchill was beside himself with joy. Before he met Cockran, whatever Churchill knew about public speaking he had obtained from his own observation, reading and study. But now, for the first time, he was getting private instruction from an experienced orator.

Churchill asked Cockran if he would send him copies of his speeches so that he could study them carefully. Cockran promised he would, and so began a kind of correspondence course in public speaking that was to continue for several decades until Cockran died.

In their letters Churchill would evaluate Cockran's speeches and Cockran would respond to the comments. Churchill wrote, "It is one of the finest I have read . . . Of course—my dear Cockran—you will understand that we approach the subject from different points of view . . ." Cockran replied, "I was so profoundly impressed with the vigor of your language and the breadth of your views as I read your criticisms of my speech that I conceived a very high opinion of your future career."

In addition to their regular correspondence, they saw each other from time to time when Churchill visited the United States and Cockran visited England. When Churchill went on an American speaking tour in 1900, he arrived in New York for his opening lecture and stayed with Cockran, "who worked indefatigably to make the lecture a success," as Churchill wrote to his mother. Several years later Cockran gave a speech to a London audience, which included Churchill.

In Churchill's book *Thoughts and Adventures*, published in 1932, he paid this tribute to Cockran: "I must record the strong impression which this remarkable man made upon my untutored mind. I have never seen his like, or in some respects his equal . . . his conversation, in point, in pith, in rotundity, in antithesis, and in comprehension, exceeded anything I have ever heard."

In his speeches, too, Churchill expressed his gratitude for Cockran's help. In his famous "Iron Curtain" speech at Westminster College in Fulton, Missouri, in 1946, he said, "I have often used words which I learned fifty years ago from a great Irish-American orator, a friend of mine, Mr. Bourke Cockran."

Churchill repeated his appreciation in a speech at the University of Rochester, New York, in 1954, "I remember when I first came over here, in 1895, I was a guest of your great lawyer and orator, Mr. Bourke Cockran . . . he poured out all his wealth of mind and eloquence to me. Some of his sentences are deeply rooted in my mind."

Lesson number two from Churchill to public speakers: See and hear eloquent speakers in action, and study the texts of their speeches.

Stimulated by his father's career, young Churchill's ambition was to go into politics, but he worried about his stutter and lisp. He wondered, "Why can't I ever say my sibilants like other people?" Once he said, "I can only say *zest* by giving an expiratory snort. I can't make sibilants by putting my tongue against my teeth." How could he ever become a member of Parliament if he stumbled over words and couldn't say any word that began with "s" or "z"?

So he consulted a prominent throat specialist in London. The doctor found no defects of speech organs or nerves. Advising Winston that neither medicine nor surgery could correct his speech impediments, the doctor told him only "constant practice and perseverance" would help him eliminate or modify his speech defects.

NEVER SUBMIT TO FAILURE

Diligently and faithfully, Churchill practiced and persevered. He believed that people should never submit to failure. Years later he said in a speech, "Never give in! Never give in! Never, never, never, never—in nothing great or small, large or petty—never give in except to convictions of honor and good sense."

Realizing that his stuttering probably resulted from speaking too fast, he changed his involuntary stops and repetitions into deliberate pauses. With continually recurring pauses he slowed down his manner of speaking to a halting delivery. This technique made his stutter imperceptible and transformed it into a distinctive style of delivery, which became one of his trademarks. "If you have a defect, make it a prop," he once said.

Churchill discovered, however, that his lisp was more difficult to overcome, but he didn't give up trying. As a rule, he'd avoid using as much as he could words beginning with "s" or "z." He rehearsed aloud to make sure he wouldn't muff the pronunciation of such words. Whenever possible he practiced this or similar sentences, "The Spanish ships I cannot see since they are not in sight." Eventually he managed to develop a blend of the "s" and "th" sounds.

Additionally, Churchill eagerly sought opportunities to speak. He had always wanted to make speeches, but had never been asked. There had been no speechmaking at his military academy or in his regiment. Visiting the Conservative Party's headquarters one day while on home leave from the army, he introduced himself and indicated he hoped to embark on a political career. Noticing on a table a large book labeled "Speakers Wanted," he asked, "Tell me about this. Do you-mean to say there are a lot of meetings which *want* speakers?" "Yes," came the answer, "can't I book for you?"

The book showed hundreds of indoor meetings, outdoor fetes, bazaars and rallies, clamorous for speakers. Churchill said he scanned the list "with the eye of an urchin looking through a pastry cook's window." He finally selected a political rally in a park in the city of Bath.

Churchill's speech was carefully prepared over a ten-day period. He learned it "so thoroughly by heart that I could almost have said it backwards in my sleep." In his rehearsals he repeatedly experimented with a stop-watch because "above all one must not be hurried or flurried."

His theme was a favorite of his father's and the speech contained catchy phrases: "England would gain far more from the rising tide of Tory Democracy than the dried-up drainpipe of Radicalism." He was particularly pleased with that sentence and others like it. His fiery delivery showed he remembered the rhythms of Bourke Cockran's powerful voice.

DEFECTS NO PROBLEM

When his speech was over, he was ecstatic that neither his stutter nor lisp had been a problem. "The audience," he wrote, "seemed delighted. They cheered a lot at all the right places when I paused on purpose to give them a chance, and even at others which I had not foreseen. At the end they clapped loudly and for quite a long time. So I could do it after all!"

All these efforts helped Churchill to lose the inhibition that had probably caused his stammering, though he never completely lost his lisp. But even the lisp, like the stutter, he turned from a hindrance to a help. Just as he developed a distinctive style of delivery from his stammering, he put his lisp to the same constructive use.

Randolph Churchill, Winston's son, theorized that his father may have exploited the residual speech impediments to his advantage by achieving an individual style of oratory. Winston said as much when he wrote at age 23 an unpublished article on oratory titled "The Scaffolding of Rhetoric." Describing the physical attributes of orators, he wrote, "Sometimes a slight and not unpleasing stammer or impediment has been of some assistance in securing the attention of the audience."

Lesson number three from Churchill to public speakers: Endure your handicaps if they can't be cured and turn them to your advantage.

Failure in academic schooling, except for English, led young

Churchill to a military academy. Enthusiastic about his military studies, he was highly successful at the academy. In sharp contrast to his earlier school work, where he usually landed at the bottom of his class, he was close to the top of his military graduating class, ranking eight among 150. This showed, he wrote later, "that I could learn quickly enough the things that mattered."

After graduating, he received his commission as lieutenant in a cavalry regiment. Assigned to routine army duty in Bangalore, India, he found time dragged. Soon he began complaining in letters to his mother. He wrote, "The regiment is completely isolated. I find no one worth speaking to or looking at." His mother replied, "There are drawbacks to everything of course. Meanwhile enjoy the intervals of polo and military work. I hope you will find time for reading. Think how you will regret the waste of time when you are in politics and will feel your want of knowledge."

Winston already had become aware of his lack of a university education. In a letter to his younger brother Jack, he wrote, "I shall envy you the enjoyment of a liberal education, and the power to appreciate the classical works." Winston also revealed his unfulfilled longing for such an education in a letter to his mother, "What a strange inversion of fortune—that I should be a soldier and Jack at college." In his autobiography, he wrote, "The desire for learning came upon me. I began to feel myself wanting in even the vaguest knowledge about many large spheres of thought. I resolved to read history, philosophy, economics, and things like that; and I wrote to my mother asking for such books as I had heard of on these topics."

His mother was delighted and cooperated enthusiastically when he asked her to send him books in box-loads, starting with all the books by Gibbon and Macaulay, who earlier had fascinated him. She sent him eight volumes of Gibbon's *Decline and Fall of the Roman Empire* and twelve volumes of Macaulay—eight of history and four of essays.

Then came other books, including Plato's *Republic*, Aristotle's *Politics*, Adam Smith's *Wealth of Nations*, Malthus' *On Population*, Darwin's *On the Origin of Species* and Winwood Reade's *The Martyrdom of Man*. Devoting four or five hours each day to reading, he read several authors at a time rather than finishing one before starting another. He found it easier and more palatable to absorb his readings if he interspersed them. As though he were studying at a college, he assigned to himself a certain number of pages a day for each author.

Another book he read from cover to cover was John Bartlett's

Familiar Quotations. He often turned to this collection, which he said "is an admirable work, and I studied it intently." In *My Early Life*, he wrote, "It is a good thing for an uneducated man to read books of quotations. The quotations when engraved upon the memory give you good thoughts. They also make you anxious to read the authors and look for more."

Mindful of his need to know everything that went on in Parliament while he served as a soldier in India, he asked his mother to send him copies of the *Annual Register* (which corresponds to the *Congressional Record*). In his letter to his mother he wrote, "Of course the *Annual Register* is only valuable for its facts. A good knowledge of these would arm me with a sharp sword. Macaulay, Gibbon, Plato, etc. must train the muscles to wield that sword to the greatest effect."

Churchill approached all this reading, as he said, "with a hungry, empty mind, and with fairly strong jaws, and what I got I bit." One biographer writes, "Because he read—as the hungry eat—neither from habit nor from duty, but from need, these books entered into his system and became a part of him."

These efforts at self-education while in the army in India stretched his mind, widened and matured his interests, and gave him knowledge and opportunities for independent thinking. Nourished in the fertile soil of such excellent reading, ideas developed in his enriched mind.

Lesson number four from Churchill to public speakers: Read good books to broaden your mind and stimulate your thinking, since much of eloquent speaking depends on both knowledge and thought.

As a result of having closely studied and read aloud the eloquent speeches of both historic and contemporary orators, Churchill wrote his article, "The Scaffolding of Rhetoric." Although he never submitted it for publication, the manuscript survived and was printed two years after his death—some 70 years after he had written it.

In the article Churchill concluded that rhetoric is "the key to the hearts of men," oratory is an art and rhetorical power can be developed through observation, practice and perseverance. But he also believed that the rhetoric must be buttressed by the sincerity of the orator: "Before he can inspire others with any emotion he must be swayed by it himself. When he would rouse their indignation his heart is filled with anger. Before he can move their tears his own must flow. To convince them he must himself believe. His opinions may change as their impressions fade, but every orator means what he says at the moment he says it."

SIX SPEECH ELEMENTS

Churchill further discovered that constructing an oration requires six principal elements. He examined each in detail. Here's a summary:

1. *Correct Diction*—This means using the best possible word that expresses your full meaning. Avoid long words, if you can. Prefer "short, homely words of common usage," provided such words exactly fit your thoughts and feelings.

2. *Rhythm*—Create a rhythmic flow of sounds with long, rolling, sonorous sentences and balanced phrases. Rhythmic rhetoric has a tremendous effect on audiences by producing a cadence which provides prose with poetic touches.

3. *Accumulation of Argument*—Set forth a series of facts and assemble them vividly and rhythmically, pointing them all in one direction. This leads the audience to enthusiastically anticipate the conclusion as the last words are spoken "amid a thunder of assent."

4. *Analogy*—Apt analogies are effective in explaining and clarifying difficult or new ideas by comparing them with simpler concepts familiar to audiences. Churchill cited an analogy used by his father, "Our rule in India is, as it were, a sheet of oil spread over and keeping free from storms a vast and profound ocean of humanity."

5. *Examples*—These will "make or mar" a speech, so make sure your examples or instances fit the facts and thoughts.

6. *Extravagance of Language*—Some words must be found that express the speaker's emotions and excite the feelings of the audience. Churchill provided two illustrations:

To glorify the freedom of English citizens, the Earl of Chatham said, "The poorest man may in his cottage bid defiance to all the forces of the Crown. It may be frail; its roof may shake; the wind may blow through it; the storms may enter; the rain may enter—but the King of England cannot enter! All his forces dare not cross the threshold of the ruined tenement."

William Jennings Bryan, extolling a silver standard over a gold standard, said, "You shall not press down upon the brow of labor this crown of thorns; you shall not crucify mankind upon a cross of gold."

"The effect of such extravagances on a political struggle is tremendous," wrote Churchill. And he was right. Bryan's eloquent "Cross of Gold" speech so electrified the delegates of a national political convention that they nominated him for president of the United States.

When Churchill wrote his article on oratory, he also had begun to write his only novel, *Savrola*, published three years later. He worked much of the article into the novel and described additional oratorical techniques. Although fiction, the novel's central character, Savrola, is unmistakably the author's self-portrait. Many things about Savrola—talents, thinking, books he reads, methods he uses to prepare and deliver speeches—are exactly like Churchill's. The author describes at length both the composition and delivery of Savrola's speeches, including all the essential elements covered in "The Scaffolding of Rhetoric" plus other techniques such as simile, alliteration, pausing, repetition, and voice modulation.

PREPARING AND DELIVERING SPEECHES

Here's an excerpt from *Savrola* on how the hero prepares a speech:

> What was there to say? . . . he saw a peroration which would cut deeply into the hearts of a crowd; a high thought, a fine simile, expressed in that correct diction which is comprehensible even to the most illiterate and appeals to the most simple; something to lift their minds from the material cares of life and to awake sentiment. His ideas began to take the form of words, to group themselves into sentences; he murmured to himself; the rhythm of his own language swayed him; instinctively he alliterated. Ideas succeeded one another . . . He seized a piece of paper and began hurriedly to pencil notes. That was a point; could not tautology accentuate it? He scribbled down a rough sentence, scratched it out, polished it, and wrote it in again.

Here's an excerpt on how Savrola delivers a speech:

> He began to speak . . . very quietly and slowly, his words reached the furthest ends at the hall . . . here and there in his sentences he paused as if he searched for a word . . . His passions, his emotions, his very soul appeared to be communicated to the 7,000 people who heard his words; and they mutually inspired each other . . . Then he raised his voice, and in a resonant, powerful, penetrating tone which thrilled the listeners, began the peroration. The effect of his change of manner was electrical . . . The excitement of the audience became indescribable . . . His sentences grew longer, more rolling and sonorous. He reached the conclusion. The people saw it coming, and when the last words fell, they were greeted with thunders of assent.

Both "The Scaffolding of Rhetoric" and *Savrola* show young Churchill's deepest interest in oratory. From the time he recited poetry as a schoolboy to the end of his working days, the power of words fascinated him. Lord Moran, his physician and friend, wrote in his published diaries that Churchill had once said to him, "It was my ambition all my life to be master of the spoken word."

So Churchill learned how great orators impress audiences. He discovered the necessary elements and techniques that help listeners understand, feel, remember and act upon what speakers convey. What he learned he consistently put into practice during half a century of eloquent speechmaking.

Lesson number five from Churchill to public speakers: Be sincere and use rhetorical devices to help your audiences understand and remember what you say, and to stir their emotions.

While in the army Churchill maintained his keen interest in politics and avidly read Parliament's *Annual Register* as well as newspapers to keep abreast of public affairs. After four years, he resigned his commission to enter politics. He lost his first election campaign, but won the next year. He was 26 when elected to a seat in the House of Commons.

Commenting on his first speech in the House of Commons, Churchill wrote in his autobiography, "I need not recount the pains I had taken to prepare, nor the efforts I had made to hide the work of preparation." For his third speech he explained, "I took six weeks to prepare this speech, and learned it so thoroughly by heart that it hardly mattered where I began it or how I turned it."

Throughout his long career of eloquent speechmaking, whether in Parliament or on the public platform, he always depended on thorough preparation. He worked as hard to prepare a speech in his seventies as he did in his twenties. Insistent on meeting his own exacting standards, he never left his choice of words to chance. A speech, he believed, must be in both substance and form a work of art. That requires much time and effort. He once said, "I take the very greatest pains with the style and composition. I do not compose quickly. Everything is worked out by hard labor and frequent polishing. I intend to polish till it glitters."

So Churchill's eloquence as an orator didn't come effortlessly. Only by the sweat of his brow did he achieve brilliance.

In the beginning he wrote out his speeches in longhand. Later, he dictated every word to a secretary, who took it in shorthand or on the typewriter. One of his secretaries once described that he paced "slowly up and down the room, his hands clasped behind his back, his shoulders hunched, his head sunk forward in deep thought, slowly and haltingly dictating . . . Sometimes there are long halts, during which he patiently sounds out a phrase a dozen times."

He put his ideas to rhetoric as composers set theirs to music. The cigar in his hand served as a baton to punctuate the rhythm of his words. He tested words and phrases: muttering to himself; weighing them; striving to balance his thoughts; making sure he liked the sound, rhythm and harmony. Then he came out loudly with his choice and his secretary took it all down. At times he said, "Scrub that and start again" or "Gimme!" as he snatched the paper from the typewriter to scan a phrase.

Finally, he sat down at his desk and revised the triple-spaced typewritten draft. With pen in hand, he would read the draft as many as half a dozen times. Final alterations, substitutions, insertions, deletions—he applied them all like the finishing touches to a painting.

REHEARSING SPEECHES

Next came rehearsals of his written speeches. He practiced by reciting them aloud. As he boomed away in his room, his words could be heard along with crashing knocks on the furniture. No opportunity to rehearse was overlooked, even while taking a bath. As he got into the tub he would start murmuring. The first time this happened his valet asked, "Were you speaking to me, sir?" "No," came the reply, "I was addressing the House of Commons." At private showings of films in his house he enjoyed the movie and at the same time rehearsed his speech in a low rumble with gestures. As a result of such diligent rehearsing, when he gave his speeches his delivery was so natural it seemed spontaneous.

Lesson number six from Churchill to public speakers: Put forth your best efforts to prepare your speeches and seize every possible opportunity to practice them.

When 2,500 of Churchill's speeches were published in an eight-volume set, a critical review at the time of publication stated, "The speeches, of course, are pure gold interlarded now and then with just the least bit of dross. The biggest nuggets—the 'Finest Hour,' for example—are beyond price."

Edward Heath, a former leader of Britain's Conservative Party and Prime Minister of England, also commented on the speeches, saying that "Churchill's words will live on when the statues erected in his memory have crumbled."

Churchill's written words alone, however, can't do what he did when he spoke them. Aneurin Bevan, British Socialist leader, said, "Nobody could have listened and not been moved . . ." Even if delivered verbatim by someone else, Churchill's speeches could not have had the same effect on audiences.

Always resolutely assured, Churchill felt with his whole being that he knew what he was talking about. He put the stamp of his personality on all his speeches, delivering them in his own distinct style.

"What kind of a people do they think we are?" he asked of the enemy. The incisive, intense, affronted tone of his voice as he said those words told eloquently of his anger, disgust and determination to fight on. Didn't the enemy realize the English were a people who would never cease to persevere—who would rather see their country a shambles than give in to the enemy? He transmitted that determination to his people through one eloquent speech after another until they all caught his spirit.

Churchill's loathing for the enemy, especially Adolf Hitler, had him almost foaming at the mouth. He drove a truckload of sarcasm and scorn into his description of Hitler as "this bloodthirsty guttersnipe . . . a monster of wickedness, insatiable in his lust for blood and plunder . . ." or whenever he rolled the word "Nazi" slowly off his tongue as "Nahhzzee."

To ridicule the enemy and show his utter contempt, Churchill made his words sound as corrupt and shameless as he could.

MASTER OF THE PAUSE

An important feature of the Churchillian style of delivery was the dramatic pause. He was a master at this. He said once, "I . . . made a pause to allow the House to take it in . . . As this soaked in, there was something like a gasp." He relied on timing to assure heightened effect because it made silence even more eloquent than words and allowed his listeners time to digest what they heard and get ready for what would be said next. His use of the dramatic pause forced any restless members of his audience to look at him and listen. Even his "gar-rumphs" and throat clearings came at the right moments.

FACIAL EXPRESSIONS

Those who saw him say that Churchill's facial expressions as he worked through and up to his main points were something to see. While merely reading his words you can almost see his anger, contempt and defiance as he reveals how passionately he despised Hitler and his cohorts. He snarled and scowled as he spoke of the "clanking, heel-clicking, dandified Prussian officers" and "the dull, drilled, docile, brutish masses of the Hun soldiery, plodding on like a swarm of crawling locusts" and of "Mussolini, this whipped jackal . . . frisking up by the side of the German tiger with yelps . . ." His manner was stern yet stimulating as he growled, "I have nothing to offer but blood, toil, tears and sweat."

Even in his most serious speeches he sprinkled jokes, quips and other humor. While German bombers were devastating London he quipped, "At the present rate it would take them about ten years to burn down one-half of London's buildings. After that, of course, progress would be much slower."

In one speech he said, "We are expecting the coming invasion; so are the fishes." In another, "We have a higher standard of living than ever before. We are eating more." Then, gazing at his ample round belly, and with his eyes twinkling, he added, "And that is very important."

Although his voice wasn't especially appealing, it carried conviction and his delivery gave the impression of power and sincerity. He combined flashy oratory with sudden shifts into intimate, conversational speaking. Each change of pace, each pause, each rhetorical flourish—all were carefully orchestrated. He roared like a lion and cooed like a dove with hand and facial gestures to suit.

Effective delivery, however, is more than voice and gestures. It is also the impact of personality on the listeners. In his autobiography Churchill writes, "Mr. Gladstone's reputation as an orator depends less upon his published speeches than upon the effect they produced at the time upon the audience. Lord Randolph Churchill's place in our political history is measured not by his words and actions, but by the impression which his personality made upon his contemporaries."

Although Winston Churchill was always carefully prepared, his delivery never lacked spontaneity. He put feelings into his words. He made them breathe with life through his exhilarating and forceful personality. This uniqueness as a person made the difference in his speech delivery, and in his effect on the audience.

Lesson number seven from Churchill to public speakers: Let your feelings and personality show in your speeches.

SUMMING UP

Winston Churchill wasn't a natural orator. Like most public speakers, he began his speaking career unsure of his ability to face large audiences. But he was highly motivated.

Lacking a university education, he enriched himself with a wealth of knowledge, enlarged his vocabulary, and overcame speech defects by turning them to his advantage. He also thoroughly studied the speeches and methods of eloquent speakers and diligently applied their techniques to his own speeches.

His speech mentor, Bourke Cockran, once told him, "Only a speaker who is sincere can be eloquent because sincerity is the name of eloquence." Sincerity is one thing, however, Churchill didn't have to learn or develop. That came to him naturally.

He always believed without reservations or misgivings what he said and was eager to say it in speeches as often as the occasion arose. His rise to world fame is directly attributable to his speechmaking. From his life and speeches, seven lessons emerge for other public speakers:

1. Know, respect and love the English language.
2. See and hear eloquent speakers in action, and study the texts of their speeches.
3. Endure your handicaps if they can't be cured and turn them to your advantage.
4. Read good books to broaden your mind and stimulate your thinking, since much of eloquent speaking depends on both knowledge and thought.
5. Be sincere and use rhetorical devices to help your audiences understand and remember what you say, and to stir their emotions.
6. Put forth your best efforts to prepare your speeches and seize every possible opportunity to practice them.
7. Let your feelings and personality show in your speeches.

All his life Winston Churchill aimed for the highest glory. From the beginning, personal distinction was his goal. Above all, he had set his heart on becoming an orator because he believed that an orator wields tremendous power over people. That's why, in spite of his handicaps, or perhaps because of them, he took infinite pains to develop himself into one of history's most eloquent orators. Even if you don't have his lofty aspirations, the seven lessons from his life and speeches can help you achieve eloquence in your own public speaking.

CHAPTER 14

Enhance Your Eloquence with Wit and Humor

WIT AND HUMOR HAVE A LONG HISTORY. The ancient Greeks and Romans laughed at the banquet table because they thought it helped them to digest your food. And they were right. Today after-dinner speeches are commonplace. At breakfast, luncheon and dinner clubs as well as at conventions, speakers follow the food and serve wit and humor on almost any subject.

But wit and humor are more than aids to digestion. The orator Cicero said, "Joking and humor are pleasant, and often of extreme utility." Horace, the Roman poet, believed that "a man learns more quickly and remembers more easily that which he laughs at than that which he approves and reveres." For those general reasons professional public speakers use wit and humor in their speeches and so do preachers in their sermons. Specifically, they use wit and humor to:

1. Establish harmonious relations between speaker and audience at the start of the speech.
2. Enable the speaker to proceed in a more relaxed and natural manner.
3. Show the audience that the speaker is not stuffy or preoccupied with self-importance.
4. Create a receptive audience to diminish any possible resistance to the speaker's ideas.
5. Serve as glue that makes dry facts and figures stick with the audience.
6. Provide relief from emotional or intellectual tension as do the comic interludes in plays and musical compositions.

7. Connect, like steppingstones, one part or point of the speech with the next.
8. Change the pace to bring back the attention of the audience or to lay the groundwork for a serious message.
9. Help explain dull but essential points or those not readily understood.
10. Liven up the speech and give it zest.
11. Conclude the speech.

The use of wit and humor for some of those purposes was covered, with examples, you'll remember, in parts of previous chapters in this book:

—Chapter 5, "Excite Your Audience With Eloquent Openings."

—Chapter 6, "Wrap Up Your Talks With Eloquent Closings."

—Chapter 7, "Strengthen Your Eloquence With Transitions."

—Chapter 9, "Shape Your Eloquence With the Rule of Three."

—Chapter 11, "Enrich Your Speech With Eloquent Quotations."

—Chapter 13, "The Anatomy of a Master of Eloquence."

This entire chapter will cover with examples all the other aspects of wit and humor in both serious and humorous speeches.

Wit and humor certainly can enhance any speech no matter what the subject. While there's no doubt that you can use both to your advantage in speeches, the question is, "What makes wit and humor funny?"

The American humorist Josh Billings said, "There are very few good judges of humor and they don't agree." Shakespeare believed the audience is the final judge of whether or not a joke is funny. He said, "A jest's prosperity lies in the ear of him that hears it, never in the tongue of him that makes it."

Nevertheless, various groups of people have different values and tensions. What's funny to one audience may not be funny to another. What's funny to some members of an audience may not be funny to other members of the same audience. What's funny to one person may not be funny to a second person and to a third person it may be an insult.

SOURCE OF LAUGHTER

Wit and humor should be adapted to the particular audience you're addressing. The witty French playwright Marcel Pagnol suggested that the source of laughter is not in comic things or situations themselves but in the experience, knowledge and education of the person who laughs. That observation underscores the importance of public speakers knowing the background of their audiences.

Writer E. B. White once said, "Humor can be dissected, as a frog can, but the thing dies in the process." Even humorists and comics themselves don't know or have different ideas as to what makes wit and humor funny. Here are comments from some of them:

Will Rogers: "I don't know what humor is. Anything that's funny—tragedy or anything, it don't make no difference, so you happen to hit it just right. But there's one thing I'm proud of—I ain't got it in for anybody. I don't like to make jokes that hurt anybody."

Mark Twain: "Humor is only a fragrance, a decoration." At another time he said, "Everything human is pathetic. The secret source of humor itself is not joy but sorrow."

Charlie Chaplin: "Playful pain—that's what humor is."

Groucho Marx: "There are all kinds of humor. Some is derisive, some sympathetic, and some merely whimsical. That is just what makes comedy so much harder to create than serious drama; people laugh in many different ways, and they cry only in one."

Abraham Lincoln: "I laugh because I must not cry—that's all, that's all."

Stephen Leacock: "The savage who cracked his enemy over the head with a tomahawk and shouted 'Ha! Ha!' was the first humorist. Here began, so to speak, 'the merry ha! ha!' the oldest and most primitive form of humor. It seems odd to think that even today when we give our acquaintances the 'merry ha! ha!' over their minor discomfitures, we are reproducing true to type, the original form of humor."

Eddie Cantor: "What is the cause of laughter? Frankly, I don't know . . . The theory that there is hostility, or a feeling of superiority in all laughter, that all jokes are 'on' somebody and that all laughter is ridicule, I believe to be a mistaken idea. This is not to say that at some time or other laughter does not assume the form of ridicule. Therein, I think, lies the difference between satire and humor. Satire is barbed and malicious, and likely to hurt, whereas, the genuine quality of humor is founded on tenderness and gentleness."

The above quotation from Eddie Cantor contrasting satire and humor brings to mind the distinction between wit and humor. We often speak loosely of wit as being the same as humor. They're not actually the same. Orator Robert G. Ingersoll said, "Wit comes from the brain, humor from the heart." Wit suggests intellectual brilliance, or subtlety, often sharp and biting. Humor implies tolerance, kindliness or pathos.

The difference between wit and humor, then, is the same as the difference between satire and humor described by Eddie Cantor. Humor is more tolerant and kindlier than wit, satire, sarcasm and irony. Yet all these terms are close cousins. So are the words jest, joke, quip, witticism and wisecrack, each of which means saying something to evoke laughter. Each applies to any utterance not seriously intended whether sarcastic, ironic, witty or merely playful.

In the final analysis, all of those terms are the opposite of seriousness. All mean to say something amusing. Unless you're a specialist in semantics, little purpose is served to concern yourself with a fine distinction in meaning among them. In fact, the wit and the humorist are often the same person. That's certainly true of both Mark Twain and Will Rogers, whose laugh-provoking expressions are interchangeably humorous or witty. The use of either humor or wit can be equally effective in your speech.

More important for the public speaker is to know what makes wit or humor funny. What are the ingredients? Here are some:

1. Surprise

This is the principal ingredient of almost any type of humor. To surprise is to lead your audience to believe you're going to say something normal, then saying something unexpected, as in the following examples:

—A speaker gave a speech at a prison to 2,000 inmates. He began, "Now, gentlemen, there's one big difference between all of you and me—*you got caught*."

—Mark Twain said in a speech, "I've tried all sorts of things and that is why I want to try the great position of ruler of a country. I have been in turn reporter, editor, publisher, author, lawyer, *burglar*.

—Two men met outside a municipal bathhouse in Europe. "Have you taken a bath?" asked one. "Why?" replied the other, "*Is one missing*?"

—"The only sure way to double your money in these inflationary times is to *fold it*."

—The famous after-dinner speaker Chauncey Depew said in a speech, "It is expected that the mayor of New York should have the fluency of Henry Clay, the solidity of Daniel Webster, the firmness of Andrew Jackson, and *the digestion of an ostrich*."

—"I'm not sure I believe in an afterlife, but just to make sure, I always carry *a change of underwear*."

In each of the above examples, you notice a juxtaposition of incongruous ideas. That phrase is surely a mouthful but it describes exactly what produces a laugh, chuckle or smile. "Juxtaposition" places two or more things side by side; "incongruous" means out of place, inconsistent, illogical. The last thing—the italicized word or phrase in the foregoing examples—doesn't seem to belong with the other things; so its sudden and unexpected appearance takes us by surprise and makes us laugh.

The speaker in each of the examples above has been leading us on to expect something else but in the end frustrates our expectation by saying something that's not consistent, proper or logical with what precedes it. The joke, being a trick on the listener's mind, is kept up the speaker's sleeve and then suddenly released. The ending word or phrase in the above examples takes us unawares, impresses itself forcibly upon us through surprise, and amuses us.

The German philosopher Schopenhauer said, "The cause of laughter is simply the sudden perception of the incongruity between a concept and the real object." Another German philosopher, Immanuel Kant, explained, "Laughter arises from a sudden transformation of an expectation into nothing." The American philosopher, poet and essayist Ralph Waldo Emerson stated the same theory in this way, "The balking of the intellect, the frustrated expectation, the break of continuity in the intellect, is comedy and it announces itself in the pleasant spasm we call laughter." Another American, the author Max Eastman said, "A joke is not a thing but a process, a trick you play on the listener's mind, and then by a sudden twist you land him nowhere at all—or just where he didn't expect to go."

2. Exaggeration

This ingredient, often used by humorists Mark Twain and Will Rogers and other public speakers, enables you to strengthen your point by saying something that goes beyond a normal statement. Mark Twain said, "To exaggerate is the only way I can approximate the truth." You might say, "Traffic congestion is terrible—the pedestrian has the right of way only after the ambulance picks him up."

To illustrate his three-time loss as candidate for president, William Jennings Bryan used this humorous anecdote: a woman who was so fat that she was obliged to get off a streetcar backward had tried three times to leave it but each time to her consternation was helped on again by someone who thought she was entering instead of leaving.

Telling about a jackrabbit he shot at, Mark Twain said, "He dropped his ears, set up his tail, and left for San Francisco at a speed which can only be described as a flash and a vanish! Long after he was out of sight we could hear him whiz."

3. Understatement

Understatement is, of course, the opposite of exaggeration and another way to get your point across humorously. Mark Twain said, "Water, in moderation, cannot hurt anybody." Will Rogers said, "One of our pigs swallowed a stick of dynamite. Later he rubbed against a building. This caused an explosion that razed four city blocks. It sure inconvenienced us."

Or you can take a famous quotation like this one from Rudyard Kipling, "If you can keep your head when all about you are losing theirs and blaming it on you," and replace the last five words with an understatement such as "maybe you just don't understand the situation."

An example of Winston Churchill's humorous use of the understatement technique in his speech to the U.S. Congress was his reference to the Japanese attack on Pearl Harbor: "They have certainly embarked upon a very considerable undertaking."

4. The pun

The pun is a play on the sound and meaning of words. You use a word in such a way as to suggest a different meaning or words that sound like each other but have different meanings. From the earliest times to the present day the pun has been regarded as the "lowest form of humor." You can never be quite sure of a pun. A pun may be fun to some and punishment to others. Yet it persists and is still widely used. In Shakespeare's plays you'll find thousands of puns. He was very fond of them. So was Adlai Stevenson, though he didn't use as many as Shakespeare.

Here are some examples of the pun from Stevenson's speeches:

"They pick a president and then for four years they pick on him."

"The power of positive brinking," referring to the foreign policy of President Dwight Eisenhower and Secretary of State John Foster Dulles.

"A man who thinks everything will be better in the rear future," describing a presidential nominee.

"I was a little baffled by the emergence of that word 'egghead' to describe some of my supporters. I am happy to note you have refrained from saying of the eggheads that the yolk was on them." (Addressing the annual meeting of Washington reporters at the Gridiron Club a month after he was defeated in his first campaign for president.)

5. Irony

Irony is a witty expression in which your intended meaning is the opposite of what you're apparently saying. It's a form of ridicule—making fun of something or someone. Notice in the following examples from Mark Twain's speeches how each contains a contradiction between the literal and intended meaning—saying one thing and obviously meaning another:

"It's very easy to give up smoking. I've done it a thousand times."

After commenting on the great number of people killed in railroad accidents, Mark Twain added: "But, thank Heaven, the railway companies are generally disposed to do the right and kindly thing without compulsion. I know of an instance which greatly touched me at the time. After an accident, the company sent home the remains of a dear distant relative of mine in a basket, with the remark, 'Please state what figure you hold him at—and return the basket.' Now there couldn't be anything friendlier than that."

6. Sarcasm

This ingredient is almost the same as irony but the ridicule may be stronger. The following excerpt from a Franklin D. Roosevelt presidential campaign speech is an eloquent example of sarcastic humor which demolished the argument over the issue involved:

> "These Republican leaders have not been content with attacks on me, or my wife, or on my sons. No, not content with that, they now include my little dog, Fala. Well, of course, I don't resent attacks, and my family doesn't resent attacks, but Fala *does* resent them.

"You know, Fala is Scotch, and being a Scottie, as soon as he learned that the Republican fiction writers in Congress and out had concocted a story that I had left him on the Aleutian Islands and had sent a destroyer back to find him—at a cost to the taxpayers of two or three, or eight or twenty million dollars—his Scotch soul was furious. He has not been the same dog since.

"I am accustomed to hearing malicious falsehoods about myself—such as that old, worm-eaten chestnut that I have represented myself as indispensable. But I think I have a right to resent, to object to, libelous statements about my dog."

7. Climax

In a serious speech the climax refers to a series of words, phrases or sentences arranged in *ascending* order of rhetorical forcefulness. The humorous climax technique works in the same way except that at the culminating point the last words are funny instead of dramatic. Notice the pattern in the following example in which the statements are arranged in climactic order with an unexpected twist at the end:

"The members of a small-town church tried to increase the pastor's salary from $9,000 to $9,500. But he turned them down. 'I refuse your offer,' he said, 'for three reasons. First, because you can't afford to give me more than $9,000. Second, because my services are not worth more than $9,000. Third, because the additional task of trying to collect the extra $500 from you would probably kill me."

8. Anticlimax

Anticlimax is defined in the dictionary as "The usually sudden transition in speaking from a significant idea to a trivial or ludicrous idea." In using this technique, you end a statement or a series of remarks by saying something that is strikingly less important than what has preceded it. The anticlimax works in the opposite way from the climax technique. That is, the words, phrases or statements are arranged in *descending* order of significance. The ending in the anticlimax is such a sudden and extreme reversal of roused expectancy as to be absurd enough to cause laughter. For example, you might say, "I've got a headache, my heart beats fast, my nerves are shot, my ulcer is acting up—and I don't feel well."

Here's an excerpt from Mark Twain's speech, "Advice to Youth," that shows his mastery of the anticlimax technique:

"Never handle firearms carelessly. The sorrow and suffering that have been caused through the innocent but heedless handlng of firearms by the young! Only four days ago, right in the next farmhouse to the one where I'm spending the summer, a grandmother, old and gray and sweet, one of the loveliest spirits in the land, was sitting at her work, when her grandson crept in and got down an old, battered, rusty gun which had not been touched for many years and was supposed not to be loaded, and pointed it right at her, laughing and threatening to shoot. In her fright she ran screaming and pleading toward the door on the other side of the room; but as she passed him he placed the gun almost against her very breast and pulled the trigger! He had supposed it was not loaded. And he was right—it wasn't."

WIT AND HUMOR IN SERIOUS TALKS

Like all good things, wit and humor are subject to misuse. In after-dinner speeches the purpose is to entertain, so wit and humor form the substance of the talk. In all other speeches, however, they're merely the seasoning. There the purpose is to communicate ideas and feelings. In those speeches wit and humor are not essential, though they can help make your message more palatable, just as salt and spice are added to food to heighten its flavor. (See also Chapter 7, "Strengthen Your Eloquence With Transitions," about combining humorous and serious material.)

In the speech to entertain you tell stories, anecdotes and jokes primarily to raise laughs. But in the other kinds of speeches—to inform, persuade or inspire—you don't want listeners to remember your humorous remarks as such. You'd rather they recall the wit or humor only because it illustrates the point you seek to convey. Adlai Stevenson often used wit and humor in his serious speeches for this purpose. Here are a couple of examples:

When Stevenson was Governor of Illinois, he said in a speech:

"There is a lesson for all of us in this rallying of our forces, from every corner of Illinois. Perhaps I can best illustrate it with the story of the young man who approached the father of his intended bride to seek his approval of the marriage. The father was skeptical. 'I doubt very much,' he said, 'that you would be able to support my daughter—I can hardly do it myself.' To which the young suitor offered the bright suggestion: 'We'll just have to pool our resources.' "

This next excerpt is from one of Stevenson's speeches when he was United States Ambassador to the United Nations: "You know the story about the man in the restaurant who complained to the waiter that his broiled lobster had only one claw, and the waiter said it lost the other one in a fight; so the man said, 'All right, then bring me the winner.' Well, the United States is still the winner in the United Nations."

In a bitter political campaign William Jennings Bryan defended himself against furious attacks by his opponents with this witty story:

> "Some years ago a celebrity returned to his alma mater, a small college in the west. After a speech in the chapel by the visitor, the president of the institution inquired if he would like to visit the room he had occupied while a student. The celebrity said he would be delighted to do so and the two men crossed the campus to the old dormitory, climbed to the second floor, and knocked at the door of the room.
>
> "Now it happened that the present occupant of that room was digging out his Latin with the help of a fair coed—a violation of the rule that forbade girls to visit the boys' dormitory. The boy, suspecting that his caller might be a faculty member, told the girl to step into a convenient closet, which she promptly did, and the student answered the knock.
>
> "The president presented his distinguished guest and explained the nature of the call. The celebrity looked around the room and smilingly remarked, 'The same old table, the same old chairs'; went to the window, looked out, 'Yes, and the same old tree'; turned about, 'And the same old closet into which I should like to peep,' opened the door, saw the coed and exclaimed, 'And the same old girl.' The student spoke up, 'My sister, sir.' 'And the same old lie,' rejoined the celebrity. Now my Republican friends are at it again telling the same old lies about me."

Those humorous examples from serious speeches by Adlai Stevenson and William Jennings Bryan show how you sometimes can drive home your points more sharply than you could in straight talk. Yet eloquent orators of earlier times didn't use humor at all in their speeches because they believed that audiences would brand them as frivolous or disregard their serious points. Some of today's business executives also shy away from humor in public speeches because they feel it may be undignified.

Daniel Webster, regarded by many as among the supreme orators of all time, never used humor in public speeches. Nor did Lincoln on the public platform after he became president. He had been criticized for his jokes and humorous stories in previous speeches. Bryan seldom used humorous illustration to make a point because he believed humor might set him up as a mere entertainer unqualified for public office. Mark Twain said he was sorry he had a reputation as a humorist because nobody took him seriously. But eloquent speakers such as Winston Churchill, Adlai Stevenson and John F. Kennedy used wit and humor in serious public speeches to strengthen their points.

AFTER-DINNER SPEECHES

Even after-dinner speeches, usually lightweight in content and easygoing in delivery, can be eloquent. There's little fundamental difference between the after-dinner speech and the formal platform speech. The only important distinguishing feature of the after-dinner speech is its emphasis on wit and humor, since its purpose is primarily to entertain. So the after-dinner speech differs in the way the subject is treated but is otherwise similar to other speeches. An analysis of one of Will Rogers' after-dinner speeches will illustrate this point.

While you may have no illusions about being another Will Rogers, his example can show you how to get wonderful responses from your audiences by using wit and humor. Conscious attention to his techniques will help you in your own use of wit and humor. To see how he did it, let's examine the speech he delivered at a convention of the Corset Manufacturers of America.

First of all, Rogers made sure he was given enough time to prepare. He wrote all of his own speeches and wouldn't accept any such invitation "unless they give me three weeks to figger it out." Even for him, humor wasn't easy. He said, "The guys that tell you they can be funny at any minute, without any effort, are guys that ain't funny to anybody but themselves."

Another reason for allowing himself adequate time was to learn as much as he could about the audience and organization, including its products and services. This information helped him gear his speech to the specific occasion, using material his listeners could identify with.

Next he chose his subject. Since the delegates' business was making corsets, why not speak about corsets? That subject, familiar and interesting to all of them, would provide him with a definite central theme and give his speech unity and impact. But this was a banquet requiring, as Shakespeare put it, "flashes of merriment . . . to set the table on a roar."

Despite the fact it was naturally a serious subject to an audience of corset manufacturers, corsets nevertheless could be sufficiently ridiculous to win laughs. "There is nothing yet so serious," Rogers once said, "that an American audience won't see something funny in it." It's not the subject, but how it's treated that counts. Almost any subject can be handled humorously. See the funny side of it. Look at it from every angle. Turn it on one side, then the other, and finally upside down.

To arrange his material so he could guide the corset manufacturers from beginning to end, Rogers applied a five-step plan of speech organization based on the problem-solution pattern. The following analysis of his talk, with excerpts, shows how he led his audience forward from one step to another.

Step 1: Getting Attention—To warm up his audience, he set the mood and paved the way for introducing his theme. Rogers spoke about some local happenings. He told the incidents as true stories that involved himself and took place recently in the city where the listeners were meeting. "No matter how much I may exaggerate it," he once said, "it must have a certain amount of truth." So he used the names of real organizations and actual places. Weaving them into the introduction, he began as follows:

> "There has been an awful lot of fashion shows and all their by-products held here in New York. All the out-of-town buyers from all over have been here . . . I had to help welcome them at their various banquets. There was the retail Milliners' big fashion show at the Astor ballroom where they showed 500 hats and me. Some of the hats were just as funny looking as I was . . . The next night at the Commodore Hotel I mingled with those Princes of Brigands, the Leather and Shoe men . . . we never paid more for our shoes and were nearer barefooted than we are today . . ."

Step 2: Arousing Interest—As if to answer his listeners' unasked question, "What's all that got to do with us?", Rogers soon tied those events directly to them. This he did with the simple device of a brief transitional sentence serving as a bridge between steps 1 and 2: "During this reign of indigestion I was called on to speak at a big banquet at the Waldorf to the Corset Manufacturers." Following this transitional sentence, he sharpened his audience's interest and created a sense of anticipation by suggesting mock-serious concerns and hinting what was to follow. He said:

> "This speaking calls on a fellow to learn something about articles that self-respecting man has no business knowing about . . . If a man is called on to tell in a public banquet room what he knows about corsets, there is no telling what other ladies' wearing apparel he might be called on to discuss . . ."

Step 3: Describing the Problem—His listeners now fully attentive and wanting to hear more, Rogers presented his conception of the corset problem. The difference between what they expected and what he provided brought on the laughs. What he said obviously couldn't be taken seriously. Like Mark Twain, Rogers usually based his humor on incongruities created by exaggeration. His method was to take the truth and stretch it just over the realm of possibility so that his audience could recognize the absurdity.

In his book, *Esar's Comic Dictionary*, Evan Esar defines absurdity as "anything so contrary to reason that it is laughable, like the scientist who discovered a cure for which there was no disease." Using techniques of comparison and imagery as well as exaggeration, here's how Rogers described the corset problem:

> ". . . Just imagine, if you can, if the flesh of this country were allowed to wander about promiscuously! Why, there ain't no telling where it would wind up . . . when our human bodies get beyond our control, why, we have to call on some mechanical force to help assemble them and bring back what might be called the semblance of a human frame . . . The same problem confronts Corset Builders that does the people that run the subways in New York City. They both have to get so many pounds of human flesh into a given radius."

Step 4: Presenting a Solution—With the problem described and illustrated almost to the point of burlesque, Rogers next launched into an equally preposterous solution—again using techniques of overstatement, comparison and imagery. Here's what he said:

> "The subway does it by having strong men to push and shove until they can just close the door with only the last man's foot out. But the Corset Carpenters arrive at the same thing by a series of strings . . . By judiciously holding your breath . . . you arrange yourself inside this. Then you tie the strings to the doorknob and slowly back away. When your speedometer says you have arrived at exactly 36, why, haul in your lines and tie off . . ."

To heighten the absurdity, Rogers then told a short, personalized story:

> "Of course, the fear of every fleshy lady is the broken corset string. I sat next to a catastrophe of this nature once. We didn't know it at first, the deluge seemed so gradual, till finally the gentleman on the opposite of her and myself were gradually pushed off our chairs. To show you what a wonderful thing this corseting is, that lady had come to the dinner before the broken-string episode in a small roadster. She was delivered home in a bus . . ."

Step 5: Closing—Having made all his points in the preceding steps, Rogers was ready to wrap up his speech with a final touch. Careful to avoid a long conclusion, he ended with this short, apt analogy:

> "Men have gone down in history for shaping the destinies of nations, but Corset Architects shape the destinies of women, and that is a lot more important than some of the shaping that has been done on a lot of nations that I can name offhand."

To be sure, humorous speeches sometimes look rather drab on printed pages and may not read quite as funny as they sound when delivered. The speaker's delivery makes the difference. This is especially true of Will Rogers, whose humor depended mostly on exaggeration offset by his casual manner.

Exaggeration leads to a broad kind of humor and succeeds best when your delivery underplays your words. To be successful, exaggeration must be gross enough to be absurd and original enough to appeal by its ingenuity. If you can put your story across with assurance, your audience will delight in your imagination and inventiveness.

The comic effect of Will Rogers' outrageous remarks was heightened by his easy naturalness and genial lightness of touch. His words were helped much by the way he spoke them in his distinct Southwestern drawl as well as by his precise pauses, sheepish grin, sly winks and glances from under his eyebrows. Though he had prepared most carefully, his humor sounded spontaneous because his delivery seemed as effortless and natural as breathing. He was having fun speaking to the convention delegates and he transmitted that feeling to them. Relaxed and folksy, he would always speak to 1,000 persons in a hotel ballroom as if he were talking to a visiting friend in his home. "I am just an old country boy trying to get along," he'd say.

But delivery, though important, is only one element of any speech. You can still learn a lot from the printed speeches of eloquent speakers like Will Rogers and others. Once you've examined the content and organization of their speeches for the techniques they reveal, you're on your way to using them yourself.

CONCLUDING THOUGHTS

Few things in speechmaking will grab and hold the attention of audiences as effectively as wit and humor. People like to be amused and are grateful to speakers who make them smile or laugh. Mark Twain observed that the one thing nobody will admit to not having is a sense of humor. Shakespeare was well aware of the importance of humor. That's why humor of every kind is found not only in his comedies but also in his tragedies.

In using humor, see the funny side of life's problems and troubles. But keep your humor in harmony with your audience, the occasion, and the purpose of your speech. Wit and humor in the serious speech are incidental to ideas, while in the all-humorous or after-dinner speech wit and humor dominate over ideas.

As sincerity is the top ingredient in a serious speech, surprise is the most important in the humorous speech. Laughter depends on surprise. That's why you shouldn't announce that you're about to say something funny. Too many speakers say, "Let me tell you a funny story," "I heard a good one the other day, "You'll die laughing at this one," and "That reminds me of a funny story." If it's funny, your listeners will discover it for themselves and laugh. But if you tell them in advance, you eliminate the surprise and kill the laugh.

Humor must be relevant as well as in good taste. Use only humor that relates to the points in your speech. Don't tell funny stories just to get laughs. As to good taste, avoid humor that might offend some members of your audience. Quintilian, the great Roman oratory teacher, said, "The price of a laugh is too high, if it is raised at the expense of propriety."

Although a few theorists believe that humor has no place in a serious speech, some wit or humor can be found in the most solemn and best speeches. True, just as overspicing spoils food, so can excessive wit or humor ruin a serious talk.

But just as a dash of spice flavors food, so does a bit of wit or humor enhance a serious speech. When spice is left out altogether, food tastes flat. Similarly, when wit or humor is missing, a serious speech seems dull. "A little levity will save many a speech from sinking," said the English poet Samuel Butler.

CHAPTER 15

It All Adds Up to Eloquence

WHAT DO ALL THE PRECEDING CHAPTERS ADD UP TO? They sum up the power of eloquence. The first chapter introduces the subject of eloquence by defining and illustrating it. That chapter demonstrates how little it takes to transform an ordinary passage in a speech into a powerful one. By revealing the speaker's strong ideas and feelings, a powerful passage imposes itself forcibly on the mind of the listeners and stirs them deeply.

Following the opening chapter we begin a practical step-by-step preparation of your speech, starting with what you propose to say, gathering your material and organizing it into the body of your speech, then preparing your introduction and conclusion.

The first step is creating an exciting and provocative title that arouses interest or curiosity (Chapter 2). By beginning with your title, you can prepare a speech that fits it. The title steers your thinking while developing your speech. As you work on your talk, you'll stay on the course indicated by your title in order to make it fulfill its promise or prove it out.

That first step leads directly to the content of your speech (Chapter 3). An eloquent speech has to say something, which means you should have something to say that's important and useful not only to you but also to the audience. The power of eloquence comes partly from the force of facts. Know your subject. Cicero believed you cannot be eloquent on a subject you don't understand.

Having something to say also means you've been thinking about the subject, you've taken a stand on it and you believe firmly in what you say. Emerson put it this way: "Fame of voice or of rhetoric will carry people a few times to hear a speaker; but they soon begin to ask, 'What is he driving at?' and if this man does not stand for anything, he will be deserted."

Schopenhauer said, "The first rule for good style is to have something to say; in fact, this in itself is almost enough." But not quite all. Eloquence derives part of its power from the way you put your material together. What you have to say must be properly organized into the body of your speech, as shown in Chapter 4.

The next steps needed to organize your speech are the introduction and conclusion (Chapters 5 and 6). These parts are covered in separate chapters, each about the same length as the chapter on organizing the body, despite the fact that the body occupies about 80 percent to 85 percent of the speech. The space provided in this book to the introduction and conclusion of a speech is not out of proportion because the beginning and closing, due to their strategic positions in the talk, can make or break your speech. The introduction gives your listeners their first impressions of you, while the conclusion provides the final impact.

Although the three parts of a speech—introduction, body, conclusion—are dealt with separately, they must not sound separate when you deliver the speech. Nor should your ideas and sentences within those parts sound disconnected when you face your audience. That's why a whole chapter is devoted to transitions immediately following the three chapters on organization.

TRANSITIONS GUIDE LISTENERS

Chapter 7 shows you how to use transitional devices to move smoothly from introduction to body to conclusion and from one idea or sentence to another, and to make clear the relationship between them. Transitions hold all those elements of your speech together to keep it unified. Such unity helps both you and your audience to follow the organization of your material. Without transitions, your listeners might easily get lost. They would soon stop listening or show impatience.

The next two chapters cover rhetorical devices. When properly and skillfully used, these "tricks of the trade" are language techniques which contribute much to the power of eloquence. Proof of their effectiveness is that all eloquent speakers from the earliest times to today have used the same rhetorical devices. They strengthen words and sentences by putting them together in such ways as to create force and fluency as well as graceful language.

If there's one rhetorical device that's more useful in eloquent speechmaking than any other, it would be the rule of three, also called the triad. For that reason it's not included in Chapter 8 with the other rhetorical devices but receives special prominence and attention in a chapter all its own (Chapter 9).

Eloquent content and organization of a speech are not enough to complete the job of public speaking. The speech has to be delivered—spoken and supplemented or reinforced by such speech elements as posture, eye contact, voice, gestures, pauses, bodily movement, and visual aids. These elements make delivery the most easily noticed aspect of a speech.

Yet delivery is of no greater significance than the content or organization of a speech. One speaker's excellent delivery, for example, gave the impression of a wonderful speech, but his listeners were left unsatisfied. The material showed inadequate knowledge of the subject and was poorly organized. Judging by the sloppy way the speech had been put together, it had no plan. It was just a hodgepodge of statements, mostly the speaker's opinions, with a couple of stories thrown in.

All three elements—content, organization and delivery—are needed for total eloquence. You must have something worthy to say and your material must be carefully organized. Delivery can increase the power of your eloquence. For example, the American novelist Thomas Wolfe wrote that one of his characters "pressed his arm reassuringly, and the gesture was more eloquent than any words could be." Friedrich Klopstock, the German poet, once said, "The tones of human voices are mightier than strings or brass to move the soul."

Chapter 10, which covers the principles and techniques of delivery, ends the step-by-step preparation of your speech. The next four chapters deal with different subjects touched upon in preceding chapters but covered in depth in these four separate chapters. The importance of the subjects dictates the need for extended treatment in individual chapters.

Chapter 11 analyzes the power of the quotation as a tool in speechmaking. The chapter shows you how to use the quotation as an accessory to: begin or end your speech; drive home your points; add sparkle; provide humor. Additionally, the chapter explores the ways you can use the quotation to serve as a framework in constructing a whole speech. The chapter also names sources of quotations and provides suggestions for selecting as well as for delivering them.

Quotations contribute to the eloquence of a speech because they not only contain the best thoughts of great minds but also sound impressive, since they're crafted in arresting ways. Moreover, quotations can be humorous or serious and serve the speaker accordingly. Choose quotations which apply to human lives today and are consistent in both content and purpose with the objectives of your speech.

Even though the persons you quote died years ago, their words should be as fresh and new today as in their time. Quote living men and women, too, if their thoughts and words fit your speech and add to its eloquence.

WORDS REQUIRE CARE

Chapter 12 considers a speaker's choice of words with regard to correctness, clearness and effectiveness. The language you use should be appropriate to the purpose of your speech, to the occasion and to the particular audience you're addressing. Joseph Joubert, the French philosopher, asserted that "as soon as a thought has reached its full perfection, the word springs into being, offers itself, and clothes the thought." Not so. That may happen sometimes but not often. The eloquent words of Lincoln, Churchill or Franklin D. Roosevelt did not result from chance or accident. They knew that a worthy thought must be so expressed as to compel others to listen to it as well as understand and accept it. So they searched for the right words.

In addition to the choice of the right words, Chapter 12 covers words that have different meanings, abstract words versus concrete words, and emotive words, jargon and slang that set up roadblocks to communciation.

Speaking of Winston Churchill, one of his contemporaries said, "The oldest among us can recall nothing to compare with him, and the younger ones among us, however long we live, will never see his like again." The aim of Chapter 13 in this book is to present a brief survey of Churchill's long public speaking career to answer the question, "What made him the most famous orator of the twentieth century despite such obstacles as stuttering, lisping and a raspy voice?"

When Churchill was awarded the Nobel Prize for literature, the presentation address stated, "Behind Churchill the writer is Churchill the orator—hence the resilience and pungency of his phrases . . . His eloquence in the fateful hours of freedom and human dignity was heart-stirring. With his great speeches he has, perhaps, himself erected his most enduring monument."

By going back over the evidence step by step, Chapter 13 discloses that Churchill's rise to international prominence was directly related to his eloquent speeches. In his twenties he decided to become an orator because he believed that the orator wields great power over people and resolved to do whatever was necessary to achieve his goal. What he did and how he did it are detailed in the chapter and are an inspiration to all those who seek to become eloquent public speakers.

Although several previous chapters touched on humor in speeches, Chapter 14 explores it at length. As the American humorist James Thurber once said, "Humor is a serious thing. I like to think of it as one of our greatest and earliest national resources which must be preserved at all costs." So the entire chapter is devoted to humor.

Humorous speeches of course require humor and serious ones may be enhanced by it. When you think of using humor, however, bear in mind the old proverb, "One man's meat is another man's poison." What's funny to one audience may not be to another.

In any case, the humor must always be in good taste and relevant to both the subject and the occasion. The humor must also illustrate or emphasize some point you're about to make or have just made in your speech. By rising from your material, the humor will sound genuine and appeal to your audience.

Over a hundred techniques in speechmaking have been covered throughout the previous pages of this book. Each technique was identified, described, explained and illustrated with plenty of examples. Those techniques constitute just about everything you need to know about how to make a speech. When you've learned all of them, you've learned all the tricks of the trade.

If you've already used some of the techniques, work to improve your skill in handling them. Try only one technique at a time. It's easier and more effective to concentrate on one technique than to work simultaneously on a number of techniques. Benjamin Franklin in his autobiography tells of the time he set out to achieve perfection in thirteen virtues. He wrote, "I judged it would be well not to distract my attention by attempting the whole at once, but to fix it on *one* of them at a time; and when I should be master of that, then to proceed to another, and so on, till I should have gone through the thirteen."

PRACTICE IS VITAL

As Franklin did, work with one speech technique at a time until you perfect its use, then go on to another and before long you'll be skillfully using all of them. But there's more to do. A vital part of the preparation for making a speech is practice. Knowing the techniques is not enough. As Shakespeare said, "If to do were as easy as to know, paupers' cottages would be princes' palaces." When Napoleon was asked if he would name the most essential ingredient of success, he quickly answered, "Practice, practice, practice!"

Speechmaking is a performing art and that means you have to deliver the speech to an audience. Practicing doesn't mean mumbling the speech to yourself but talking it aloud. Magicians know their tricks but they practice them constantly to improve them. Musicians know how to play their instruments but never stop practicing, no matter how good they've become. The famous pianist Ignace Paderewski once said, "If I do not practice one day, I notice it. If I do not practice two days, my friends notice it. If I do not practice three days, the public notices it."

Eloquent speakers in past and present times have felt the need of practice. Demosthenes filled his mouth with pebbles to improve his vocalizing and used the waves of the Aegean sea as his audience. Daniel Webster practiced speeches while fishing, his listeners the fish in the bottom of the boat. William Jennings Bryan practiced in a grove of trees behind buildings on a college campus. Guy Vander Jagt, who delivered the keynote address at the 1980 Republican national convention, rehearsed it with the squirrels and pine trees as his audience near his Michigan home.

JOIN A TOASTMASTERS CLUB

Solitary practice before an imaginary audience helps your development as a speaker in some respects such as breathing and voice control, but speaking to a real audience is much better for all-around improvement. An ideal way to practice in front of audiences is to join a Toastmasters Club. Members prepare speeches on subjects of their own selection and deliver them at club meetings. Each speech is then judged for its effectiveness of content, organization and delivery by an evaluator, also a club member. This feedback received by the speaker enables him or her to improve future speeches. Over 2 million men and women have become proficient at public speaking through Toastmasters Clubs.

Thousands of Toastmasters Clubs meet mornings, noon or evenings in the United States, Canada and other countries. The dues are low but the benefits gained in improved public speaking are far beyond any monetary value. For information about the Toastmasters Club nearest your home or work, write to Toastmasters International World Headquarters, 2200 N. Grand Avenue, Santa Ana, California 92711.

Following this final chapter are two appendixes, one containing eloquent quotations and the other, models of eloquent speeches. The quotations will serve as samples of the kinds you can use to drive home important points in your speeches. From the speech models you'll see how the speakers put into practice the principles and techniques offered throughout this book. If you apply them in your own speeches, you'll have many happy years as an eloquent public speaker.

APPENDIX I

Eloquent Quotations

This section consists of eloquent quotations which can strengthen the points you make in your speeches, add flavor to your talks, suggest ideas for speech topics, and inspire you as well as your audiences.

ABILITY

The winds and waves are always on the side of the ablest navigators.

Edward Gibbon

ACHIEVEMENT

Unswerving loyalty to duty, constant devotion to truth, and a clear conscience will overcome every discouragement and surely lead the way to usefulness and high achievement.

Grover Cleveland

No great thing is created suddenly, any more than a bunch of grapes or a fig. If you tell me that you desire a fig, I answer you that there must be time. Let it first blossom, then bear fruit, then ripen.

Epictetus

First say to yourself what you would be, and then do what you have to do.

Epictetus

ACTION

Things do not get better by being left alone. Unless they are adjusted, they explode with a shattering detonation.

Winston Churchill

ADVERSITY

Adversity not only draws people together but brings forth that beautiful inward friendship, just as the cold winter forms ice-figures on the window-panes which the warmth of the sun effaces.

Sören Kierkegaard

ADVICE

Many receive advice, only the wise profit by it.

Publilius Syrus

Advice is like snow: the softer it falls, the longer it dwells upon and the deeper it sinks into the mind.

Samuel Coleridge

AGE

We do not count a man's years until he has nothing else to count.

Ralph Waldo Emerson

Perhaps middle age is, or should be, a period of shedding shells: the shell of ambition, the shell of material accumulations and possessions, the shell of the ego.

Anne Morrow Lindbergh

AMBITION

The height of the pinnacle is determined by the breadth of the base.

Ralph Waldo Emerson

APATHY

By far the most dangerous foe we have to fight is apathy—indifference from whatever cause, not from a lack of knowledge, but from carelessness, from absorption in other pursuits, from a contempt bred of self-satisfaction.

Sir William Osler

ASPIRATION

Each reaching and aspiration is an instinct with which all nature consists and cooperates, and therefore it is not in vain. If a man believes and expects great things of himself it makes no odds where you put him, he will be surrounded by grandeur.

Henry D. Thoreau

ATTENTION

Observations must be continual if our ideas are to remain true. Eternal vigilance is the price of knowledge; perpetual hazard, perpetual experiment, keep quick the edge of life.

George Santayana

The one serviceable, safe, certain, remunerative, attainable quality in every study and in every pursuit is the quality of attention. My own invention, or imagination, such as it is, I can most truthfully assure you would never have served me as it has but for the habit of commonplace, humble, patient, daily, toiling, drudging attention.

Charles Dickens

BELIEF

What matters today is not the difference between those who believe and those who do not believe, but the difference between those who care and those who don't.

Abbe Pire

BOLDNESS

Whatever you can do or dream you can do, begin it. Boldness has genius, power and magic in it.

Johann von Goethe

BOOKS

In the best books great men talk to us, give us their most precious thoughts, and pour their souls into ours.

William Ellery Channing

The man who does not read good books has no advantage over the man who can't read them.

Mark Twain

BROTHERHOOD

Our prayer is that men everywhere will learn, finally, to live as brothers, to respect each other's differences, to heal each other's wounds, to promote each other's progress, and to benefit from each other's knowledge.

Adlai E. Stevenson

BUSINESS

Some people regard private enterprise as a predatory tiger to be shot. Others look on it as a cow they can milk. Not enough people see it as a healthy horse, pulling a sturdy wagon.

Winston Churchill

CHANGE

Change is the law of life. And those who look only to the past are certain to miss the future.

John F. Kennedy

CHARACTER

The Golden Rule is of no use to you whatever unless you realize that it is your move.

Frank Crane

Fame is a vapor, popularity an accident, riches take wings. Only one thing endures, and that is character.

Horace Greeley

CHOICE

The world is a looking-glass, and gives back to every man the reflection of his own face. Frown at it, and it will in turn look sourly upon you; laugh at it and with it, and it is a jolly, kind companion; and so let all young persons take their choice.

William Thackeray

CONCEIT

Conceit may puff a man up, but can never prop him up.

John Ruskin

CONSISTENCY

To hold the same views at forty as we held at twenty is to have been stupefied for a score of years and to take rank, not as a prophet, but as an unteachable brat, well birched and none the wiser.

Robert Louis Stevenson

There are those who would misteach us that to stick in a rut is consistency—and a virtue, and that to climb out of the rut is inconsistency—and a vice.

Mark Twain

True consistency, that of the prudent and the wise, is to act in conformity with circumstances, and not to act always the same way under a change of circumstances.

John C. Calhoun

DECEPTION

Falsehood is never so successful as when she baits her hook with truth, and no opinions so falsely mislead us as those that are not wholly wrong, as no watches so effectually deceive the wearer as those that are sometimes right.

Charles C. Colton

No man, for any considerable period, can wear one face to himself, and another to the multitude, without finally getting bewildered as to which may be the true.

Nathaniel Hawthorne

DECISION

Not only strike while the iron is hot, but make it hot by striking.

Oliver Cromwell

Don't be afraid to take a big step when one is indicated. You can't cross a chasm in two small jumps.

David Lloyd George

DESPAIR

Never despair, but if you do, work on in despair.

Edmund Burke

DESTINY

Destiny is not a matter of chance, it is a matter of choice; it is not a thing to be waited for, it is a thing to be achieved.

William Jennings Bryan

No trumpets sound when the important decisions of our life are made. Destiny is made known silently.

Agnes De Mille

DIFFICULTY

You cannot run away from a weakness; you must sometimes fight it out or perish; and if so, why not now, and where you stand?

Robert Louis Stevenson

Let us be of good cheer, and remember that the misfortunes hardest to bear are those which never come.

James Russell Lowell

That which we acquire with the most difficulty we retain the longest; as those who have earned a fortune are usually more careful of it than those who have inherited one.

Charles C. Colton

The greater the difficulty, the more glory in surmounting it. Skillful pilots gain their reputation from storms and tempests.

Epicurus

DIGNITY

There is a healthful hardiness about real dignity that never dreads contact and communion with others, however humble.

Washington Irving

DIPLOMACY

Let us never negotiate out of fear. But let us never fear to negotiate.

John F. Kennedy

DUTY

Our grand business is not to see what lies dimly at a distance, but to do what lies clearly at hand.

Thomas Carlyle

Let us have faith that right makes might; and in that faith let us to the end, dare to do our duty as we understand it.

Abraham Lincoln

EARNESTNESS

A man in earnest finds means or, if he cannot find, creates them.

William Ellery Channing

Honesty is one part of eloquence: we persuade others by being in earnest ourselves.

William Hazlitt

Earnestness is the salt of eloquence.

Victor Hugo

EDUCATION

The entire object of true education is to make people not merely do the right things, but enjoy the right things—not merely industrious, but to love industry—not merely learned, but to love knowledge—not merely pure, but to love purity—not merely just, but to hunger and thirst after justice.

John Ruskin

ELOQUENCE

A word fitly spoken is like apples of gold in pictures of silver.

Old Testament

Let your speech be always with grace, seasoned with salt.

New Testament

True eloquence consists in saying all that is proper and nothing more.

Francois de la Rochefoucauld

It is so plain to me that eloquence, like swimming, is an art which all men might learn, though so few do.

Ralph Waldo Emerson

ENTHUSIASM

I like the man who bubbles over with enthusiasm. Better be a geyser than a mud puddle.

John G. Shedd

Enthusiasm is the white heat which fuses all a man's business qualities—ability, initiative, knowledge, tact, industry and the rest—into one effective whole.

Hugh Chalmers

Every great and commanding movement in the annals of the world is a triumph of enthuasism. Nothing great was ever achieved without it.

Ralph Waldo Emerson

EVIL

Those who corrupt the public mind are just as evil as those who steal from the public purse.

Adlai E. Stevenson

EXPERIENCE

I know not what profit there may be in the recorded experience of the past, if it be not to guide us in the present.

Benjamin Disraeli

Take fifty of our current proverbial sayings—they are so trite, so threadbare, that we can hardly bring our lips to utter them. Nonetheless, they embody the concentrated experience of the race, and the man who orders his life according to their teaching cannot go far wrong.

Norman Douglas

Experience is not what happens to a man. It is what a man does with what happens to him.

Aldous Huxley

We should be careful to get out of an experience only the wisdom that is in it—and stop there; lest we be like the cat that sits down on a hot stove-lid. She will never sit down on the hot stove-lid again—and that is well; but also she will never sit down on a cold one anymore.

Mark Twain

To know the road ahead, ask those coming back.

Chinese Proverb

I have but one lamp by which my feet are guided, and that is the lamp of experience. I know of no way of judging the future but by the past.

Patrick Henry

FAITH

It is cynicism and fear that freeze life; it is faith that thaws it out, releases it, sets it free.

Harry Emerson Fosdick

The only limit to our realization of tomorrow will be our doubts of today. Let us move forward with strong and active faith.

Franklin D. Roosevelt

The smallest seed of faith is better than the largest fruit of happiness.

Henry D. Thoreau

FANATICISM

A fanatic is one who can't change his mind and won't change the subject.

Winston Churchill

FAULTS

The greatest of faults, I should say, is to be conscious of none.

Thomas Carlyle

FORESIGHT

If a man takes no thought about what is distant, he will find sorrow near at hand.

Confucius

FRIENDSHIP

Friendship is the only cement that will ever hold the world together.

Woodrow Wilson

GIFT

I am in the habit of looking not so much to the nature of a gift as to the spirit in which it is offered.

Robert Louis Stevenson

GOALS

To be what we are, and to become what we are capable of becoming, is the only end of life.

Benedict (Baruch) Spinoza

If a man does not know to what port he is steering, no wind is favorable to him.

Seneca

GOODNESS

Die when I may, I want it said of me by those who knew me best, that I always plucked a thistle and planted a flower where I thought a flower would grow.

Abraham Lincoln

When bad men combine, the good must associate; else they will fall, one by one, an unpitied sacrifice in a contemptible struggle.

Edmund Burke

GOVERNMENT

The legitimate object of government is to do for the people what needs to be done but which they cannot by individual effort do at all or do so well for themselves.

Abraham Lincoln

The very essence of a free government consists in considering offices as public trusts, bestowed for the good of the country, and not for the benefit of an individual or a party.

John C. Calhoun

It is the duty of the government to make it difficult for people to do wrong, easy to do right.

William E. Gladstone

GREATNESS

If I cannot do great things, I can do small things in a great way.

J. F. Clarke

The way of a superior man is threefold: virtuous, he is free from anxieties; wise, he is free from perplexities; bold, he is free from fear.

Confucius

GROWTH

Harmony makes small things grow; lack of it makes great things decay.

Sallust

HABIT

The chains of habit are generally too small to be felt, until they are too strong to be broken.

Samuel Johnson

Habit is habit, and not to be flung out of the window by any man, but coaxed downstairs a step at a time.

Mark Twain

HAPPINESS

Happiness doesn't come from doing what we like to do but from liking what we have to do.

Wilferd Peterson

HONORS

Dignity does not consist in possessing honors, but in deserving them.

Aristotle

It is better to deserve honors and not have them than to have them and not deserve them.

Mark Twain

HOPE

Hope is wanting something so eagerly that, in spite of all the evidence that you're not going to get it, you go right on wanting it. And the remarkable thing about it is that this very act of hoping produces a kind of strength of its own.

Norman Vincent Peale

I steer my bark with hope in the head, leaving fear astern.

Thomas Jefferson

HUMOR

A man without mirth is like a wagon without springs, in which one is caused disagreeably to jolt by every pebble over which it runs.

Henry Ward Beecher

Good humor is one of the best articles of dress one can wear in society.

William Thackeray

IDEALS

Ideals are like stars; you will not succeed in touching them with your hands, but, like the seafaring man on the desert of water, you choose them as your guides, and, following them, you reach your destiny.

Carl Schurz

IDEAS

A man may die, nations may rise and fall, but an idea lives on. Ideas have endurance without death.

John F. Kennedy

IMMORTALITY

I believe that man will not merely endure: he will prevail. He is immortal, not because he alone among creatures has an inexhaustible voice, but because he has a soul, a spirit capable of compassion and sacrifice and endurance.

William Faulkner

IMPOSSIBILITY

Nothing is impossible to a willing heart.

John Heywood

IMPRESSION

Nothing is truer to experience or more wholesome to recognize than that the impression we make comes from what we are, in inmost desire and habit, and not from what we may try to seem to be. Our souls are not much hidden.

Charles Horton Cooley

IMPROVEMENT

He who stops being better stops being good.

Oliver Cromwell

INDIVIDUALITY

If a man does not keep pace with his companions, perhaps it is because he hears a different drummer. Let him step to the music which he hears, however measured or far away.

Henry D. Thoreau

Individuality does not consist in the use of the very personal pronoun I; it consists in tone, in method, in attitude, in point of view; it consists in saying things in such a way that you will yourself be recognized as a force in saying them.

Woodrow Wilson

Nature never rhymes her children, nor makes two men alike.

Ralph Waldo Emerson

INFORMATION

You get a great deal more light on the street than you do in the closet. You get a good deal more light by keeping your ears open among the rank and file of your fellow citizens than you do in any private conference whatever.

Woodrow Wilson

INITIATIVE

Be not the first by whom the new is tried, nor yet the last to lay the old aside.

Alexander Pope

INSIGHT

A moment's insight is sometimes worth a life's experience.

Oliver Wendell Holmes, Sr.

INTEGRITY

Our integrity is never worth so much as when we have parted with our all to keep it.

Charles C. Colton

Integrity without knowledge is weak and useless, and knowledge without integrity is dangerous and dreadful.

Samuel Johnson

You cannot throw away words like heroism and sacrifice and nobility and honor without abandoning the qualities they express.

Marya Mannes

INTEREST

A great preservative against angry and mutinous thoughts, and all impatience and quarreling, is to have some great business and interest in your mind, which like a sponge shall suck up your attention and keep you from brooding over what displeases you.

Joseph Rickaby

JUSTICE

Justice and power must be brought together, so that whatever is just may be powerful, and whatever is powerful may be just.

Blaise Pascal

KNOWLEDGE

In order that knowledge be properly digested, it must have been swallowed with a good appetite.

Anatole France

Many men are stored full of unused knowledge. Like loaded guns that are never fired off, or military magazines in times of peace, they are stuffed with useless ammunition.

Henry Ward Beecher

The more a man knows, the more willing he is to learn. The less a man knows, the more positive he is that he knows everything.

Robert G. Ingersoll

I hold that the most important thing is not the quantity of knowledge which a man has taken in and can pour out again, but the ability he shows to use the knowledge he has acquired.

Herbert Spencer

The more extensive a man's knowledge of what has been done, the greater will be his power of knowing what to do.

Benjamin Disraeli

If a man empties his purse into his head, no one can take it away from him. An investment in knowledge always pays the best interest.

Benjamin Franklin

The greater our knowledge increases, the greater our ignorance unfolds.

John F. Kennedy

Knowledge and timber shouldn't be much used till they are seasoned.

Oliver Wendell Holmes, Sr.

LAW

Our nation is founded on the principle that observance of the law is the eternal safeguard of liberty, and defiance of the law is the surest road to tyranny.

John F. Kennedy

Let reverence for the laws be breathed by every American mother to the lisping babe that prattles on her lap. Let it be taught in schools, in seminaries, and in colleges. Let it be written in primers, spelling books, and in almanacs. Let it be preached from the pulpit, proclaimed in legislative halls, and enforced in courts of justice. And, in short, let it become the political religion of the nation.

Abraham Lincoln

LEADERSHIP

Leaders are ordinary persons with extraordinary determination.

Herbert Kaufman

LIBERTY

Liberty does not consist in doing what you like but in liking to do what you can, what you may and what you ought.

Henry Van Dyke

The shepherd drives the wolf from the sheep's throat, for which the sheep thanks the shepherd as his liberator, while the wolf denounces him for the same act as the destroyer of liberty.

Abraham Lincoln

LIFE

Well, I have found life an enjoyable, enchanting, active, and sometimes a terrifying experience, and I've enjoyed it completely. A lament in one ear, maybe, but always a song in the other. And to me life is simply an invitation to live.

Sean O'Casey

Mark how we realize the beauty and blessing of life itself only in rare, inexplicable moments, and then most keenly. It comes to us like a sudden blare of trumpets in the wind.

J. B. Priestley

Life can only be understood backwards; but it must be lived forwards.

Sören Kierkegaard

There are two things to aim at in life: first, to get what you want; and after that, to enjoy it. Only the wisest of mankind achieve the second.

Logan Pearsall Smith

There is no day born but comes like a stroke of music into the world and sings itself all the way through.

Henry Ward Beecher

Be not afraid of life. Believe that life *is* worth living, and your belief will help create the fact.

William James

MANNERS

Manners are changing but the essential need for manners of some kind remains the same. Good manners are the traffic rules for society in general—not in the purely "social" sense. Without good manners, living would be chaotic, human beings unbearable to each other.

Amy Vanderbilt

MATURITY

A mature person is one who does not think only in absolutes, who is able to be objective even when deeply stirred emotionally, who has learned that there is both good and bad in all people and in all things, and who walks humbly and deals charitably with the circumstances of life, knowing that in this world no one is all-knowing and therefore all of us need both love and charity.

Eleanor Roosevelt

MEMORY

Memory is not just the imprint of the past upon us; it is the keeper of what is meaningful for our deepest hopes and fears.

Rollo May

MIND

Our minds are like crows. They pick up everything that glitters, no matter how uncomfortable our nests get with all that metal in them.

Thomas Merton

If we work marble, it will perish; if we work upon brass, time will efface it; if we rear temples, they will crumble into dust; but if we work upon immortal minds and instill into them just principles, we are then engraving upon tablets which no time will efface, but will brighten and brighten to all eternity.

Daniel Webster

The mind is like a trunk. If well-packed, it holds almost everything; if ill-packed, next to nothing.

Augustus T. Hare

The mind of man is like a clock that is always running down, and requires to be as constantly wound up.

William Hazlitt

Our minds, like our stomachs, are whetted by change of food, and variety supplies both with fresh appetite.

Quintilian

MORALITY

Two things fill the mind with ever new and increasing wonder and awe—the starry heavens above me, and the moral law within me.

Immanuel Kant

NOISE

Noise is the most impertinent of all forms of interruption. It is not only an interruption, but also a disruption of thought.

Arthur Schopenhauer

NONCONFORMITY

Whoso would be a man, must be a nonconformist. He who would gather immortal palms must not be hindered by the name of goodness, but must explore if it be goodness. Nothing is at last sacred but the integrity of your own mind.

Ralph Waldo Emerson

OPPORTUNITY

Life is merely a series of opportunities for turning failures into successes.

Peter Cooper

While we stop to think we often miss our opportunity.

Publilius Syrus

PATRIOTISM

The anatomy of patriotism is complex. But surely intolerance and public irresponsibility cannot be cloaked in the shining armor of rectitude and of righteousness. Nor can the denial of the right to hold ideas that are different—the freedom of man to think as he pleases. To strike freedom of the mind with the fist of patriotism is an old and ugly subtlety.

Adlai E. Stevenson

PEACE

There must be, not a balance of power, but a community of power; not organized rivalries, but an organized common peace.

Woodrow Wilson

We look forward to the time when the Power of Love will replace the Love of Power. Then will our world know the blessings of Peace.

William E. Gladstone

No one can be certain about the meaning of peace. But we all can be certain about the meaning of war.

Adlai E. Stevenson

PEOPLE

I do not know the method of drawing up an indictment against a whole people.

Edmund Burke

PERSEVERANCE

Our greatest glory is not in never falling, but in rising every time we fall.

Confucius

The hen doesn't quit scratching, just because the worms are scarce.

J. P. Gerrlofs

The rung of a ladder was never meant to rest upon, but only to hold a man's foot long enough to enable him to put the other somewhat higher.

Thomas H. Huxley

When you get into a tight place and everything goes against you, till it seems you could not hold on a minute longer, never give up then, for that is just the place and time that the tide will turn.

Harriet Beecher Stowe

PLAY

When you play, play hard; when you work, don't play at all.

Theodore Roosevelt

POISE

Nothing gives one person so much advantage over another as to remain always cool and unruffled under all circumstances.

Thomas Jefferson

POWER

There is nothing, absolutely nothing which needs to be more carefully guarded against than that one man should be allowed to become more powerful than the people.

Demosthenes

The imbecility of men is always inviting the impudence of power.

Ralph Waldo Emerson

Power will intoxicate the best hearts, as wine the strongest heads. No man is wise enough, nor good enough to be trusted with unlimited power.

Charles C. Colton

PRACTICALITY

A rational man acting in the real world may be defined as one who decides where he will strike a balance between what he desires and what can be done.

Walter Lippmann

PRAISE

Praise, like gold and diamonds, owes its value only to its scarcity.

Samuel Johnson

PREJUDICE

Prejudice is a raft onto which the shipwrecked mind clambers and paddles to safety.

Ben Hecht

Prejudices, it is well known, are most difficult to eradicate from the heart whose soil has never been loosened or fertilized by education; they grow there, firm as weeds among stones.

Charlotte Bronte

Ignorance is stubborn and prejudice dies hard.

Adlai E. Stevenson

It is never too late to give up our prejudices.

Henry D. Thoreau

A great many people think they are thinking when they are merely rearranging their prejudices.

William James

PRINCIPLES

Get your principles right; and the rest is a mere matter of detail.

Napoleon Bonaparte

PRIORITY

You can't move so fast that you try to change the mores faster than people can accept it. That doesn't mean you do nothing, but it means that you do the things that need to be done according to priority.

Eleanor Roosevelt

PROGRESS

Every step of progress which the world has made has been from scaffold to scaffold, and from stake to stake.

Wendell Phillips

The test of our progress is not whether we add more to the abundance of those who have much; it is whether we provide enough for those who have too little.

Franklin D. Roosevelt

The art of progress is to preserve order amid change and to preserve change amid order.

Alfred North Whitehead

PROMPTNESS

Know the true value of time; snatch, seize, and enjoy every moment of it. No idleness, no laziness, no procrastination; never put off till tomorrow what you can do today.

Lord Chesterfield

PURPOSE

To be what we are, and to become what we are capable of becoming, is the only end of life.

Robert Louis Stevenson

QUOTAS

Within us all there are wells of thought and dynamos of energy which are not suspected until emergencies arise. Then oftentimes we find that it is comparatively simple to double or treble our former capacities and to amaze ourselves by the results achieved. Quotas, when set up for us by others, are challenges which goad us on to surpass ourselves. The outstanding leaders of every age are those who set up their own quotas and constantly exceed them.

Thomas J. Watson

READING

Read not to contradict and confute; nor to believe and take for granted; nor to find talk and discourse; but to weigh and consider.

Francis Bacon

To read without reflecting is like eating without digesting.

Edmund Burke

Reading is to the mind what exercise is to the body. As by the one, health is preserved, strengthened, and invigorated; by the other, virtue, which is the health of the mind, is kept alive, cherished, and confirmed.

Joseph Addison

RESULTS

The art of using moderate abilities to advantage often brings greater results than actual brilliance.

Francois de la Rochefoucauld

REVENGE

In taking revenge, a man is but even with his enemy; but in passing it over, he is superior.

Francis Bacon

REWARD

The highest reward for man's toil is not what he gets for it but what he becomes by it.

John Ruskin

The reward of a thing well done is to have done it.

Ralph Waldo Emerson

RICHES

One is not rich by what one owns, but more by what one is able to do without, with dignity.

Immanuel Kant

RIGHTEOUSNESS

The humblest citizen of all the land, when clad in the armor of a righteous cause, is stronger than all the hosts of Error.

William Jennings Bryan

SELF-CONFIDENCE

Self-confidence comes to you every time you are knocked down and get up. A little boy was asked how he learned to skate. "Oh, by getting up every time I fell down," he replied.

Ralph Waldo Emerson

SPEAKING

It has been well observed that the tongue discloses the state of mind no less than that of the body; but, in either case, before the philosopher or physician can judge, the patient must open his mouth.

Charles C. Colton

To talk much and arrive nowhere is the same as climbing a tree to catch a fish.

Chinese Proverb

As a vessel is known by the sound, whether it is cracked or not, so men are proved by their speeches whether they be wise or foolish.

Demosthenes

He knows not when to be silent who knows not when to speak.

Publilius Syrus

SUCCESS

The secret of success is constancy to purpose.

Benjamin Disraeli

If you wish to succeed in life, make perseverance your bosom friend, experience your wise couselor, caution your elder brother, and hope your guardian genius.

Joseph Addison

SURVIVAL

A nation without the means of reform is without means of survival.

Edmund Burke

TACT

Tact is the ability to remove the sting from a dangerous stinger without getting stung.

James Bryce

TALENT

Use what talents you possess: the woods would be very silent if no birds sang there except those that sang best.

Henry Van Dyke

TIME

There is one kind of robber whom the law does not strike at, and who steals what is most precious to men: time.

Napoleon Bonaparte

Time heals what reason cannot.

Seneca

The past, the present and the future are really one—they are today.

Harriet Beecher Stowe

Yesterday is not ours to recover, but tomorrow is ours to win or lose.

Lyndon B. Johnson

The value of time is in everybody's mouth, but in few people's practice.

Lord Chesterfield

Time, whose tooth gnaws away at everything else, is powerless against truth.

Thomas H. Huxley

The farther backward you can look, the farther forward you are likely to see.

Winston Churchill

TOLERANCE

Tolerance is the oil which takes the friction out of life.

Wilbert E. Scheer

The responsibility of tolerance lies in those who have the wider vision.

George Eliot

TRAVEL

The world is a great book of which they that never stir from home read only a page.

St. Augustine

TRUTH

Truth may be stretched, but cannot be broken, and always gets above falsehood, as oil does above water.

Miguel de Cervantes

The truth is found when men are free to pursue it.

Franklin D. Roosevelt

The truth is incontrovertible. Panic may resent it; ignorance may deride it; malice may distort it, but there it is.

Winston Churchill

TYRANNY

Unlimited power corrupts the possessor; and this I know, that where law ends, there tyranny begins.

William Pitt, the Elder

VARIETY

Variety's the very spice of life that gives it all its flavor.

William Cowper

VIRTUE

Search others for their virtues, thyself for thy vices.

Benjamin Franklin

The strength of a man's virtue should not be measured by his special exertions but by his habitual acts.

Blaise Pascal

Virtue consists not in abstaining from vice, but in not desiring it.

George Bernard Shaw

WAR

Mankind must put an end to war, or war will put an end to mankind.

John F. Kennedy

WIT

Wit ought to be a glorious treat, like caviar; never spread it about like marmalade.

Noel Coward

WORDS

A word is not a crystal, transparent and unchanging; it is the skin of a living thought and may vary greatly in color and content according to the circumstances and time in which it is used.

Oliver Wendell Holmes, Jr.

If you would be pungent, be brief; for it is with words as with sunbeams—the more they are condensed, the deeper they burn.

Robert Southey

WORK

When men are rightly occupied, their amusement grows out of their work, as the color petals out of a fruitful flower; when they are faithfully helpful and compassionate, all their emotions are steady, deep, perpetual and vivifying to the soul as is the natural pulse to the body.

John Ruskin

If you have built castles in the air, your work need not be lost—that is where they should be: now put foundations under them.

Henry D. Thoreau

If a man loves his work, no matter what it may be, that is the work he is best fitted for.

Edward Bok

ZEAL

Zeal without knowledge is fire without light.

Thomas Fuller

Through zeal, knowledge is gotten; through lack of zeal, knowledge is lost; let a man who knows this double path of gain and loss so place himself that knowledge may grow.

Buddha

Experience shows that success is due less to ability than to zeal. The winner is he who gives himself to his work, body and soul.

Charles Buxton

APPENDIX II

Models of Eloquent Speeches

This section fulfills a function different from that of the speech excerpts quoted throughout the main part of this book. Those are examples to illustrate particular principles and techniques of speechmaking. They are necessarily only portions of speeches. Here, speeches are presented in their entirety to show their continuity and overall effect.

These speeches were delivered by past or present-day speakers on various occasions to inform, persuade, inspire or entertain. You can read and reread both the old and new speeches with profit and satisfaction. All of them put into practice the speechmaking theories advocated in this book.

By studying the eloquent speeches which follow, you'll enlarge your stock of ideas and information and observe how the speakers skillfully organized their speeches and put their thoughts into impressive language. You'll also intensify your enthusiasm for creating your own eloquent speeches.

Speech to Inspire
"Good News About Failure"
by Eugene W. Brice
Delivered in 1983

It was the biggest moment of his young career. Every eye was on him as he stood in that packed auditorium to announce his school's vote on a new president for the State Student Council Convention. A representative from each school across the state would stand and shout out, "Mr. President,

Central High casts its vote for . . . ," and then announce the city or school it was voting for. His own school was near the end of the alphabet, and a close race had developed between Amarillo and Galveston as the next president. The lead seesawed regularly, and each vote was listened to anxiously. Finally it came to his school, and he was the spokesman. Would they vote for Amarillo or Galveston? He stood nervously, and said strongly, "Mr. President, Sulphur Springs casts its vote for Sulphur Springs." He knew at once that he had misstated himself, and tried quickly to correct it, but a roar of confusion and laughter went up from the 1500 who were there. The correction was finally made, and the world went on as before.

That incident happened 36 years ago in May, and I can remember it in incredible detail. I do not remember for whom we were voting, or who finally won. I *can* remember my moment of failure with a vividness that astonishes. And I would wager that you, too, can remember some moment in your life in which you failed, and brought embarrassment to yourself. And this is why most of us identify with such moments, and respond to them.

I think of two stories I've stumbled across in the last week or two. One was a newspaper feature about an unbelievably successful person for whom nothing ever went wrong. The article described a man who had made a fortune in computer hardware. On arriving home, he goes to his grand piano and plays Chopin while his attractive wife puts the finishing touches on the gourmet French cuisine she has been preparing. Sometimes the man's playing is loud enough to disturb their fifteen-year-old son who has set up his own meteorology lab in the basement, says the article. The couple's daughter is away, being in a beauty contest at a local school. The whole article reads like the mimeographed Christmas letter your brother-in-law sends out.

About the same time, I read about an incident in President Truman's life after he retired and was back in Independence. He was at the Truman library, talking with some elementary school students, and answering their questions. Finally, a question came from an owlish little boy. "Mr. President," he asked, "was you popular when you was a boy?" The President looked at the boy, and answered, "Why no, I was never popular. The popular boys were the ones who were good at games and had big tight fists. I was never like that. Without my glasses, I was blind as a bat, and to tell the truth, I was kind of a sissy. If there was any danger of getting into a fight, I took off. I guess that's why I'm here today." The little boy started to applaud and then everyone else did, too.

And so did I, as I read the story, for it is a reminder that all of us experience failure in different ways. That's why Paul's words in Corinthians have always hooked themselves onto my mind. "We are afflicted in every way, but not crushed; perplexed, but not driven to despair; persecuted but not forsaken; knocked down, but not knocked out." (II Cor. 4:8–9) Because such moments come to us, we acknowledge the bad times failure brings, and we look for good news. Then some observations about failure.

I. Start by saying that *failure is something we can avoid. That's* good news, isn't it? Or is it? Failure is something we can avoid by saying nothing, doing nothing and being nothing.

Let me brag on myself a bit. I have never in my life choked up while singing a solo. I have never lost a match in a tennis tournament. I have never had a poem rejected by a literary magazine. I have never been defeated in a race for public office. Inasmuch as I am one who loves music and tennis and poetry and politics, that's an amazing record. But you see, I have never sung a solo, or played in tournament tennis, or submitted a poem to a magazine, or run for public office. I have never failed at any of these things because I have never tried.

Only those people who try something run the risk of failure. The main choice most of us make, the most important choice is, at what level shall we fail? I read recently of a speech given at Texas Christian University. The title of the speech reached out and grabbed my attention. "On Failing at a Very High Level." Each of us chooses the level of his or her failure. In baseball, some make major league errors, some make minor league errors, and some make no errors at all, as they don't play the game.

In life itself, the same options are open. Paul confessed that many times in his life he was afflicted, perplexed, persecuted, and knocked down. But many in Paul's day suffered none of those discouragements. Safely living tight little lives, they never offered themselves for any great new truth, and they lived and died with nothing more than kitchen failures and backyard defeats. What small battles most of us limit ourselves to: some successes, but at a very low level. Never any great commitment. Never a hard promise made. Never a challenging job taken.

Imagine, if you will, a friend getting interested in mountain climbing. He buys all the best equipment, boots and ice axes and crampons and nylon rope. He gets arctic parkas for the cold, and a four-wheel drive vehicle to get him to inaccessible trail heads. Then the day comes, and he loads all his equipment up and drives up Main Street to attempt to climb Signboard Hill.

Sometimes our churches are like that. Sometimes our civic clubs are like that. What tremendous resources we have! What incredible talent and influence and ability and power are gathered here every Thursday at noon, year round—enough to revitalize and re-energize our community. And from time to time we organize all this into a gigantic effort to scale Signboard Hill. Succeeding at a Very Low Level! Start, then, by being honest about failure. If you are able to be satisfied in life with saying nothing, doing nothing, and being nothing, failure is avoidable.

II. Move on from there to note that *failure is a teacher*, the best one we'll ever have. Consider this: the only way you ever learned to walk was by failure. If your first step had waited until you were sure you would not fall, you would still be wearing high-topped white shoes with unscarred soles.

The only way you ever learned to read, or add, or play the piano, or run an adding machine was by trying it and failing, and then trying it again.

Last summer at Estes Park, in a court next to ours, some 9-year-olds were trying to play tennis. It wasn't going too well for them. One of the 9-year-olds swung at the ball and hit it clear over the fence just as his mother walked by. "Throw the ball to us, will you, Mom," the boy said. The mother replied, "Why did you hit it over the fence? You've had a tennis lesson!"

It takes more than a lesson in tennis to learn how not to hit it over the fence. It takes long practice and frequent failure. You don't learn to hit it in until you've hit it out many a time. In any area of life, failure is a first-rate teacher. Sir Humphrey Davy, 19th century physicist, put it like this: "The most important of my discoveries have been suggested to me by my failures."

For years, astronomers knew the planet Neptune existed, but couldn't find it. They applied the math of Isaac Newton, and found it. Then they were stymied in their search for Pluto. According to Newton's physics, it ought to be there, but it was not in place. For forty years, the search was unproductive, and Albert Einstein used the failure of Newtonian physics in this search for Pluto as a clue to help him devise the theory of relativity. Failure led to success.

Failure teaches us. If, in our work, something is going badly, something we need to learn is offering itself to us. There must be a better way to do this. In this situation, I am failing! What am I doing wrong, and where do I go from here? If, at home, things are going badly, we have the opportunity to learn, and to proceed stronger than before. Every marriage should expect moments of failure; the strong marriages are not those which never fail, but those which learn from their failures. Through learning in marriage to treat all disasters as incidents and none of the incidents as disasters, the bond between husband and wife grows ever stronger.

Failure is a teacher, and it becomes an asset to us if we learn from it. We may learn that our present strategy won't work. We may learn that our goal itself wasn't good. We may learn that our inner problems interfere with our outer work. We may learn that we quit too soon. Whatever it is, failure teaches us if we will let it.

III. Therefore, failure need never be final! To fail is not to be defeated. Mary Pickford said, "If you have made mistakes, even serious ones, there is always another chance for you. What we call *real* failure is not the falling down, but the staying down." Someone tells of the young Methodist minister who went from Seminary to his first church, and proceeded to fail miserably. The Bishop came out, talked with the lay people, discovered that indeed the young minister *had* botched the job completely. Invited to preach on Sunday, the Bishop publicly criticized the young man for his poor job. Everyone wondered what the young man would say the next Sunday after having been publicly humiliated. He rose to the pulpit the next Sunday and said quietly: "I can sin, you can sin, and the Bishop can sin. I can make mistakes, you can make mistakes, and the Bishop can make mistakes. I could go to hell, you could go to hell, and the Bishop can go to hell!" No failure ever need be final!

And that's the attractiveness of Paul's word here. Afflicted, he was, but not crushed. Perplexed, yes, but not driven to despair. Surely he was persecuted, but he was not forsaken. He was knocked down, he said, but never knocked out! What a word that is for all of us who ride this roller coaster of life, enjoying fine, high moments at one time, and then cascading down to low moments of failure. Ups and downs, victories and defeats, successes and failures—they come in dizzy cycles. But no failure ever need be final.

In a bit of whimsy, Neil Postman quotes a letter written by a high school senior who had received a letter of rejection from the college he wanted to attend. "Dear Admissions Officer," the student wrote, "I am in receipt of your rejection of my application. As much as I would like to accommodate you, I find I cannot accept it. I have already received four rejections from other colleges, and this number is, in fact, over my limit. Therefore, I must reject your rejection, and will appear for classes on September 18." (Neil Postman, *Crazy Talk*)

Crazy as it is, *I like that*! It may not have worked for that student, but it has worked and it works in many a life. That's just what Paul did. The world stamped "failure" on his hand, and Paul erased it. "Perplexed, but not despairing. Knocked down, but not knocked out." "*I reject your rejection*!"

Any one of us can say that, too. So many have said it, and have risen from failure to real achievement. In 1902, the poetry editor of Atlantic Monthly returned a sheaf of poems to a 28-year-old poet with this curt note: "Our magazine has no room for your vigorous verse." The poet was Robert Frost, who rejected the rejection. In 1905, the University of Bern turned down a Ph.D. dissertation as being irrelevant and fanciful. The young physics student who wrote the dissertation was Albert Einstein, who rejected the rejection. In 1890 a teacher at Harrow in England wrote on a 16-year-old's report card, "a conspicuous lack of success." The 16-year-old was Winston Churchill, who rejected the rejection.

Go ahead and complete the list. "In 1982, John Doe failed in the effort to (and you fill in the blanks): keep a job, expand the business, make a good marriage, head a community project, be a good father." *Name your own failure*. How long the list might be! But John Doe rejected the rejection, and tried yet again. One of God's best gifts to us is the joy of trying again, for no failure ever need be final.

Then sum it up with this. A small boy had been looking through a stationer's stock of greeting cards when a clerk asked, "Can I help you find what you're looking for, son? Birthday card? Get well card? Anniversary card for Mom and Dad?" "Not exactly," said the little boy, shaking his head. Then he added wistfully, "You got anything in the line of blank report cards?"

Life does; God does. Especially at the beginning of every new year those new report cards are available to us, and we ourselves fill them in by how we respond to the D's and F's of life. With God's help, we rise up from failure, afflicted but not crushed, perplexed, but not despairing, knocked down, but by the grace of God, never knocked out! And that, my frequently failing friends, is good news indeed!

Acceptance of Award Speech
"Let Candles Be Brought"
by Sol M. Linowitz
Delivered in 1977

As I look around this room and see so many who have done so much over the years for so many, I must admit that I have a sense of kinship with William Howard Taft's great-granddaughter who in her third-grade autobiography wrote: "My great-grandfather was President of the United States, my grandfather was a United States Senator, my father is an ambassador, and I am a Brownie."

I want you to know that in your presence, I am a Brownie.

I am truly grateful to you for the award this evening, for the spirit in which you have tendered it, and for the auspices under which you have presented it. Let me express my special appreciation to the General Electric Company for the generous contribution which they have made on my behalf in the name of that distinguished American, Charles E. Wilson.

With your permission I would like to take a few minutes just to say a few things which are on my mind and my heart.

We are met at a moment in history which is uncertain, fearful and indeed, dangerous. While it is true as Professor Whitehead once said that "it is the business of the future to be dangerous," nonetheless, there is reason for concern as we look about us.

We are at a time that has been called both the Age of Anxiety and the Age of Science and Technology. Both are accurate, for indeed one feeds upon the other. As our scientific and technological competence has increased, so have our fear and anxiety.

In a real sense we are at a time of paradox—a time when we have learned to achieve most and to fear most. It is a time when we seem to know much more about how to make war than how to make peace, more about killing than we do about living. It is a time of unprecedented need and unparalleled plenty, a time when great advances in medicine and science and technology are overshadowed by incredible achievements in instruments of destruction. It is a time when the world fears not the primitive or the ignorant man, but the educated, the technically competent man, who has it in his power to destroy civilization.

It is a time when malaise hangs heavy, when we can send men up to walk the moon yet hauntingly recall Santayana's words that people have come to power who "having no stomach for the ultimate, burrow themselves downward toward the primitive."

No one needs to remind us that this moment may be the most fateful in all the long history of mankind. And that the outcome will depend on whether the human intellect which has invented such total instruments of destruction, can now develop ways of peace that will keep any man, no matter what his ideology, his race or his nation, from pushing the fatal button.

In the past men have warred over frontiers, they have come into conflict over ideologies. And they have fought over ideologies. And they have fought to better their daily lives. But today each crisis seems to overlap the other and we are engaged in a vast human upheaval that touches upon every phase of our existence—national and international, religious and racial.

Part of that upheaval is as old as hunger. Part is as new as a walk in lunar space. The overriding fact is that today we are all part of a global society in which there no longer is any such thing as a separate or isolated concern, in which peace is truly indivisible.

And the fact is that whether we like it or not, either we will all survive together or none of us will. Either we will all share the world's bounty, or none of us will.

We must, therefore, ask what chance we have of accepting our shrinking world with its fewer and fewer natural frontiers, or of transcending our ideological struggles unless we are prepared finally to get to the roots of the problem—the roots that are dug so deep in injustice and resentment in a worldwide contrast between wealth and misery. And the answers are vital not only to a sound foreign policy, but to a compassionate domestic policy. Indeed, both are interrelated in an interdependent world. For there is no escape any longer from what I believe is surely the central fact of our time: That whether it be Africa or Asia or Latin America or New York or Detroit or Washington—human beings can no longer be condemned to hunger and disease and to the indignity of a life without hope.

Who are these human beings that make up this world in which we live—the millions upon millions no longer thousands of miles away, but now just down the runway? Here they are in microcosm: During the next 60 seconds, 200 human beings will be born on this earth. About 160 of them will be black, brown, yellow or red. Of these 200 youngsters now being born, about half will be dead before they are a year old. Of those that survive, another half will be dead before they are sixteen. The 50 of the 200 who live past their sixteenth birthday, multiplied by thousands and millions, represent the people of this earth.

They, like their fathers and forefathers before them, will till the soil working for landlords, living in tents or mud huts. Most of them will never learn to read or write. Most of them will be poor and tired and hungry most of their lives. Most of them—like their fathers and their forefathers—will lie under the open skies of Asia, Africa and Latin America watching, waiting, hoping. These are our brothers and sisters, our fellow human beings on this earth.

What kind of a tomorrow does the world offer these, the people of this earth? Two diametrically opposed philosophies are being presented. One we call Communism—the other Democracy. Each asks acceptance of a basic idea; each offers a larger slice of bread.

Make common cause with us, say the Communists, and accept three basic premises: First, *dialectical materialism*—all that matters is matter itself. Second, *godlessness*—accept the notion that there is no spiritual being who determines your destiny. Third, accept the idea that the *State is supreme* and determines the will of the individual. Believe these things and accept them, say the Communists, and we promise you more food in your stomachs, more clothes on your backs, a firmer roof over your heads.

And what about Democracy? Because Democracy rejects absolutes, it tends also to resist precise definition. But when you and I think of Democracy, we think of a system dedicated to the preservation of the *integrity, dignity* and *decency* of the individual person.

We talk of all men being created equal but what we really mean is that all men are created with an equal right to become unequal—to achieve the glorious inequality of their individual talent, their individual capacity, their individual genius. We don't talk of the common man because what we believe in is not man as common, but with a common right to become uncommon—to think uncommon thoughts, to believe uncommon beliefs, to be an uncommon man.

We like to say that in a Democracy every person has a right to life, a right to a decent life, which comes not from government, not from his fellow citizens, but from God. We say that in a Democracy it is the individual who matters; and because we count by ones and not by masses or by mobs, we believe that in a Democracy each human being, regardless of his race, his creed, his color, has the right—the God-given right—to stand erect with dignity as a child of God.

I submit to you that that is the essence of what we really mean when we talk about the impact of religion on American life—our deep faith in *every man's* right to stand erect and with dignity as a child of God. That is the basic principle to which we are committed as a nation and as a people; that is the foundation on which our system rests; and that is what distinguishes us in the eyes of the world—in the eyes of those millions who are searching for hope of a better *future*.

From the beginning there has been an expectation about us as a nation. From the beginning the world has looked to us to live up to certain standards of integrity, decency, dignity and humanity—to involve ourselves deeply in moving humankind toward a more humane world of freedom and justice.

Archibald MacLeish once wrote: “America is promises.” America is, indeed, promises. We started with a promise over two hundred years ago. At the time when we were but a loose group of weak and scattered colonies of 3 million people, we lit up the western sky with a promise based on faith and hope—the promise of a free and compassionate society committed to the preservation of fundamental human values.

From the beginning we have always treasured the human and the humane and we have always cared about what happened to other human beings. The promise we held out to the world—saying we did so “out of a decent respect to the opinions of mankind”—is still the promise of America to the millions on this earth.

And today as never before in our history we have the opportunity to redeem that promise. Today we have the science and the technology, the skills and the resources to make it happen, to put an end to the hunger and disease and privation that have for so long been the scourge of mankind.

The question is whether we have the will, whether we are prepared to do what we should and must if we are to be the kind of nation we have said we are.

We have a great responsibility to ourselves, to our heritage and to our children. We are not going to discharge that responsibility by building larger missiles or making more powerful warheads. We will not do it by issuing new and eloquent statements.

We will only do it by remembering who we are and what we are—by tapping the very deepest within us as a people—by dedicating ourselves to the fulfillment of our mission as a beacon of hope for ourselves and for the other people of this world, not only as Americans but also as Christians and Jews, drawing upon the richest within our faiths.

As I indicated earlier, this is a time of uncertainty, of deep concern. But there is a moment in our history which I think suggests the temper in which we must approach whatever challenge is before us.

On May 19, 1780, the Connecticut State Legislature was in session. For days there had been prophecies that it was to be the day of doom. Then suddenly in mid-morning the sky turned from blue to gray to black. Men fell on their knees in fear and in prayer and there were many shouts for adjournment.

Then a state Senator, Abraham Davenport, came forward to the podium, banged the gavel and said, “Gentlemen, either the day of judgment is approaching or it is not. If it is not, then there is no need to adjourn, and if it is, I choose to be found doing my duty. I therefore ask, let candles be brought”.

I suggest this is a time for all of us to make that commitment. Let us also determine that no matter what lies ahead we will be found doing our duty to God and our country. Let us together ask that candles be brought.

Speech to Inform
"A Day of Infamy"
by Franklin D. Roosevelt
Delivered in 1941

Yesterday, December 7, 1941—a date which will live in infamy—the United States of America was suddenly and deliberately attacked by naval and air forces of the empire of Japan.

The United States was at peace with that nation, and, at the solicitation of Japan, was still in conversation with its government and its Emperor looking toward the maintenance of peace in the Pacific.

Indeed, one hour after Japanese air squadrons had commenced bombing in the American island of Oahu the Japanese Ambassador to the United States and his colleague delivered to our Secretary of State a formal reply to a recent American message. And, while this reply stated that it seemed useless to continue the existing diplomatic negotiations, it contained no threat or hint of war or of armed attack.

It will be recorded that the distance of Hawaii from Japan makes it obvious that the attack was deliberately planned many days or even weeks ago. During the intervening time the Japanese Government has deliberately sought to deceive the United States by false statements and expressions of hope for continued peace.

The attack yesterday on the Hawaiian Islands has caused severe damage to American naval and military forces. I regret to tell you that very many American lives have been lost. In addition, American ships have been reported torpedoed on the high seas between San Francisco and Honolulu.

Yesterday the Japanese Government also launched an attack against Malaya.

Last night Japanese forces attacked Hong Kong.

Last night Japanese forces attacked Guam.

Last night Japanese forces attacked the Philippine Islands.

Last night the Japanese attacked Wake Island.

And this morning the Japanese attacked Midway Island.

Japan has, therefore, undertaken a surprise offensive extending throughout the Pacific area. The facts of yesterday and today speak for themselves. The people of the United States have already formed their opinions and well understand the implications to the very life and safety of our nation.

As Commander in Chief of the Army and Navy I have directed that all measures be taken for our defense. Always will we remember the character of the onslaught against us.

No matter how long it may take us to overcome this premeditated invasion, the American people in their righteous might will win through to absolute victory.

I believe I interpret the will of the Congress and of the people when I assert that we will not only defend ourselves to the uttermost but will make very certain that this form of treachery shall never endanger us again.

Hostilities exist. There is no blinking at the fact that our people, our territory and our interests are in grave danger.

With confidence in our armed forces—with the unbounding determination of our people—we will gain the inevitable triumph—so help us God.

I ask that the Congress declare that since the unprovoked and dastardly attack by Japan on Sunday, December 7, 1941, a state of war has existed between the United States and the Japanese Empire.

Anniversary Speech
"Washington's Birthday"
by Jane Addams
Delivered in 1903

We meet together upon these birthdays of our great men, not only to review their lives, but to revive and cherish our own patriotism. This matter is a difficult task. In the first place, we are prone to think that by merely reciting these great deeds we get a reflected glory, and that the future is secure to us because the past has been so fine.

In the second place, we are apt to think that we inherit the fine qualities of those great men, simply because we have had a common descent and are living in the same territory.

As for the latter, we know full well that the patriotism of common descent is the mere patriotism of the clan—the early patriotism of the tribe. We know that the possession of a like territory is merely an advance upon that, and that both of them are unworthy to be the patriotism of a great cosmopolitan nation whose patriotism must be large enough to obliterate racial distinction and to forget that there are such things as surveyor's lines. Then when we come to the study of great men it is easy to think only of their great deeds, and not to think enough of their spirit.

What is a great man who has made his mark upon history? Every time, if we think far enough, he is a man who has looked through the confusion of the moment and has seen the moral issue involved; he is a man who has refused to have his sense of justice distorted; he has listened to his conscience until conscience becomes a trumpet call to like-minded men, so that they gather about him and together, with mutual purpose and mutual aid, they make a new period in history.

Let us assume for a moment that if we are going to make this day of advantage to us, we will have to take this definition of a great man. We will have to appeal to the present as well as to the past. We will have to rouse our national consciences as well as our national pride, and we will all have to remember that it lies with the young people of this nation whether or not it is going to go on to a finish in any wise worthy of its beginning.

If we go back to George Washington, and ask what he would be doing were he bearing our burdens now, and facing our problems at this moment, we would, of course, have to study his life bit by bit; his life as a soldier, as a statesman, and as a simple Virginia planter.

First, as a soldier. What is it that we admire about the soldier? It certainly is not that he goes into battle; what we admire about the soldier is that he has the power of losing his own life for the life of a larger cause; that he holds his personal sufferings of no account; that he flings down in the gage of battle his all, and says, "I will stand or fall with this cause." That, it seems to me, is the glorious thing we most admire, and if we are going to preserve that same spirit of the soldier, we will have to found a similar spirit in the civil life of the people, the same pride in civil warfare, the spirit of courage, and the spirit of self-surrender which lies back of this.

If we look out upon our national perspective, do we not see certainly one great menace which calls for patriotism? We see all around us a spirit of materialism—an undue emphasis put upon material possessions; an inordinate desire to win wealth; an inordinate fear of losing wealth; an inordinate desire to please those who are the possessors of wealth.

Now, let us say, if we feel that this is a menace, that with all our power, with all the spirit of a soldier, we will arouse high-minded youth of this country against this spirit of materialism. We will say today that we will not count the opening of markets the one great field which our nation is concerned in, but that when our flag flies anywhere it shall fly for righteousness as well as for increased commercial prosperity; that we will see to it that no sin of commercial robbery shall be committed where it floats; that we shall see to it that nothing in our commercial history will not bear the most careful scrutiny and investigation; that we will restore commercial life, however complicated, to such honor and simple honesty as George Washington expressed in his business dealings.

Let us take, for a moment, George Washington as a statesman. What was it he did, during those days when they were framing a constitution, when they were meeting together night after night, and trying to adjust the rights and privileges of every class in the community? What was it that sustained him during all those days, all those weeks, during all those months and years? It was the belief that they were founding a nation on the axiom that all men are created free and equal.

What would George Washington say if he found that among us there were causes constantly operating against that equality? If he knew that any child which is thrust prematurely into industry has no chance in life with children who are preserved from that pain and sorrow; if he knew that every insanitary street, and every insanitary house, cripples a man so that he has no health and no vigor with which to carry on his life labor; if he knew that all about us are forces making against skill, making against the best manhood and womanhood, what would he say? He would say that if the spirit of equality means anything, it means like opportunity, and if we once lose like opportunity we lose the only chance we have toward equality throughout the nation.

Let us take George Washington as a citizen. What did he do when he retired from office, because he was afraid holding office any longer might bring a wrong to himself and harm to his beloved nation?

We say that he went back to his plantation on the Potomac. What were his thoughts during the all too short days that he lived there? He thought of many possibilities, but, looking out over his country, did he fear that there should rise up a crowd of men who held office, not for their country's good, but for their own good? Would he not have foreboded evil if he had known that among us were groups and hordes of professional politicians, who, without any blinking or without any pretense that they did otherwise, apportioned the spoils of office, and considered an independent man as a mere intruder, as a mere outsider; if he had seen that the original meaning of office-holding and the function of government had become indifferent to us, that we were not using our foresight and our conscience in order to find out this great wrong which was sapping the foundations of self-government?

He would tell us that anything which makes for better civic service, which makes for a merit system, which makes for fitness for office, is the only thing which will tell against this wrong, and that this course is the wisest patriotism. What did he write in his last correspondence? He wrote that he felt very unhappy on the subject of slavery, that there was, to his mind, a great menace in the holding of slaves. We know that he neither bought nor sold slaves himself, and that he freed his own slaves in his will. That was a century ago.

A man who a century ago could do that, would he, do you think, be indifferent now to the great questions of social maladjustment which we feel all around us? His letters breathe a yearning for a better condition for the slaves as the letters of all great men among us breathe a yearning for the better condition of the unskilled and underpaid. A wise patriotism, which will take hold of these questions by careful legal enactment, by constant and vigorous enforcement, because of the belief that if the meanest man in the republic is deprived of his rights, then every man in the republic is deprived of his rights, is the only patriotism by which public-spirited men and women, with a thoroughly aroused conscience, can worthily serve this republic.

Let us say again that the lessons of great men are lost unless they reinforce upon our minds the highest demands which we make upon ourselves; that they are lost unless they drive our sluggish wills forward in the direction of their highest ideals.

Speech to Entertain "New England Weather" by Mark Twain Delivered in 1876

I reverently believe that the Maker who made us all, makes everything in New England—but the weather. I don't know who makes that, but I think it must be raw apprentices in the Weather Clerk's factory, who experiment and learn how in New England for board and clothes, and then are promoted to make weather for countries that require a good article, and will take their custom elsewhere if they don't get it.

There is a sumptuous variety about the New England weather that compels the stranger's admiration—and regret. The weather is always doing something there; always attending strictly to business; always getting up new designs and trying them on the people to see how they will go. But it gets through more business in spring than in any other season. In the spring I have counted one hundred and thirty-six different kinds of weather inside of twenty-four hours. It was I that made the fame and fortune of that man who had that marvelous collection of weather on exhibition at the Centennial that so astounded the foreigners. He was going to travel all over the world and get specimens from all the climes. I said, "Don't you do it; you come to New England on a favorable spring day." I told him what we could do in the way of style, variety, and quantity.

Well, he came and he made his collection in four days. As to variety—why, he confessed that he got hundreds of kinds of weather that he had never heard of before. And as to quantity—well, after he had picked out and discarded all that was blemished in any way, he not only had weather enough, but weather to spare; weather to hire out; weather to sell; to deposit; weather to invest; weather to give to the poor.

The people of New England are by nature patient and forbearing; but there are some things which they will not stand. Every year they kill a lot of poets for writing about "Beautiful Spring." These are generally casual visitors, who bring their notions of spring from somewhere else, and cannot, of course, know how the natives feel about spring. And so, the first thing they know, the opportunity to inquire how they feel has permanently gone by.

Old Probabilities has a mighty reputation for accurate prophecy, and thoroughly well deserves it. You take up the papers and observe how crisply and confidently he checks off what today's weather is going to be on the Pacific, down South, in the Middle States, in the Wisconsin region. See him sail along in the joy and pride of his power till he gets to New England, and then—see his tail drop. He doesn't know what the weather is going to be in New England. Well, he mulls over it, and by and by he gets out something about like this:

Probable northeast to southwest winds, varying to the southward and westward and eastward and points between; high and low barometer sweeping around from place to place; probable areas of rain, snow, hail, and drought, succeeded or preceded by earthquakes, with thunder and lightning. Then he jots down this postscript from his wandering mind to cover accidents: "But it is possible that the program may be wholly changed in the meantime."

Yes, one of the brightest gems in the New England weather is the dazzling uncertainty of it. There is only one thing certain about it: you are certain there is going to be plenty of weather—a perfect grand review; but you never can tell which end of the procession is going to move first. You fix up for the drought; you leave your umbrella in the house and sally out with your sprinkling pot, and ten to one you get drowned.

You make up your mind that the earthquake is due; you stand from under, and take hold of something to steady yourself, and the first thing you know you get struck by lightning. These are great disappointments. But they can't be helped. The lightning there is peculiar; it is so convincing! When it strikes a thing, it doesn't leave enough of that thing behind for you to tell whether—well, you'd think it was something valuable, and a Congressman had been there.

And the thunder. When the thunder begins to merely tune up and scrape and saw, and key up the instruments for the performance, strangers say, "Why, what awful thunder you have here!" But when the baton is raised and the real concert begins, you'll find that stranger down in the cellar with his head in the ash-barrel.

Now as to the size of the weather in New England—lengthways, I mean. It is utterly disproportioned to the size of that little country. Half the time, when it is packed as full as it can stick, you will see that New England weather sticking out beyond the edges and projecting around hundreds and hundreds of miles over the neighboring States. She can't hold a tenth part of her weather. You can see cracks all about where she has strained herself trying to do it.

I could speak volumes about the inhuman perversity of the New England weather, but I will give but a single specimen. I like to hear rain on a tin roof. So I covered part of my roof with tin, with an eye to that luxury. Well, do you think it ever rains on that tin? No; skips it every time.

Mind, in this speech I have been trying merely to do honor to the New England weather—no language could do it justice. But, after all, there are at least one or two things about that weather (or, if you please, effects produced by it) which we residents would not like to part with.

If we hadn't our bewitching autumn foliage, we should still have to credit the weather with one feature which compensates for all its bullying vagaries—the ice storm—when a leafless tree is clothed with ice from the bottom to the top—ice that is as bright and clear as crystal; when every bough and twig is strung with ice beads, frozen dewdrops, and the whole tree sparkles cold and white like the Shah of Persia's diamond plume.

Then the wind waves the branches and the sun comes out and turns all those myriads of beads and drops to prisms that glow and burn and flash with all manner of colored fires, which change and change again with inconceivable rapidity, from blue to red, from red to green, and green to gold—the tree becomes a sparkling fountain, a very explosion of dazzling jewels; and it stands there the acme, the climax, the supremest possibility in art or nature, of bewildering, intoxicating, intolerable magnificence! One cannot make the words too strong.

Month after month I lay up hate and grudge against the New England weather; but when the ice storm comes at last, I say: "There, I forgive you now; the books are square between us; you don't owe me a cent; go and sin some more; your little faults and foibles count for nothing; you are the most enchanting weather in the world!"

Speech to Persuade
"On Woman's Right to Suffrage"
by Susan B. Anthony
Delivered in 1873

I stand before you tonight under indictment for the alleged crime of having voted at the last presidential election, without having a lawful right to vote. It shall be my work this evening to prove to you that in thus voting, I not only committed no crime, but, instead, simply exercised my *citizen's rights*, guaranteed to me and all United States citizens by the National Constitution, beyond the power of any State to deny.

The preamble of the Federal Constitution says:

"We, the people of the United States, in order to form a more perfect union, establish justice, insure *domestic* tranquillity, provide for the common defense, promote the general welfare, and secure the blessings of liberty to ourselves and our posterity, do ordain and establish this Constitution for the United States of America."

It was we, the people; not we, the white male citizens; nor yet we, the male citizens; but we, the whole people, who formed the Union. And we formed it, not to give the blessings of liberty, but to secure them; not to the half of ourselves and the half of our posterity, but to the whole people—women as well as men. And it is a downright mockery to talk to women of their enjoyment of the blessings of liberty while they are denied the use of the only means of securing them provided by this democratic-republican government—the ballot.

For any State to make sex a qualification that must ever result in the disfranchisement of one entire half of the people is to pass a bill of attainder, or an *ex post facto* law, and is therefore a violation of the supreme law of the land. By it the blessings of liberty are forever withheld from women and their female posterity. To them this government has no just powers derived from the consent of the governed. To them this government is not a democracy. It is not a republic. It is an odious aristocracy; a hateful oligarchy of sex; the most hateful aristocracy ever established on the face of the globe.

An oligarchy of wealth, where the rich govern the poor, an oligarchy of learning, where the educated govern the ignorant, or even an oligarchy of race, where the Saxon rules the African, might be endured; but this obligarchy of sex, which makes father, brothers, husband, sons, the oligarchs over the mother and sisters, the wife and daughters of every household—which ordains all men sovereigns, all women subjects, carries dissension, discord and rebellion into every home of the nation.

Webster, Worcester and Bouvier all define a citizen to be a person in the United States, entitled to vote and hold office.

The only question left to be settled now is: Are women persons? And I hardly believe any of our opponents will have the hardihood to say they are not. Being persons, then, women are citizens; and no State has a right to make any law, or to enforce any old law, that shall abridge their privileges or immunities. Hence, every discrimination against women in the constitutions and laws of the several States is today null and void, precisely as is every one against negroes.

INDEX

A

B

C

R

S